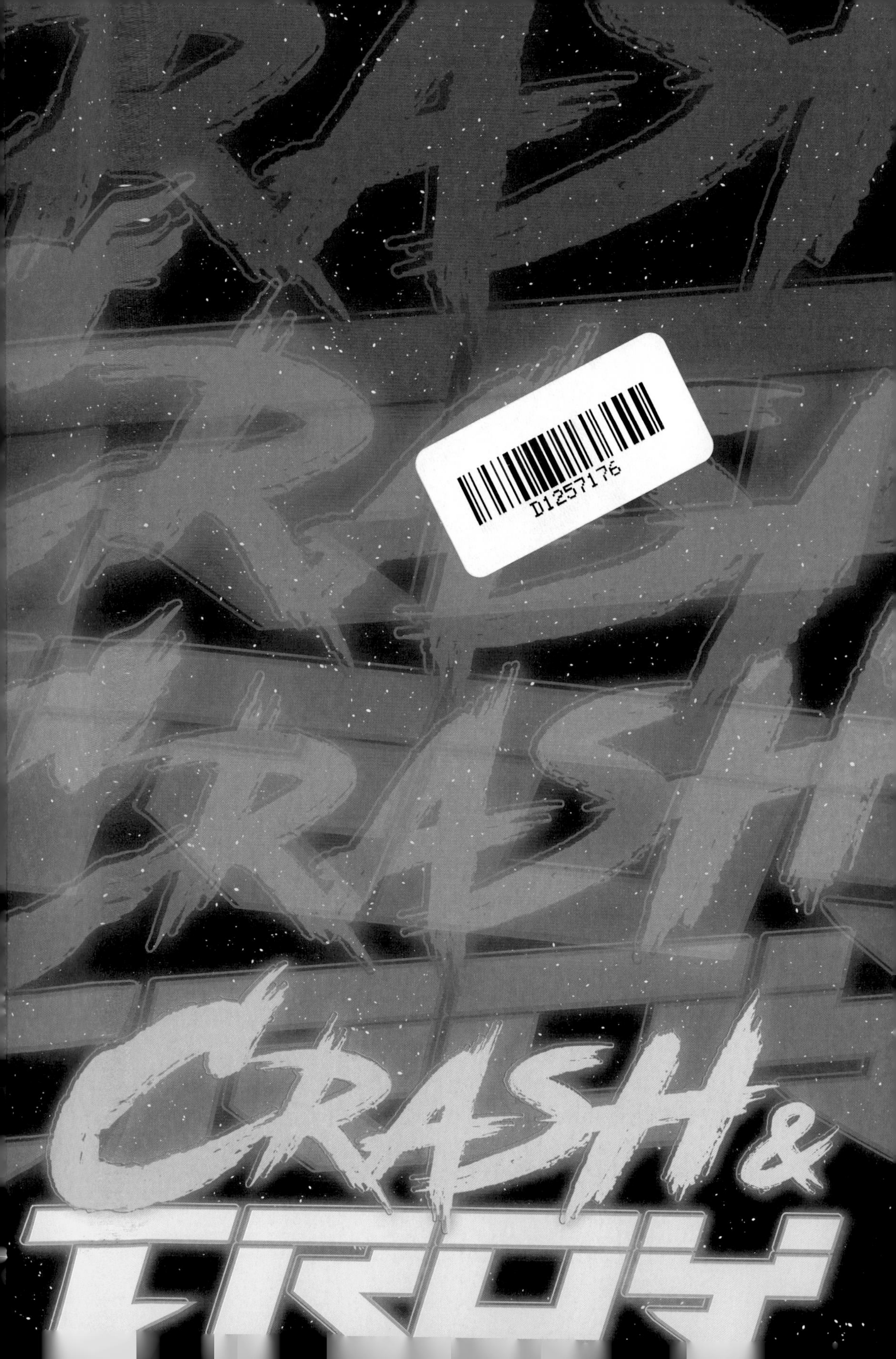
CRASH &

When the galaxy
needed HEROES,
it got stuck with...

CRASH & TROY

created by

WRITER – Jarred Luján
ARTIST – Kyler Clodfelter
COLORIST – Bruno Furlani
LETTERER – Buddy Beaudoin
EDITOR – Hernán Guarderas

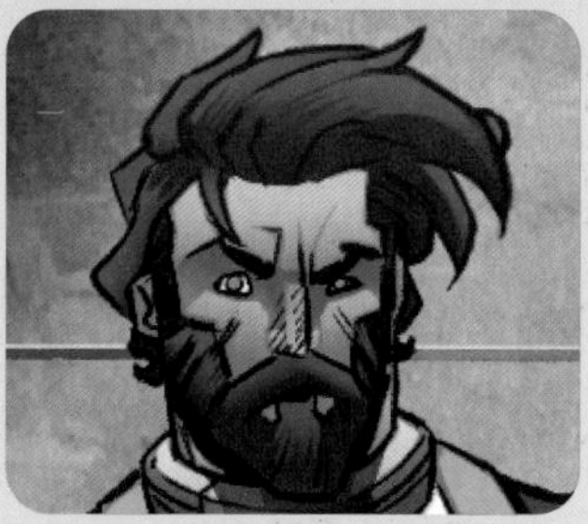

Rex "Crash" Ballard -

A human mutant who can turn his exterior form to Rose Gold, yielding impenetrable skin and gaining superhuman strength. After escaping mutant quarantine on Earth two decades ago, Crash now makes his living as a mercenary for hire. He should be considered extremely dangerous... and rude.

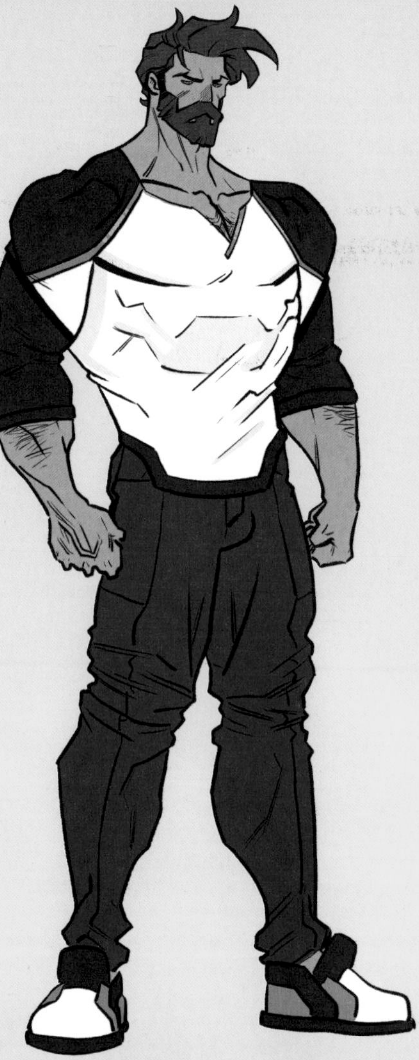

ISBN: 978-1-949518-23-8 Printed in Canada

AWBW.com

Cover Illustration by
*Kyler Clodfelter &
Bruno Furlani*

Logo by
Lettersquids

Book Design by
Pete Carlsson

Tyler Chin-Tanner
Co-Publisher

Wendy Chin-Tanner
Co-Publisher

Pete Carlsson
Production Designer

Diana Kou
Director of Marketing

Jesse Post
Book Publicist

Hazel Newlevant
Social Media Coordinator

Megan Marsden
Sales Development Manager

Troy 3.0 -

Formerly human, Troy's consciousness now exists as a software program that can be uploaded into all kinds of technology. He's rumored to have robotic husks stashed all across the galaxy. As a long-time fan of historical icon Meryl Streep, Troy isn't just a member of the fan club, he's also the president!

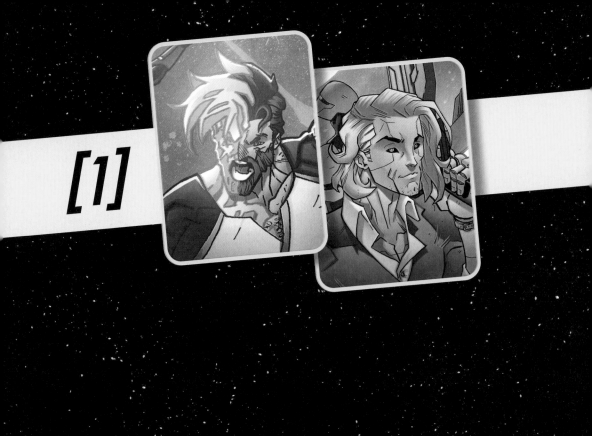

[1]

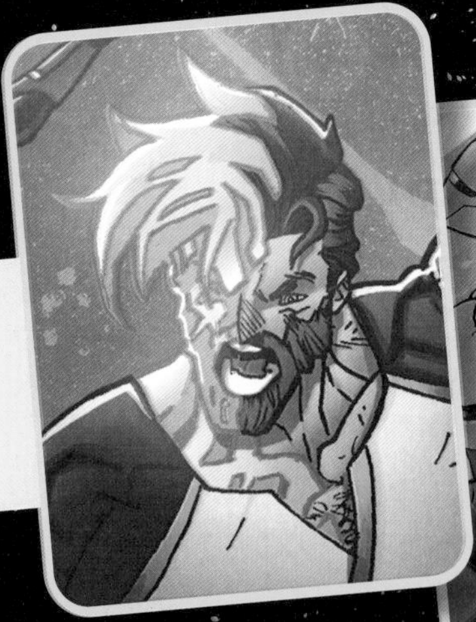

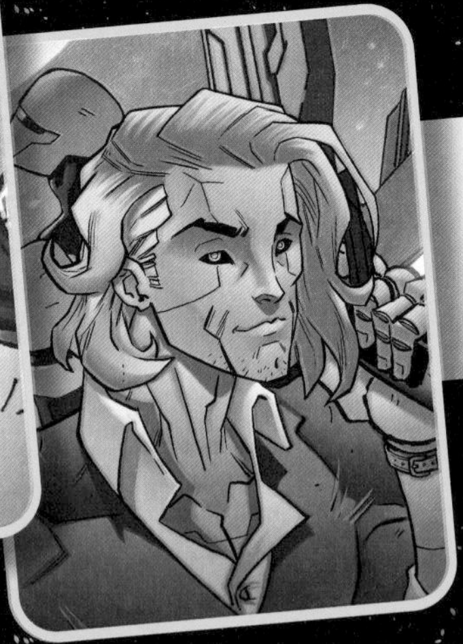

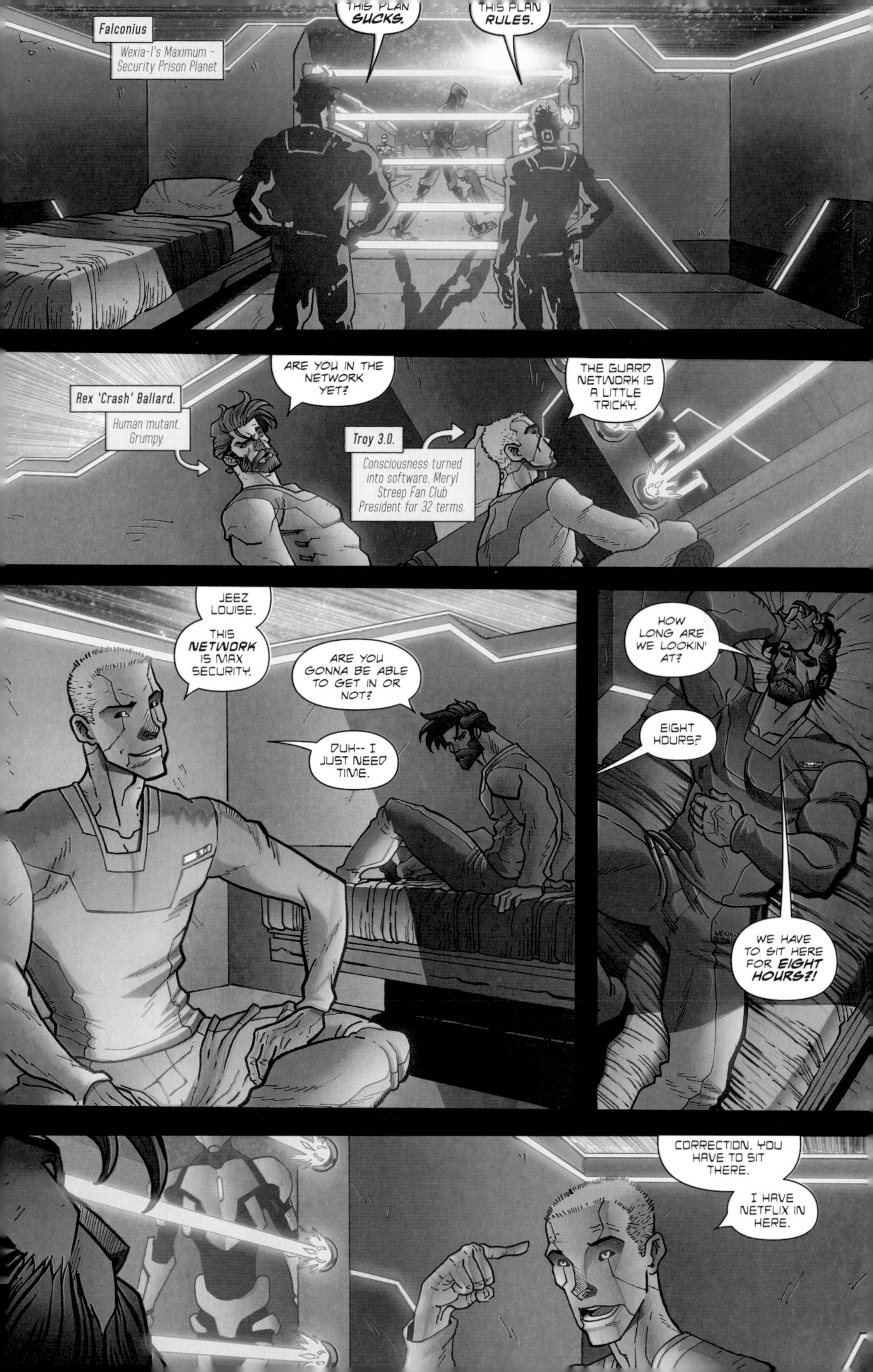
Falconius
Wexia-1's Maximum-Security Prison Planet
THIS PLAN SUCKS.
THIS PLAN RULES.
ARE YOU IN THE NETWORK YET?
THE GUARD NETWORK IS A LITTLE TRICKY.
Rex 'Crash' Ballard.
Human mutant. Grumpy.
Troy 3.0.
Consciousness turned into software. Meryl Streep Fan Club President for 32 terms.
JEEZ LOUISE.
THIS NETWORK IS MAX SECURITY.
ARE YOU GONNA BE ABLE TO GET IN OR NOT?
DUH-- I JUST NEED TIME.
HOW LONG ARE WE LOOKIN' AT?
EIGHT HOURS?
WE HAVE TO SIT HERE FOR EIGHT HOURS?!
CORRECTION. YOU HAVE TO SIT THERE.
I HAVE NETFLIX IN HERE.

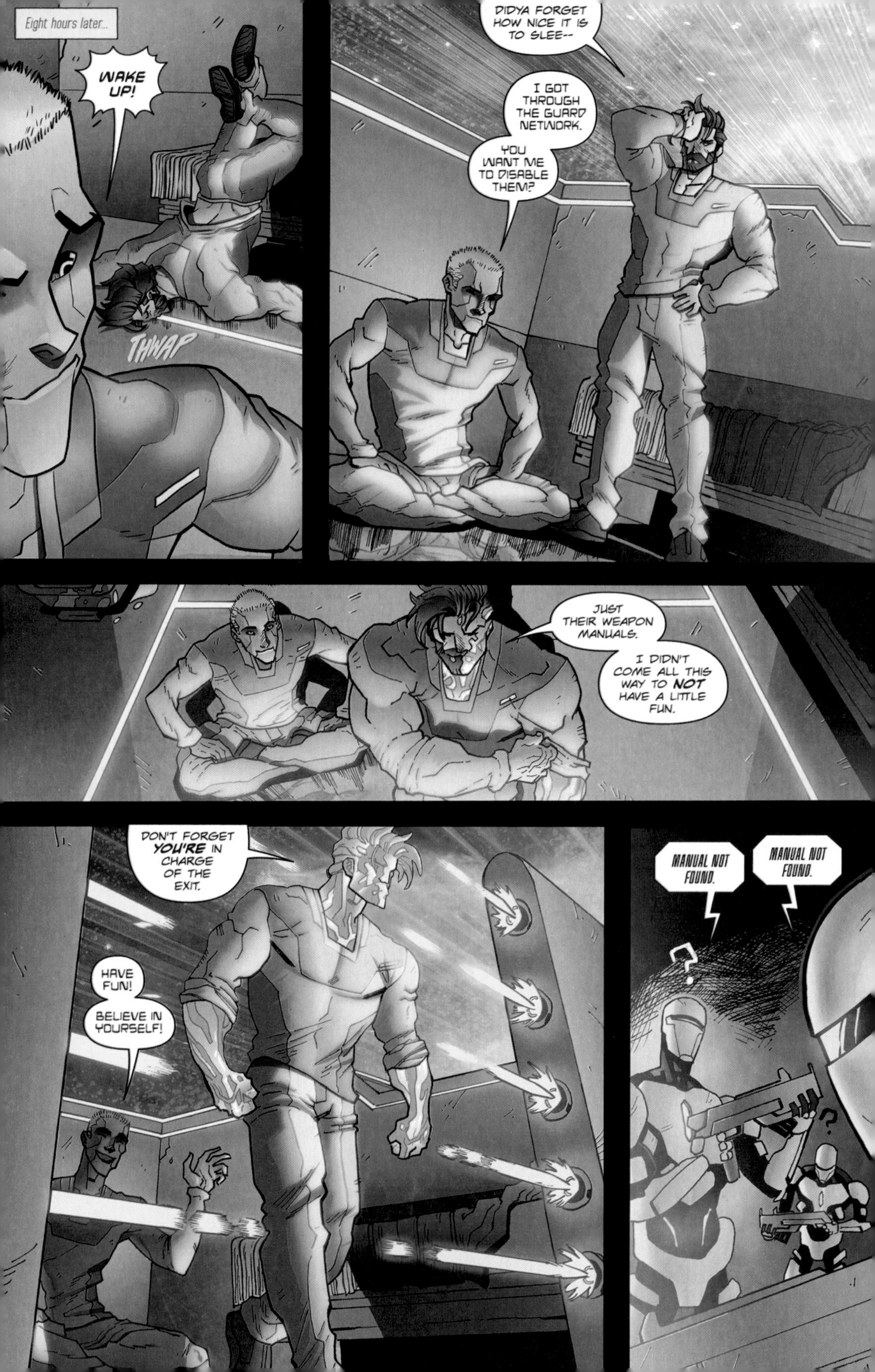
Eight hours later...
WAKE UP!
THWAP
DIDYA FORGET HOW NICE IT IS TO SLEE--
I GOT THROUGH THE GUARD NETWORK.
YOU WANT ME TO DISABLE THEM?
JUST THEIR WEAPON MANUALS.
I DIDN'T COME ALL THIS WAY TO NOT HAVE A LITTLE FUN.
DON'T FORGET YOU'RE IN CHARGE OF THE EXIT.
HAVE FUN!
BELIEVE IN YOURSELF!
MANUAL NOT FOUND.
MANUAL NOT FOUND.

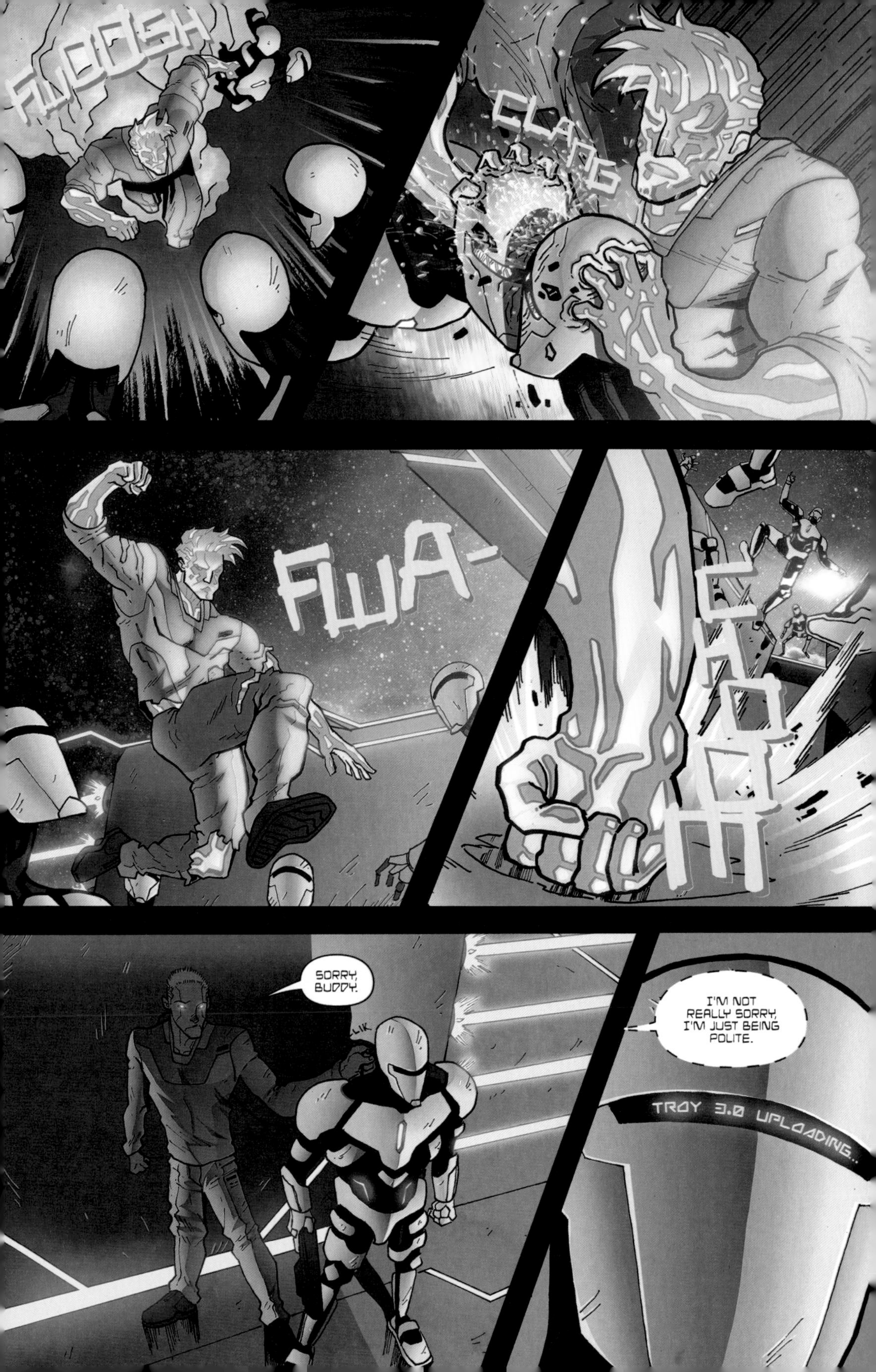
FWOOSH
CLANG
FWA-
CHOOM
SORRY, BUDDY.
LIK
I'M NOT REALLY SORRY, I'M JUST BEING POLITE.
TROY 3.0 UPLOADING...

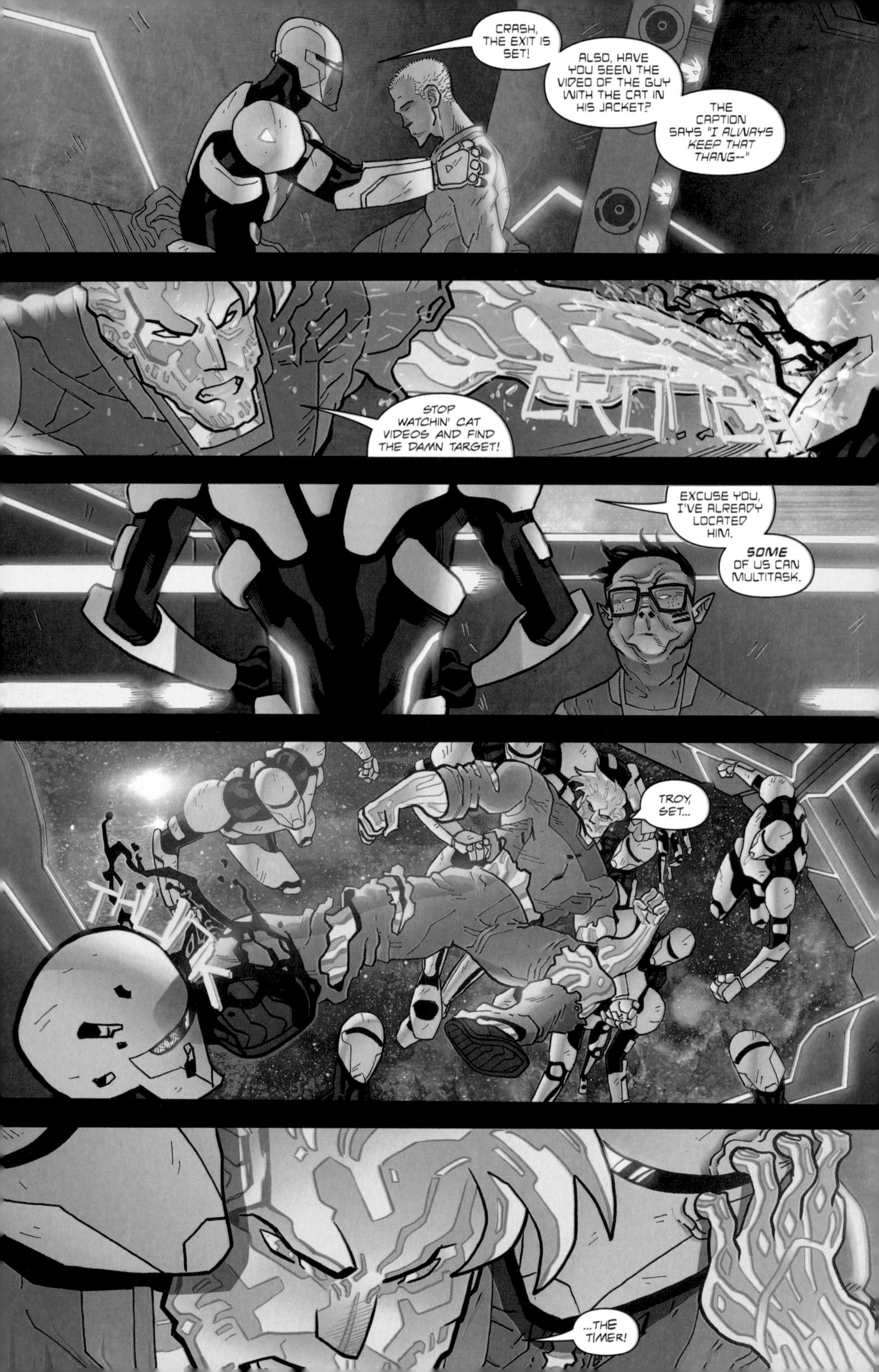
CRASH, THE EXIT IS SET!
ALSO, HAVE YOU SEEN THE VIDEO OF THE GUY WITH THE CAT IN HIS JACKET?
THE CAPTION SAYS "I ALWAYS KEEP THAT THANG--"
CRONCH
STOP WATCHIN' CAT VIDEOS AND FIND THE DAMN TARGET!
EXCUSE YOU, I'VE ALREADY LOCATED HIM.
SOME OF US CAN MULTITASK.
TROY, SET...
THUK
...THE TIMER!

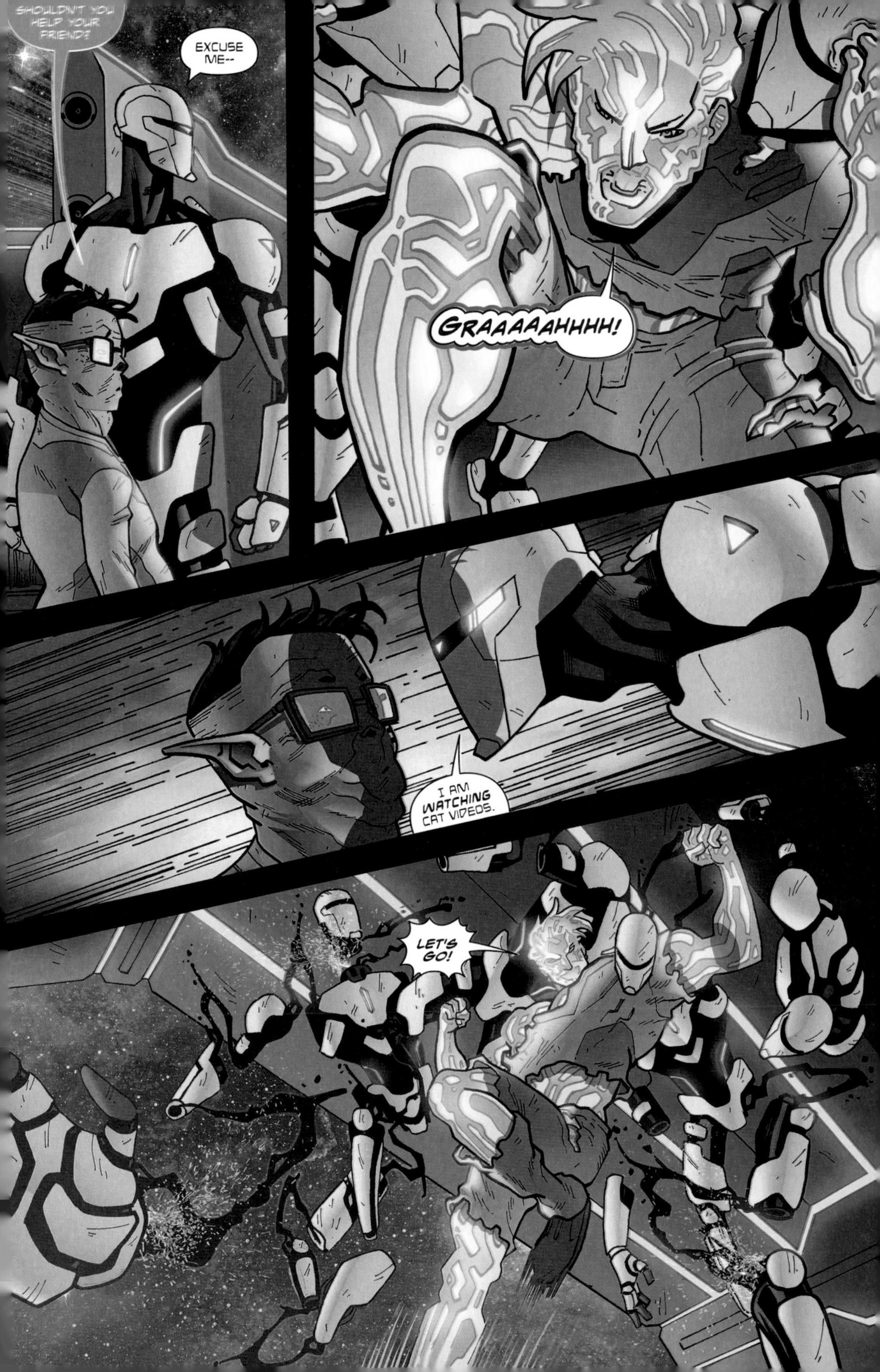
SHOULDN'T YOU HELP YOUR FRIEND?
EXCUSE ME--
GRAAAAAHHHH!
I AM WATCHING CAT VIDEOS.
LET'S GO!

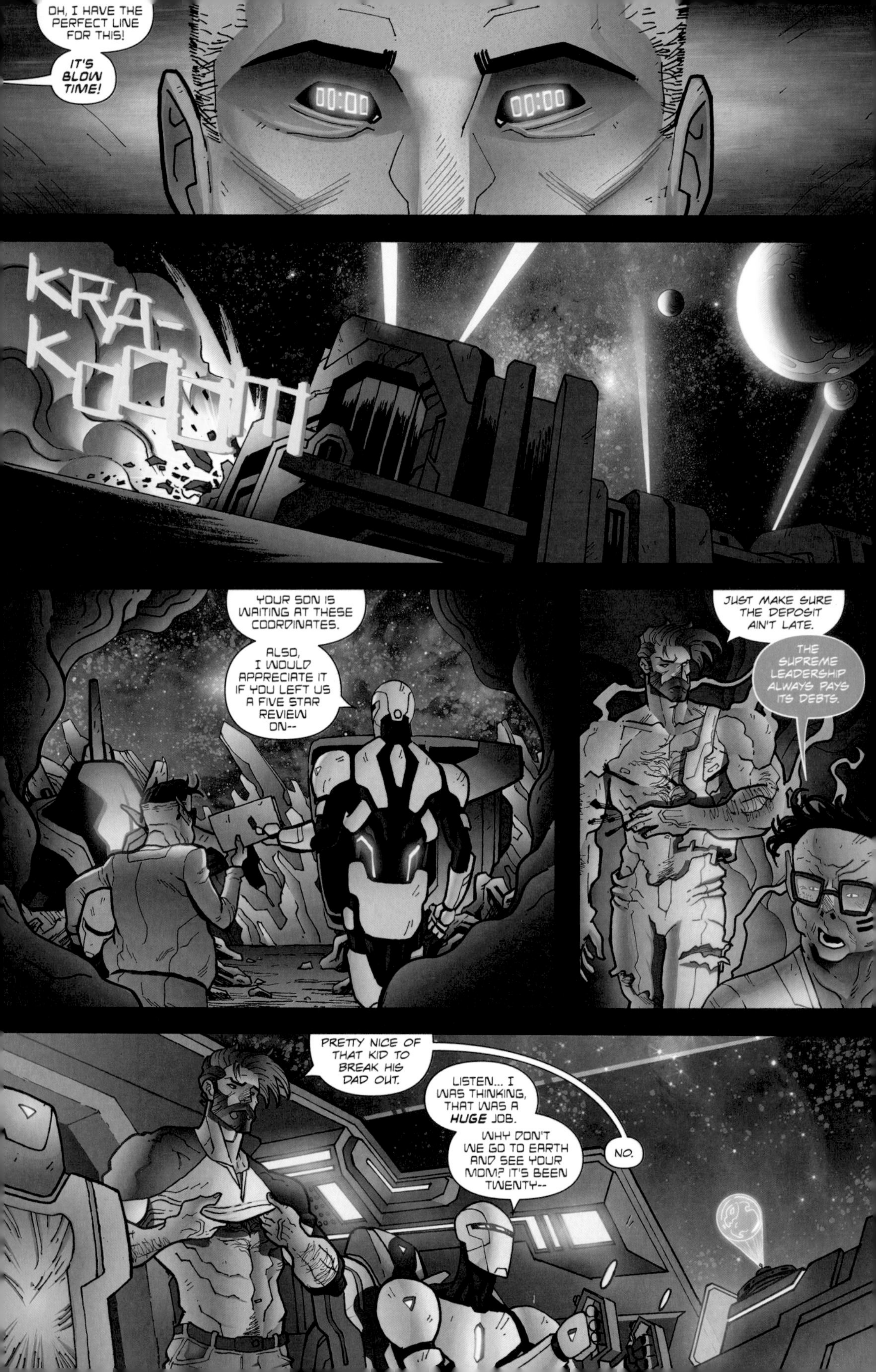
OH, I HAVE THE PERFECT LINE FOR THIS!
IT'S BLOW TIME!
KRA-KOOOM
YOUR SON IS WAITING AT THESE COORDINATES.
ALSO, I WOULD APPRECIATE IT IF YOU LEFT US A FIVE STAR REVIEW ON--
JUST MAKE SURE THE DEPOSIT AIN'T LATE.
THE SUPREME LEADERSHIP ALWAYS PAYS ITS DEBTS.
PRETTY NICE OF THAT KID TO BREAK HIS DAD OUT.
LISTEN... I WAS THINKING, THAT WAS A HUGE JOB.
WHY DON'T WE GO TO EARTH AND SEE YOUR MOM? IT'S BEEN TWENTY--
NO.

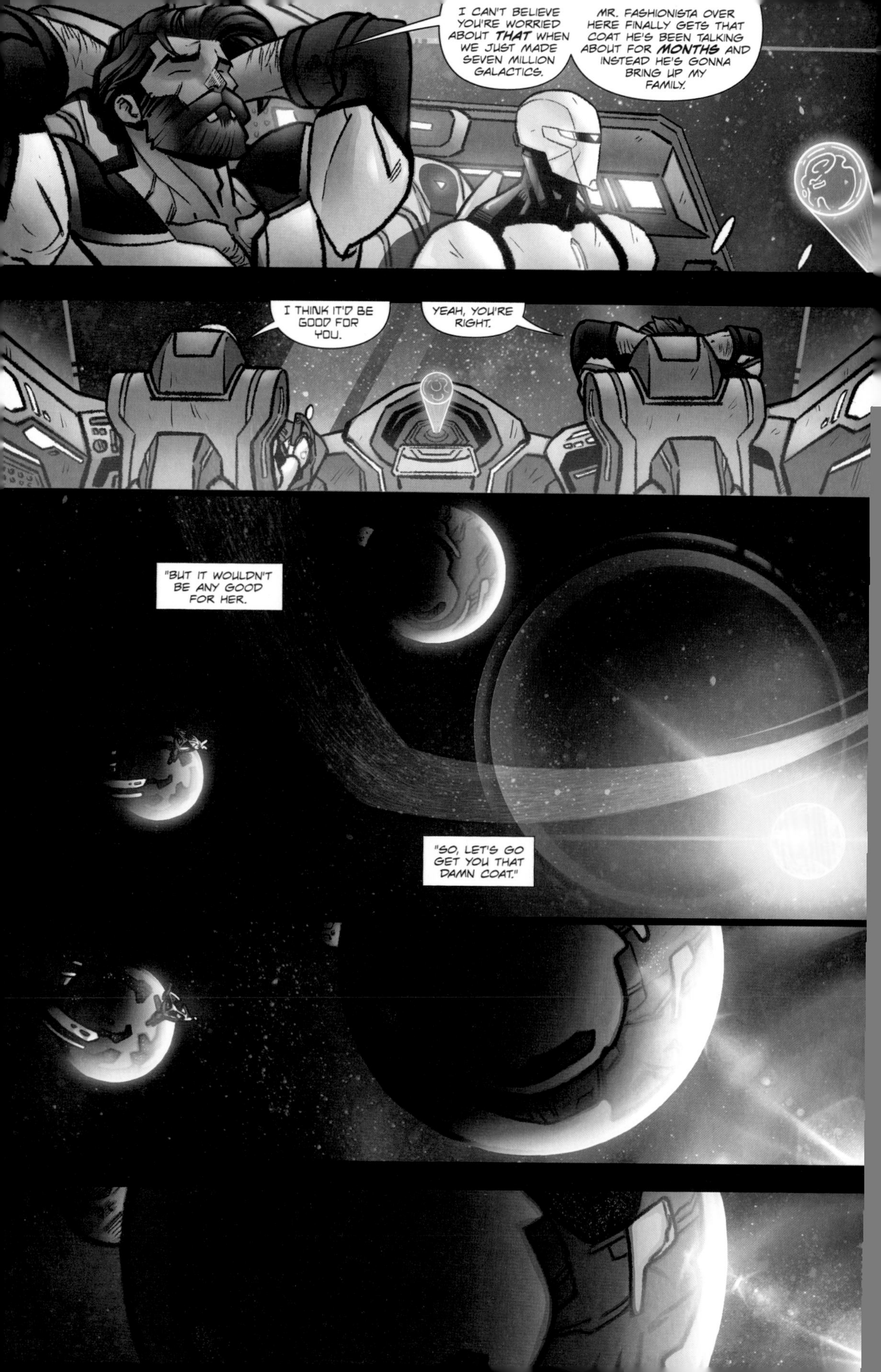
I CAN'T BELIEVE YOU'RE WORRIED ABOUT THAT WHEN WE JUST MADE SEVEN MILLION GALACTICS.
MR. FASHIONISTA OVER HERE FINALLY GETS THAT COAT HE'S BEEN TALKING ABOUT FOR MONTHS AND INSTEAD HE'S GONNA BRING UP MY FAMILY.
I THINK IT'D BE GOOD FOR YOU.
YEAH, YOU'RE RIGHT.
"BUT IT WOULDN'T BE ANY GOOD FOR HER.
"SO, LET'S GO GET YOU THAT DAMN COAT."

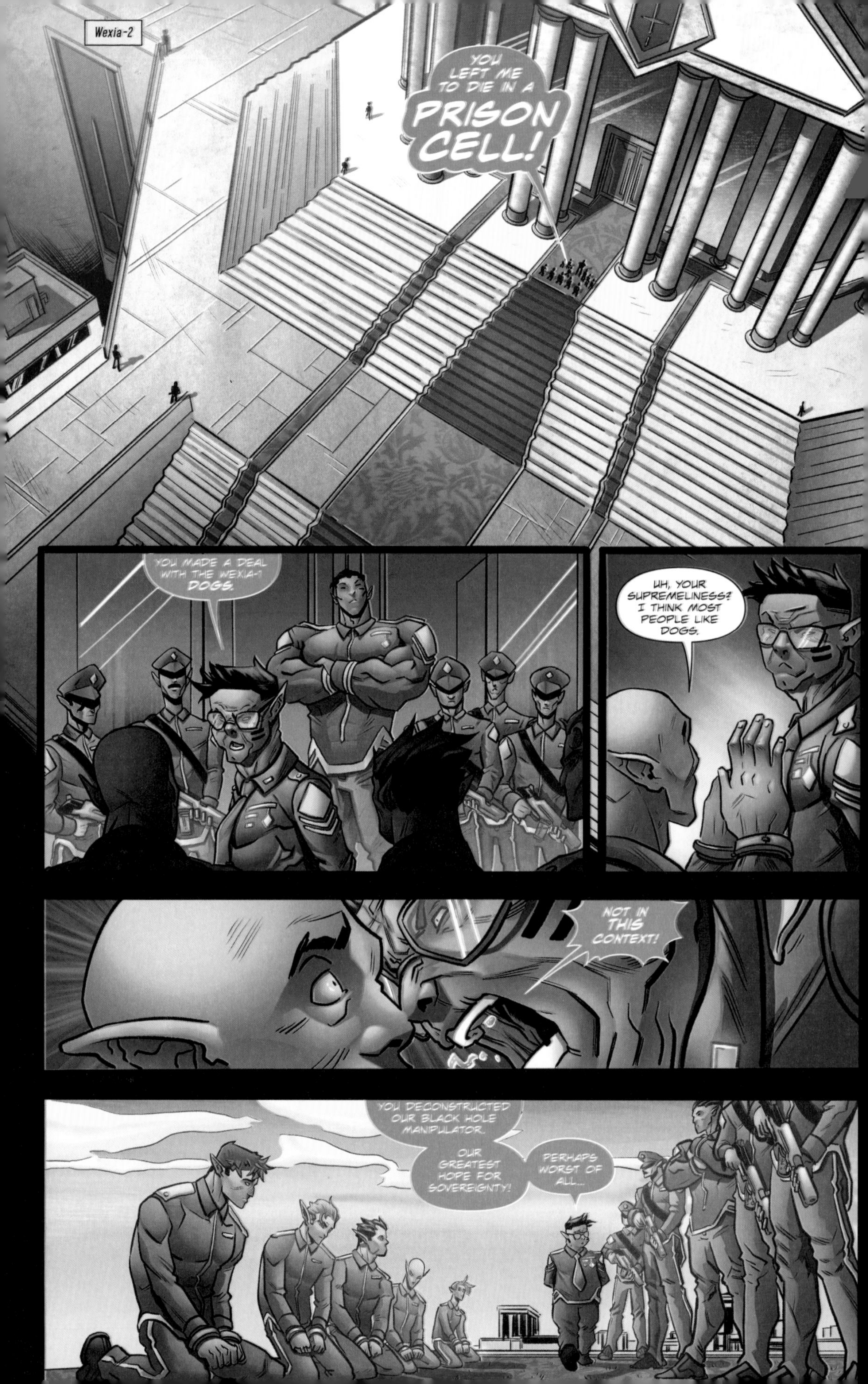
Wexia-2
YOU LEFT ME TO DIE IN A PRISON CELL!
YOU MADE A DEAL WITH THE WEXIA-1 DOGS.
UH, YOUR SUPREMELINESS? I THINK MOST PEOPLE LIKE DOGS.
NOT IN THIS CONTEXT!
YOU DECONSTRUCTED OUR BLACK HOLE MANIPULATOR.
OUR GREATEST HOPE FOR SOVEREIGNTY!
PERHAPS WORST OF ALL...

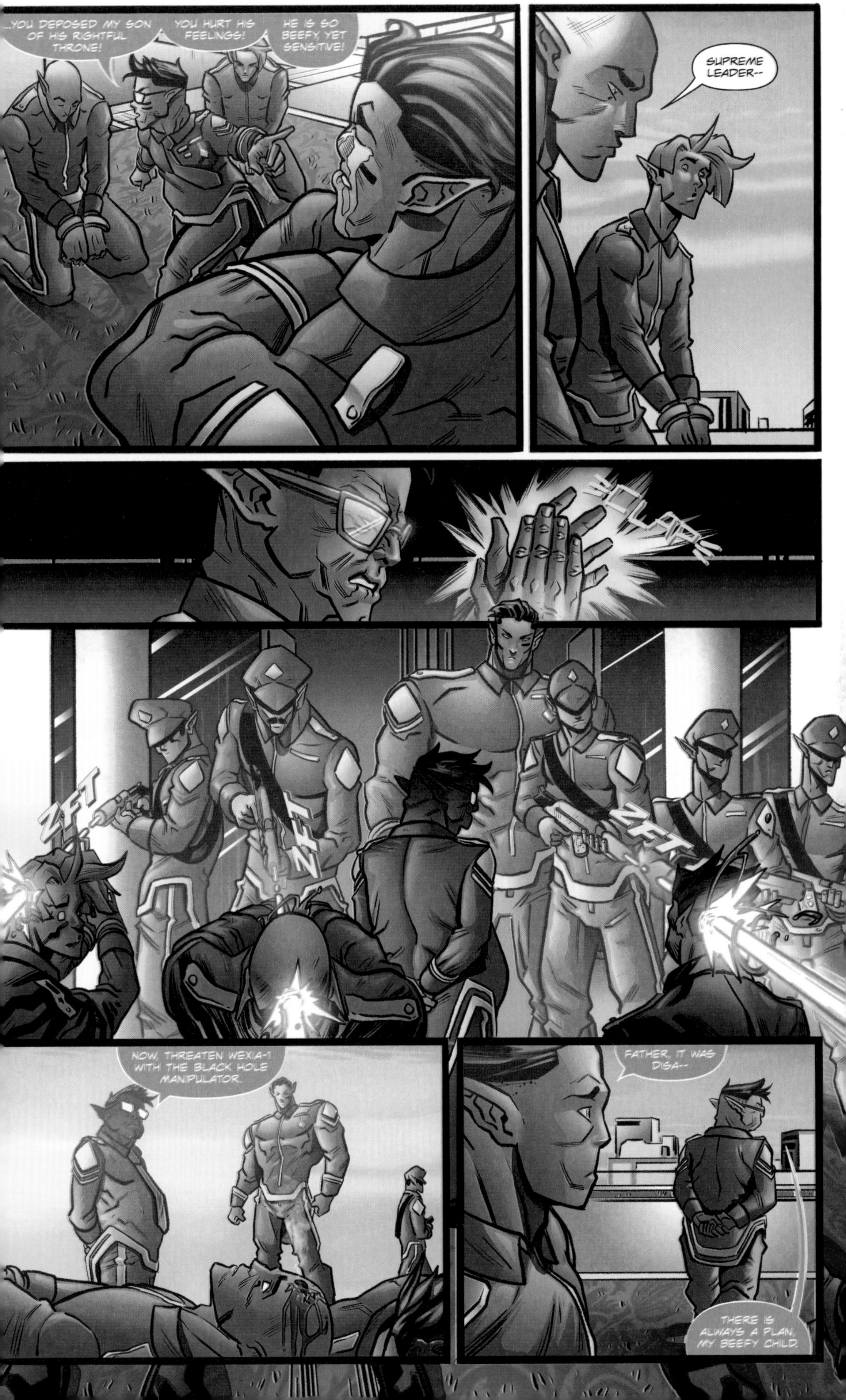
...YOU DEPOSED MY SON OF HIS RIGHTFUL THRONE!
YOU HURT HIS FEELINGS!
HE IS SO BEEFY, YET SENSITIVE!
SUPREME LEADER--
SCLAP
ZFT
ZFT
ZFT
NOW, THREATEN WEXIA-1 WITH THE BLACK HOLE MANIPULATOR.
FATHER, IT WAS DISA--
THERE IS ALWAYS A PLAN, MY BEEFY CHILD.

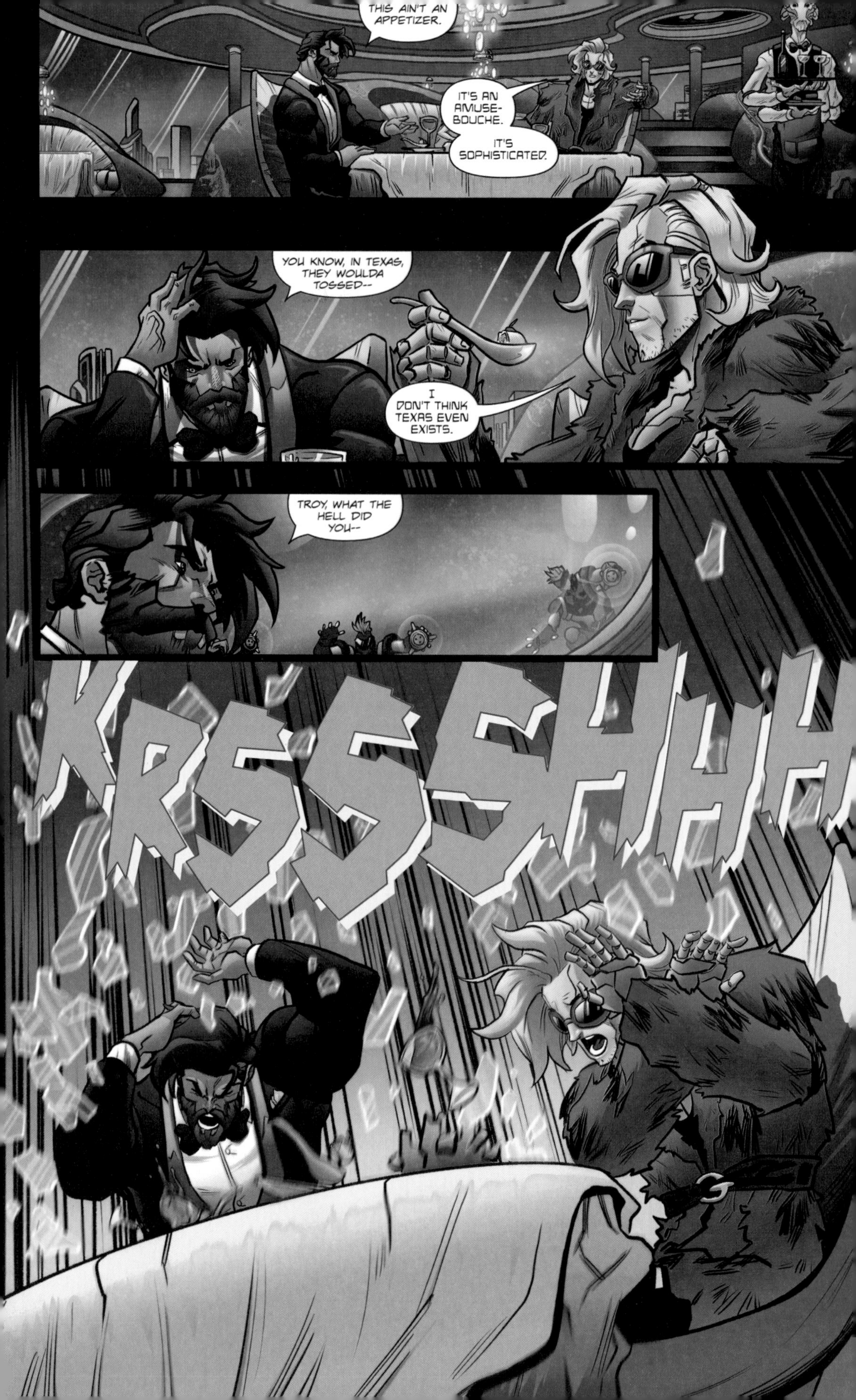
THIS AIN'T AN APPETIZER.
IT'S AN AMUSE-BOUCHE.
IT'S SOPHISTICATED.
YOU KNOW, IN TEXAS, THEY WOULDA TOSSED--
I DON'T THINK TEXAS EVEN EXISTS.
TROY, WHAT THE HELL DID YOU--
KRSS-SHHH

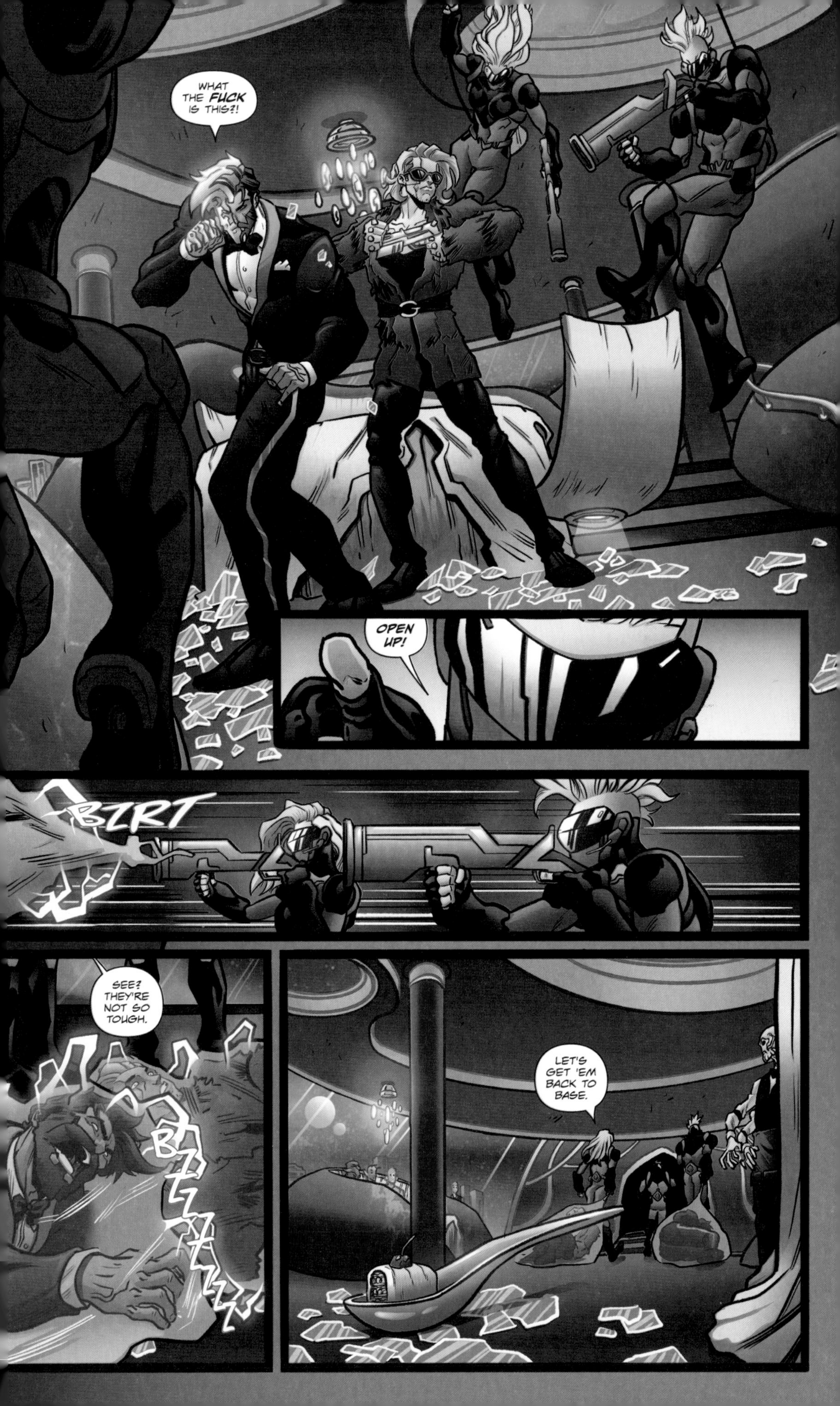
WHAT THE FUCK IS THIS?!
OPEN UP!
BZRT
SEE? THEY'RE NOT SO TOUGH.
LET'S GET 'EM BACK TO BASE.

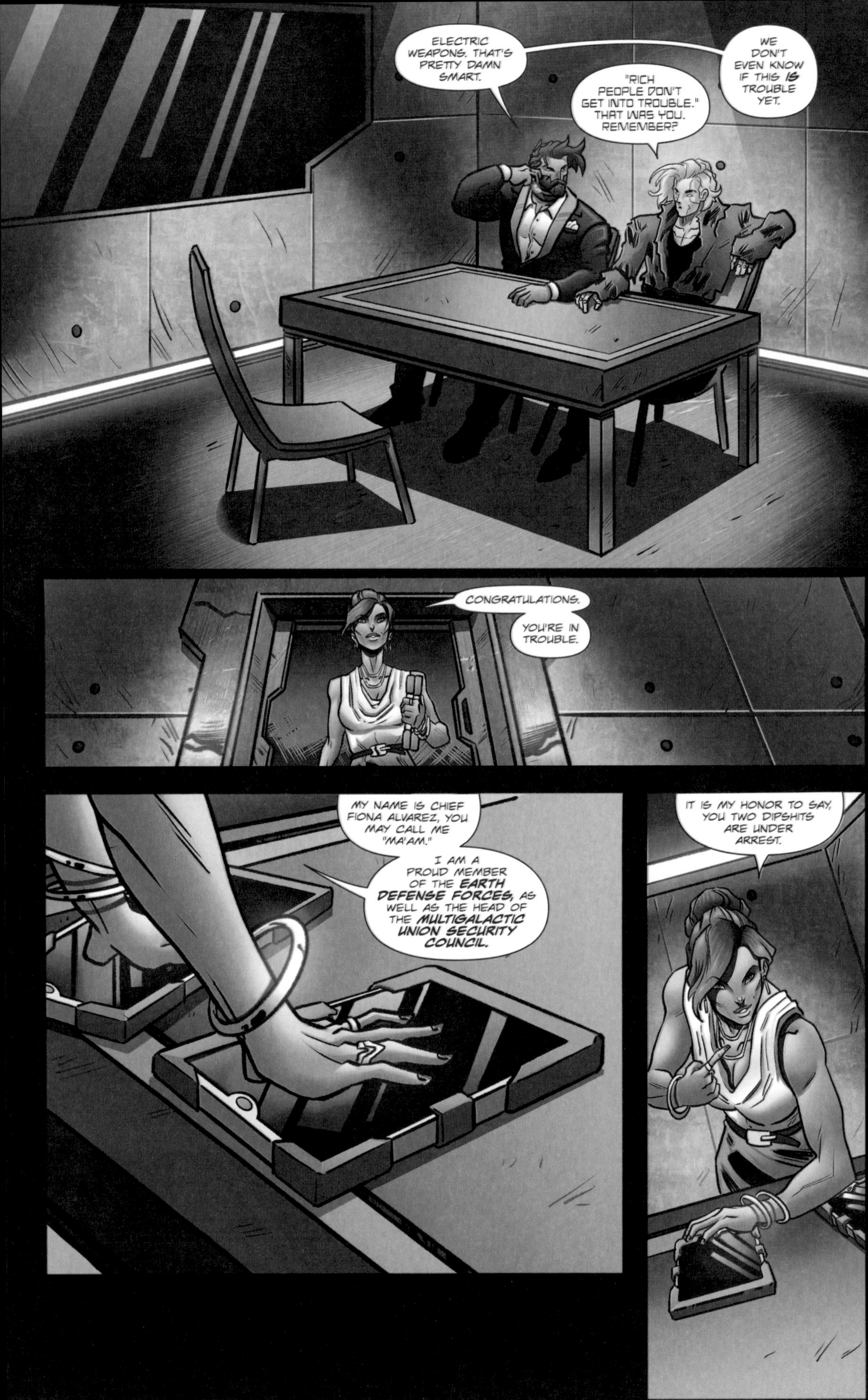
ELECTRIC WEAPONS. THAT'S PRETTY DAMN SMART.
"RICH PEOPLE DON'T GET INTO TROUBLE." THAT WAS YOU. REMEMBER?
WE DON'T EVEN KNOW IF THIS ***IS*** TROUBLE YET.
CONGRATULATIONS.
YOU'RE IN TROUBLE.
MY NAME IS CHIEF FIONA ALVAREZ, YOU MAY CALL ME "MA'AM."
I AM A PROUD MEMBER OF THE ***EARTH DEFENSE FORCES,*** AS WELL AS THE HEAD OF THE ***MULTIGALACTIC UNION SECURITY COUNCIL.***
IT IS MY HONOR TO SAY, YOU TWO DIPSHITS ARE UNDER ARREST.

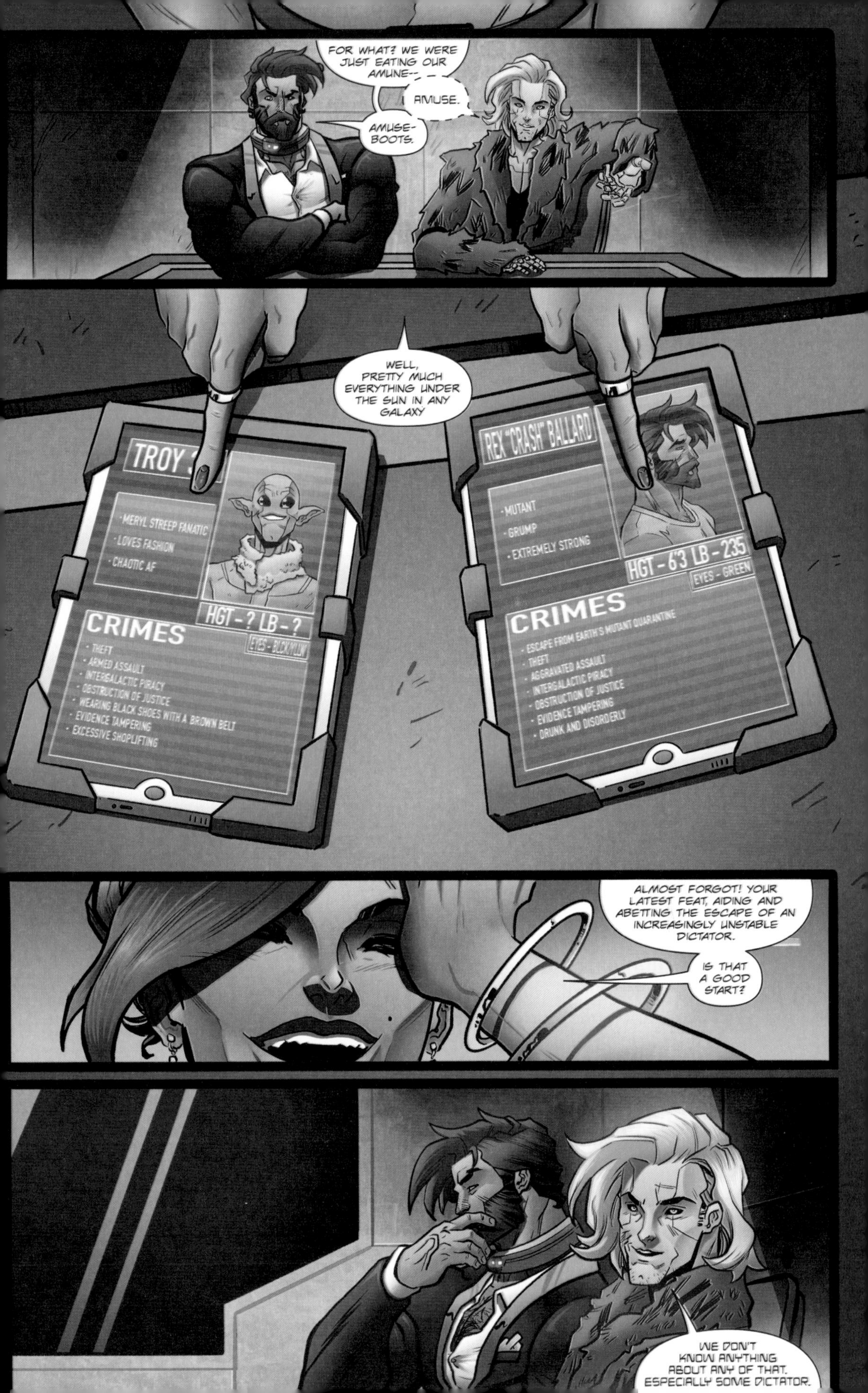
FOR WHAT? WE WERE JUST EATING OUR AMUNE--
AMUSE.
AMUSE-BOOTS.
WELL, PRETTY MUCH EVERYTHING UNDER THE SUN IN ANY GALAXY
TROY
MERYL STREEP FANATIC
LOVES FASHION
CHAOTIC AF
HGT - ? LB - ?
CRIMES
THEFT
ARMED ASSAULT
INTERGALACTIC PIRACY
OBSTRUCTION OF JUSTICE
WEARING BLACK SHOES WITH A BROWN BELT
EVIDENCE TAMPERING
EXCESSIVE SHOPLIFTING
REX "CRASH" BALLARD
MUTANT
GRUMP
EXTREMELY STRONG
HGT - 6'3 LB - 235
EYES - GREEN
CRIMES
ESCAPE FROM EARTH'S MUTANT QUARANTINE
THEFT
AGGRAVATED ASSAULT
INTERGALACTIC PIRACY
OBSTRUCTION OF JUSTICE
EVIDENCE TAMPERING
DRUNK AND DISORDERLY
ALMOST FORGOT! YOUR LATEST FEAT, AIDING AND ABETTING THE ESCAPE OF AN INCREASINGLY UNSTABLE DICTATOR.
IS THAT A GOOD START?
WE DON'T KNOW ANYTHING ABOUT ANY OF THAT. ESPECIALLY SOME DICTATOR.

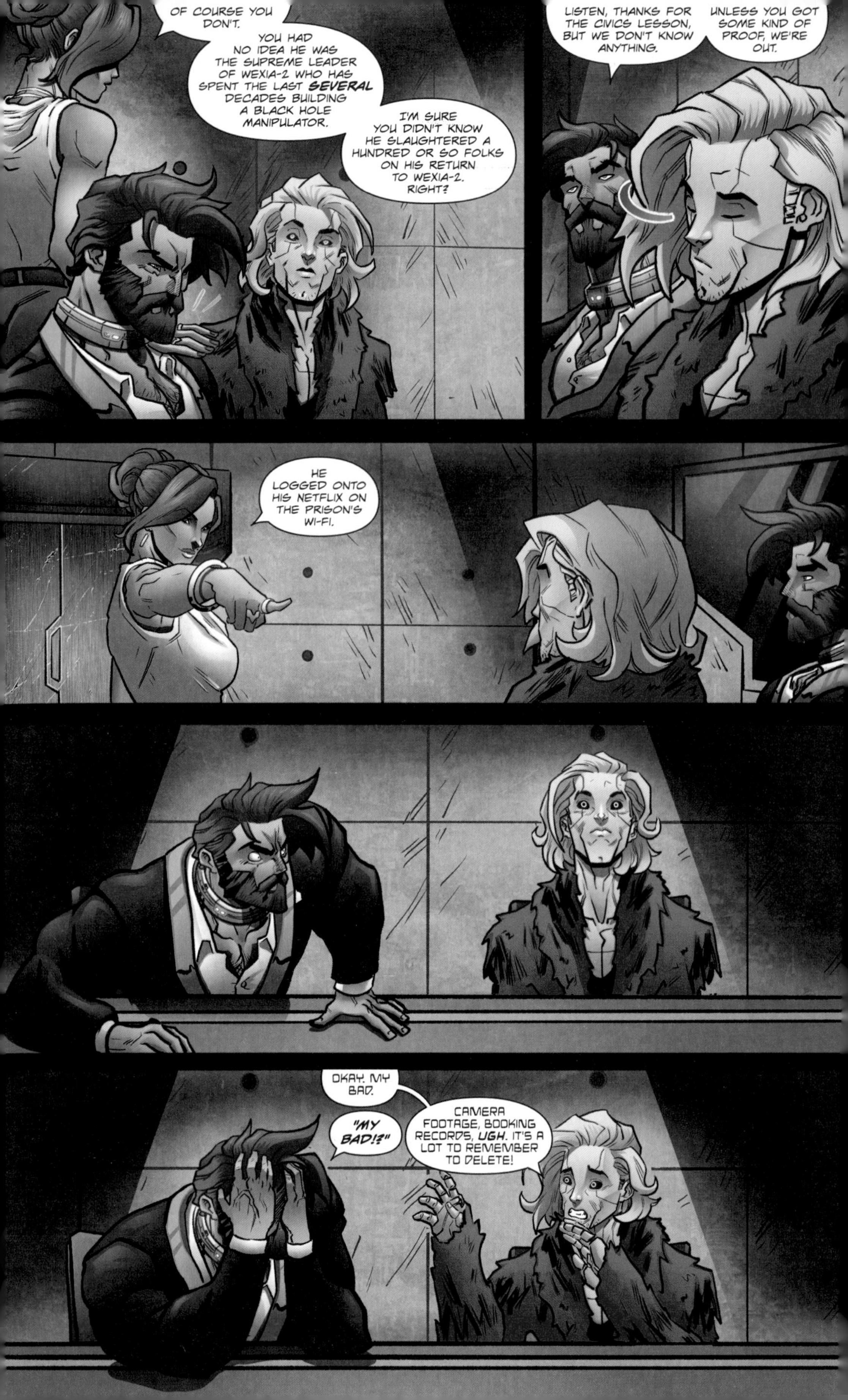
OF COURSE YOU DON'T.
YOU HAD NO IDEA HE WAS THE SUPREME LEADER OF WEXIA-2 WHO HAS SPENT THE LAST SEVERAL DECADES BUILDING A BLACK HOLE MANIPULATOR.
I'M SURE YOU DIDN'T KNOW HE SLAUGHTERED A HUNDRED OR SO FOLKS ON HIS RETURN TO WEXIA-2. RIGHT?
LISTEN, THANKS FOR THE CIVICS LESSON, BUT WE DON'T KNOW ANYTHING.
UNLESS YOU GOT SOME KIND OF PROOF, WE'RE OUT.
HE LOGGED ONTO HIS NETFLIX ON THE PRISON'S WI-FI.
OKAY. MY BAD.
"MY BAD!?"
CAMERA FOOTAGE, BOOKING RECORDS, UGH. IT'S A LOT TO REMEMBER TO DELETE!

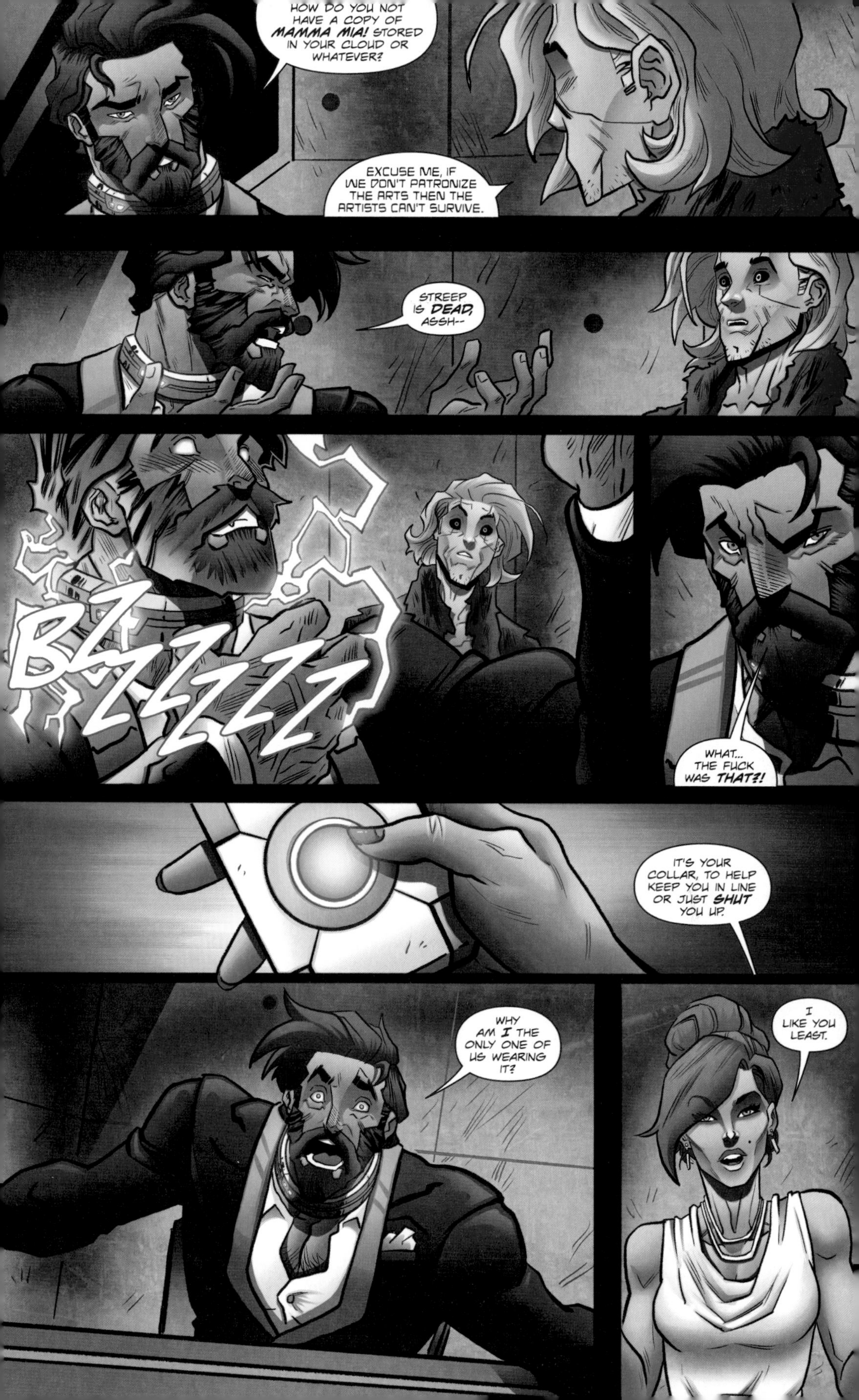
HOW DO YOU NOT HAVE A COPY OF MAMMA MIA! STORED IN YOUR CLOUD OR WHATEVER?
EXCUSE ME, IF WE DON'T PATRONIZE THE ARTS THEN THE ARTISTS CAN'T SURVIVE.
STREEP IS DEAD, ASSH--
BZZZZZZZ
WHAT... THE FUCK WAS THAT?!
IT'S YOUR COLLAR, TO HELP KEEP YOU IN LINE OR JUST SHUT YOU UP.
WHY AM I THE ONLY ONE OF US WEARING IT?
I LIKE YOU LEAST.

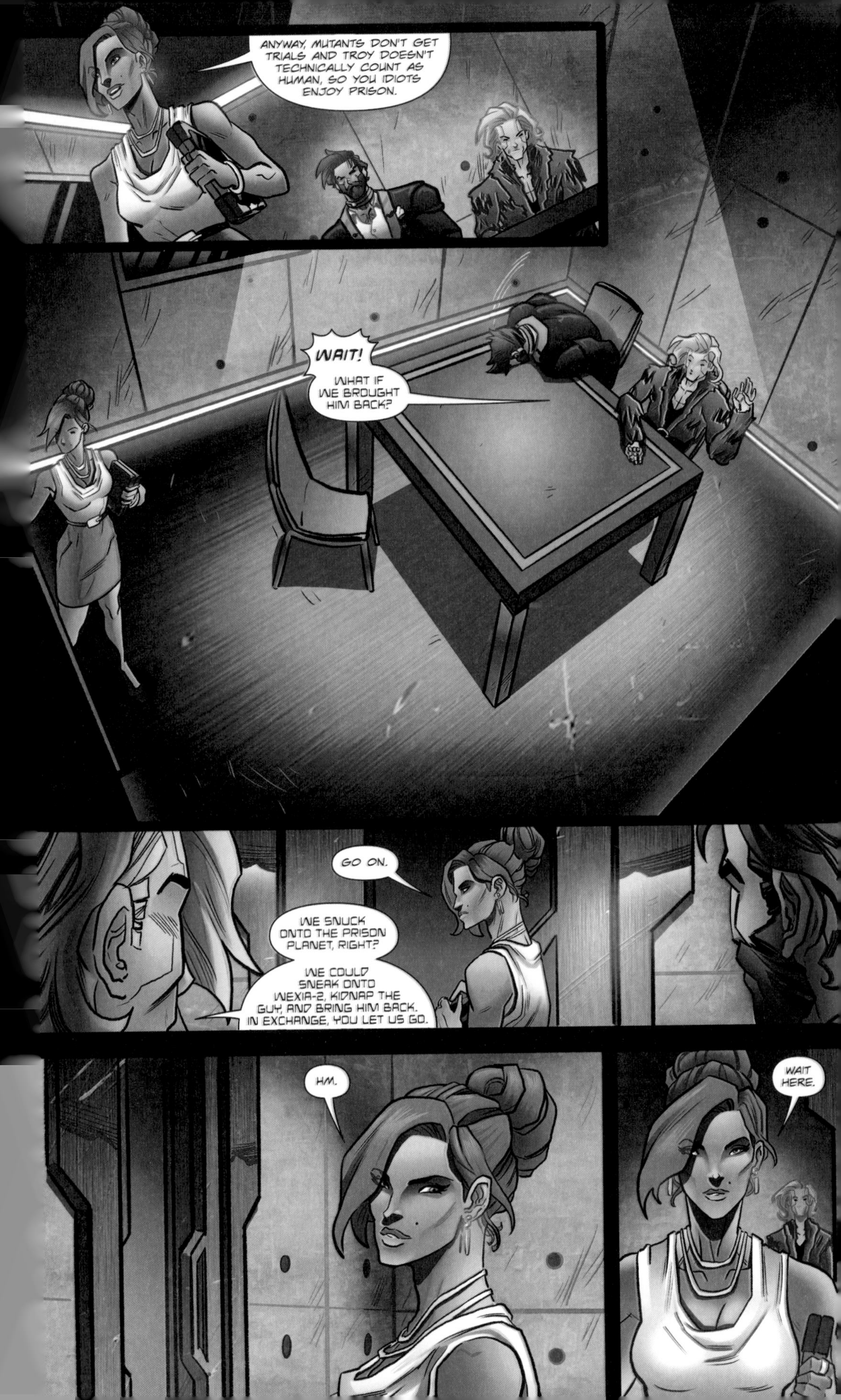
ANYWAY, MUTANTS DON'T GET TRIALS AND TROY DOESN'T TECHNICALLY COUNT AS HUMAN, SO YOU IDIOTS ENJOY PRISON.
WAIT!
WHAT IF WE BROUGHT HIM BACK?
GO ON.
WE SNUCK ONTO THE PRISON PLANET, RIGHT?
WE COULD SNEAK ONTO WEXIA-2, KIDNAP THE GUY, AND BRING HIM BACK. IN EXCHANGE, YOU LET US GO.
HM.
WAIT HERE.

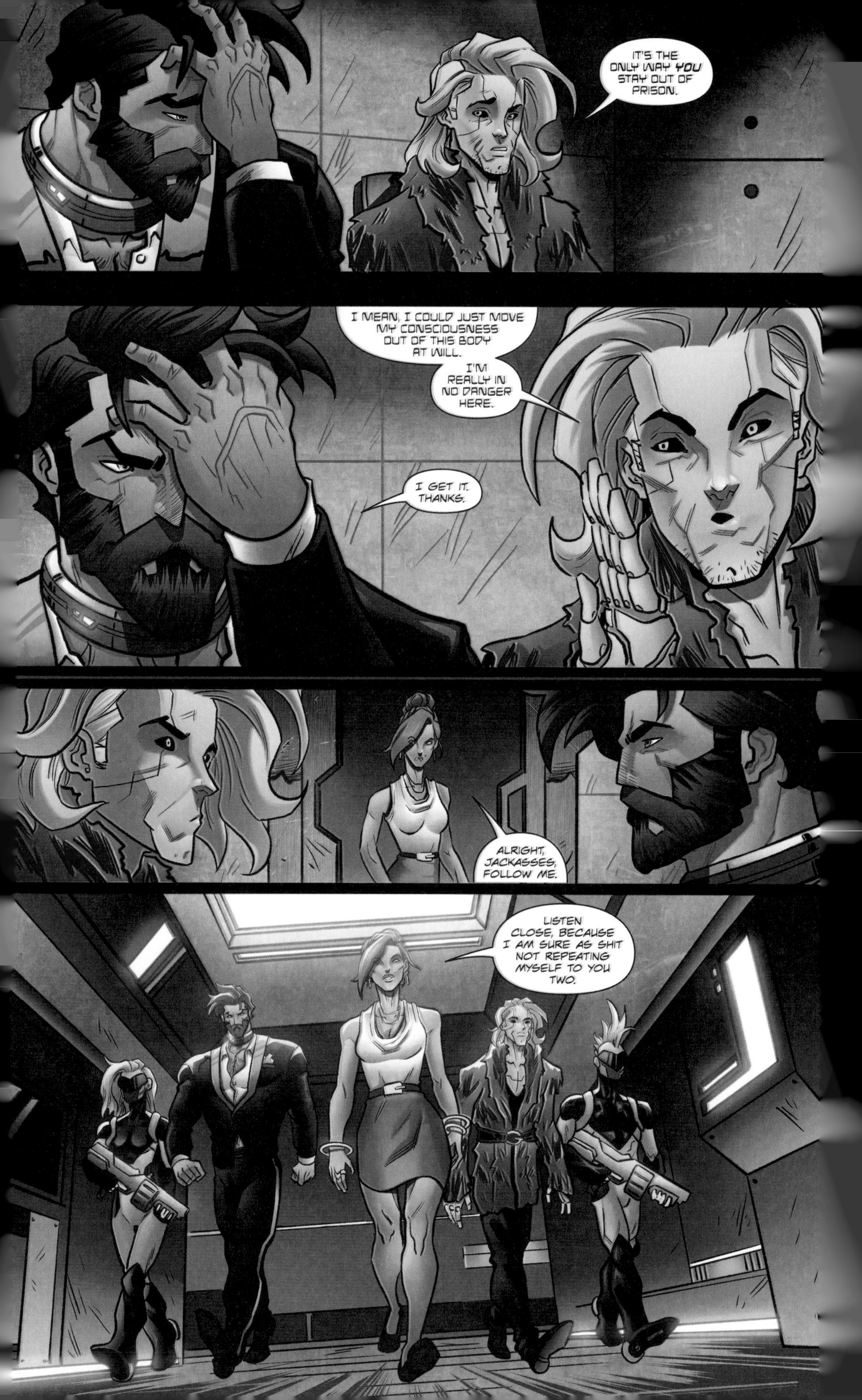
IT'S THE ONLY WAY YOU STAY OUT OF PRISON.
I MEAN, I COULD JUST MOVE MY CONSCIOUSNESS OUT OF THIS BODY AT WILL.
I'M REALLY IN NO DANGER HERE.
I GET IT. THANKS.
ALRIGHT, JACKASSES, FOLLOW ME.
LISTEN CLOSE, BECAUSE I AM SURE AS SHIT NOT REPEATING MYSELF TO YOU TWO.

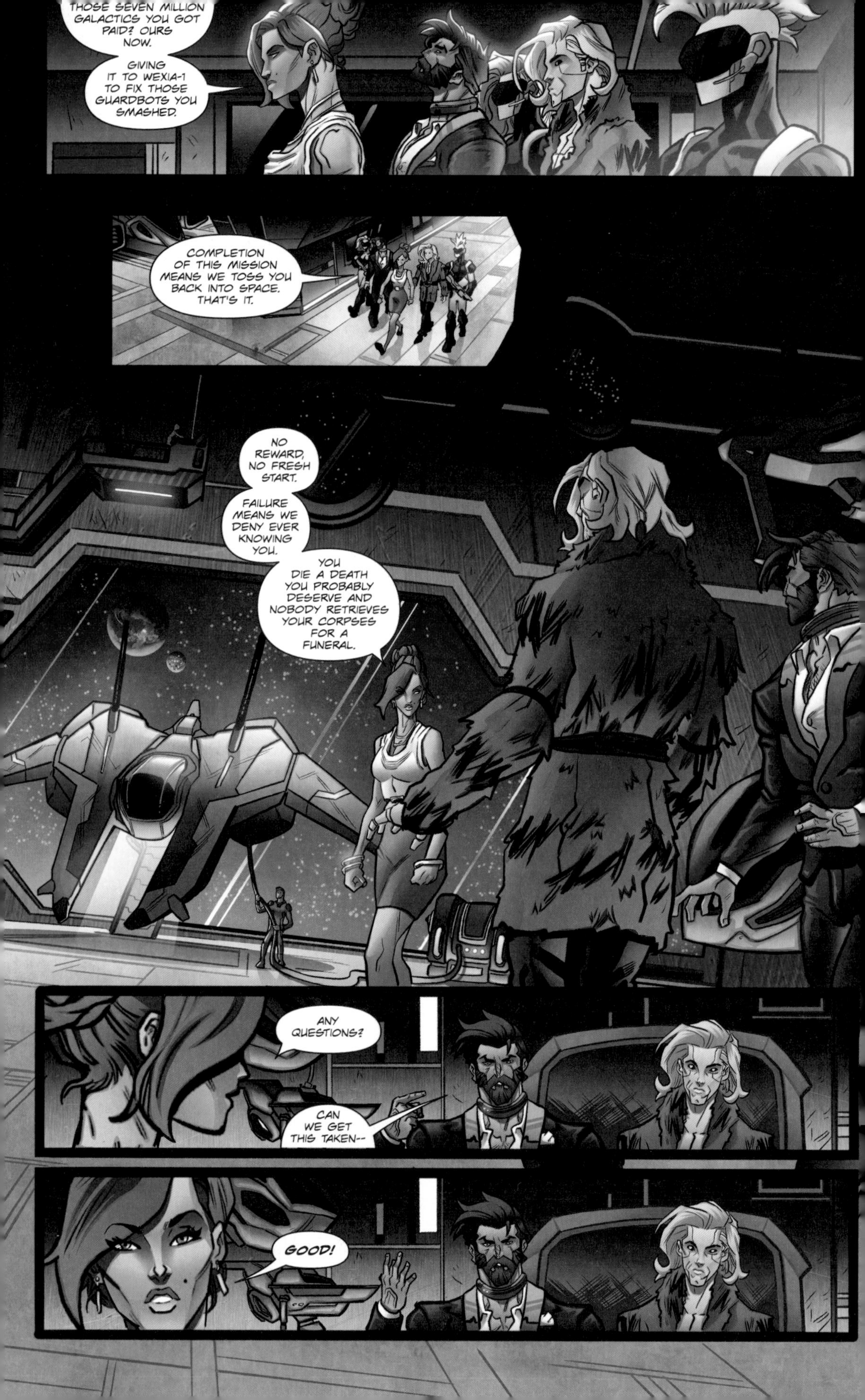
THOSE SEVEN MILLION GALACTICS YOU GOT PAID? OURS NOW.
GIVING IT TO WEXIA-1 TO FIX THOSE GUARDBOTS YOU SMASHED.
COMPLETION OF THIS MISSION MEANS WE TOSS YOU BACK INTO SPACE. THAT'S IT.
NO REWARD, NO FRESH START.
FAILURE MEANS WE DENY EVER KNOWING YOU.
YOU DIE A DEATH YOU PROBABLY DESERVE AND NOBODY RETRIEVES YOUR CORPSES FOR A FUNERAL.
ANY QUESTIONS?
CAN WE GET THIS TAKEN--
GOOD!

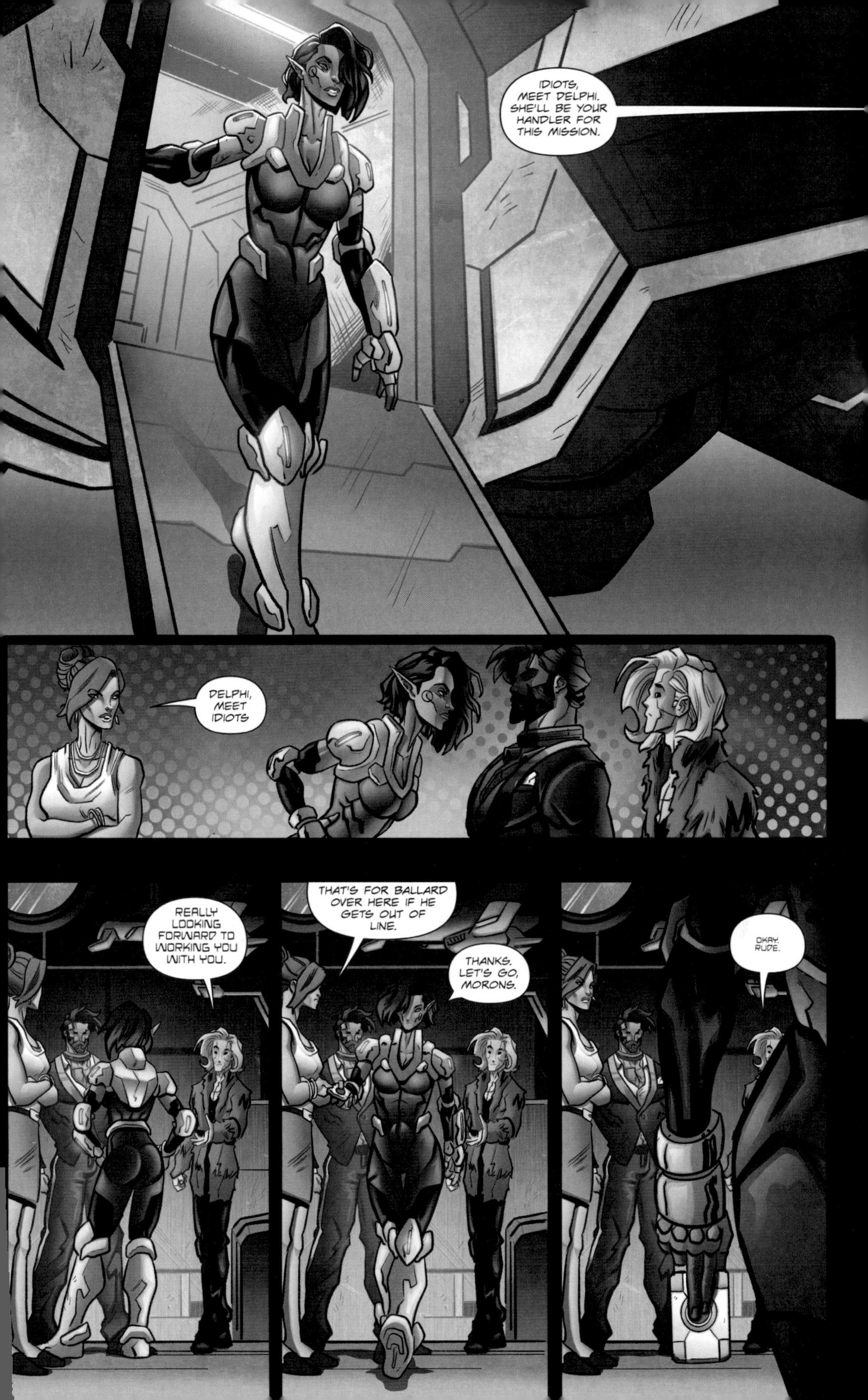
IDIOTS, MEET DELPHI. SHE'LL BE YOUR HANDLER FOR THIS MISSION.
DELPHI, MEET IDIOTS
REALLY LOOKING FORWARD TO WORKING YOU WITH YOU.
THAT'S FOR BALLARD OVER HERE IF HE GETS OUT OF LINE.
THANKS. LET'S GO, MORONS.
OKAY. RUDE.

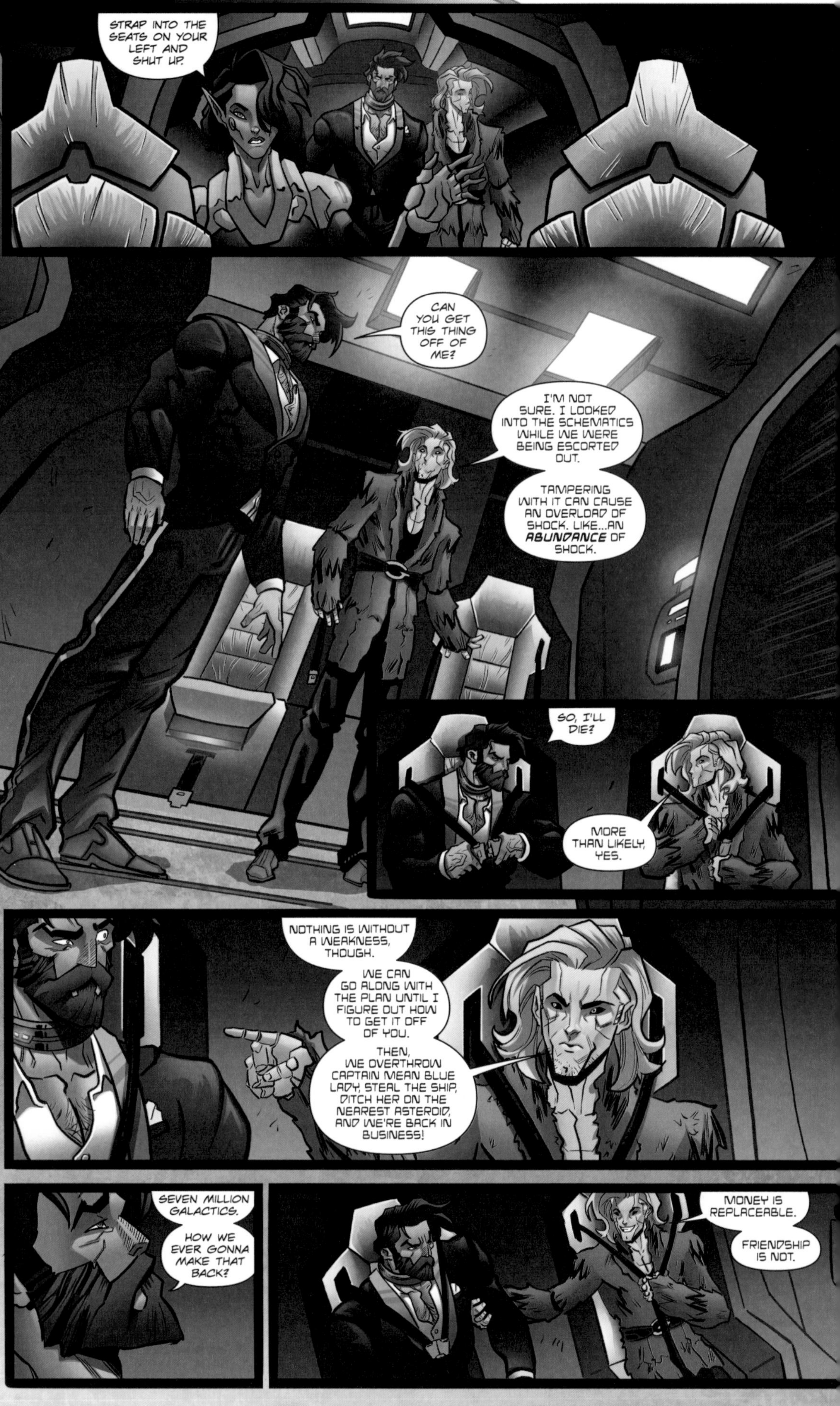
STRAP INTO THE SEATS ON YOUR LEFT AND SHUT UP.
CAN YOU GET THIS THING OFF OF ME?
I'M NOT SURE. I LOOKED INTO THE SCHEMATICS WHILE WE WERE BEING ESCORTED OUT.
TAMPERING WITH IT CAN CAUSE AN OVERLOAD OF SHOCK. LIKE...AN ABUNDANCE OF SHOCK.
SO, I'LL DIE?
MORE THAN LIKELY, YES.
NOTHING IS WITHOUT A WEAKNESS, THOUGH.
WE CAN GO ALONG WITH THE PLAN UNTIL I FIGURE OUT HOW TO GET IT OFF OF YOU.
THEN, WE OVERTHROW CAPTAIN MEAN BLUE LADY, STEAL THE SHIP, DITCH HER ON THE NEAREST ASTEROID, AND WE'RE BACK IN BUSINESS!
SEVEN MILLION GALACTICS.
HOW WE EVER GONNA MAKE THAT BACK?
MONEY IS REPLACEABLE.
FRIENDSHIP IS NOT.

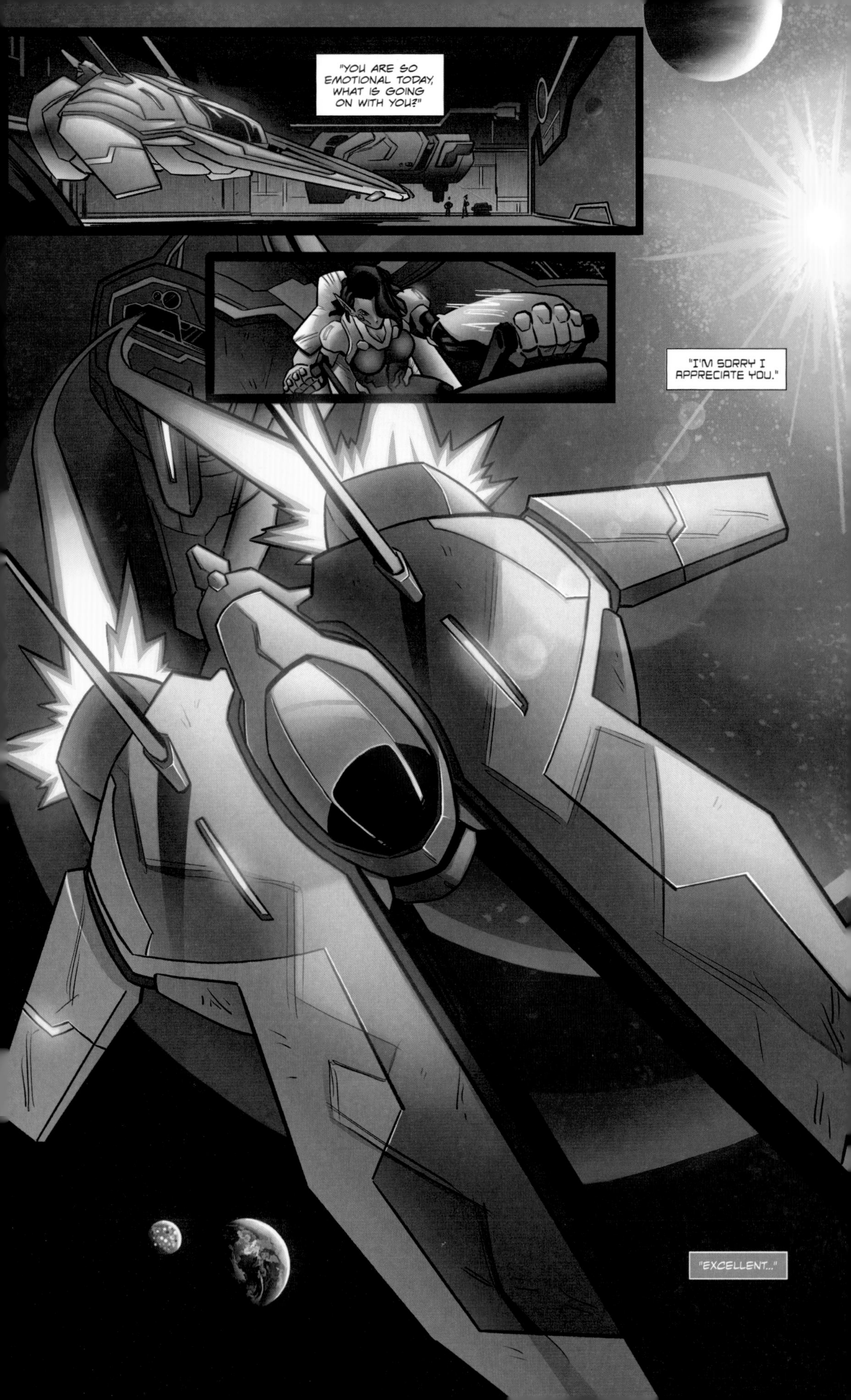
"YOU ARE SO EMOTIONAL TODAY, WHAT IS GOING ON WITH YOU?"
"I'M SORRY I APPRECIATE YOU."
"EXCELLENT..."

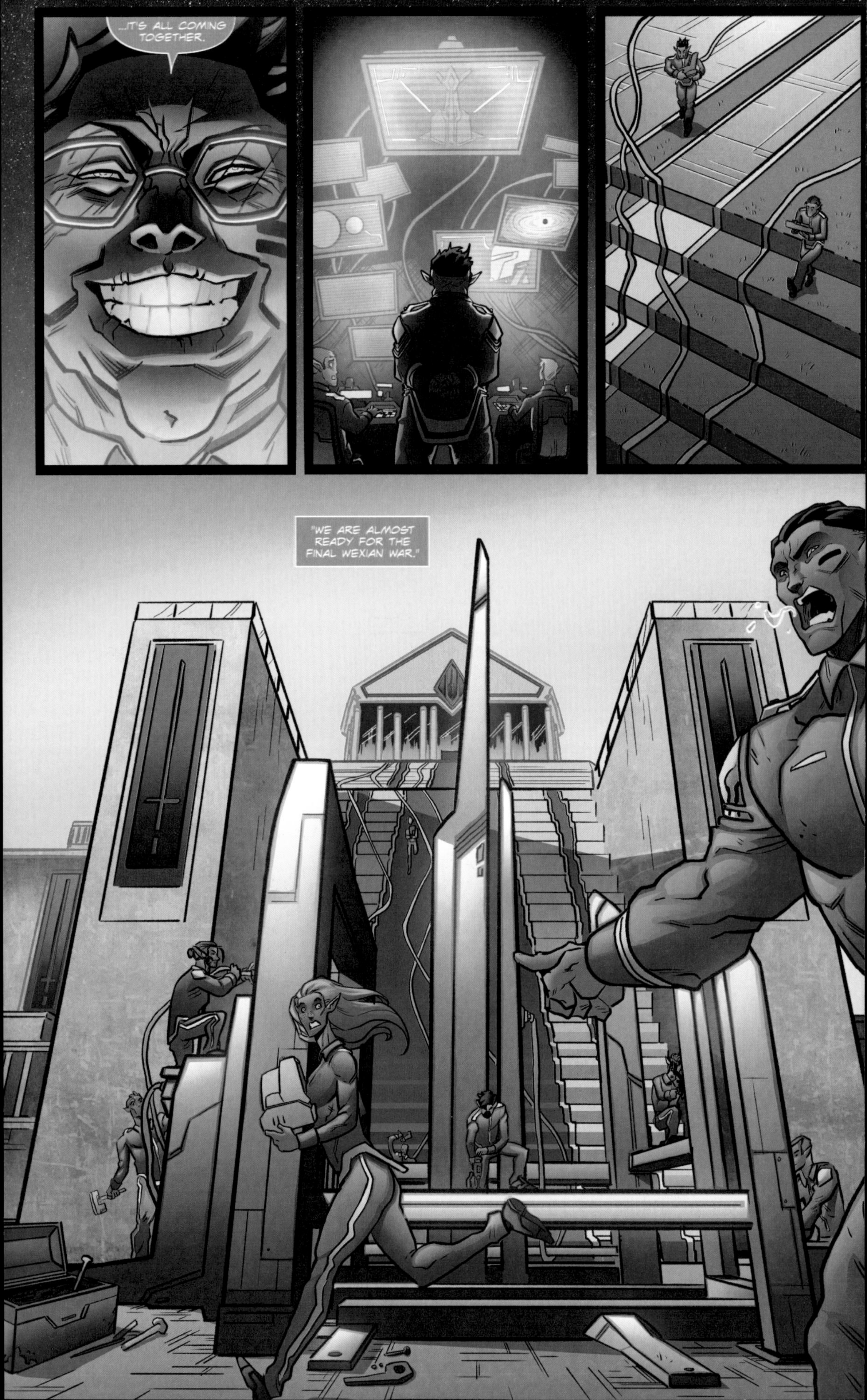
...IT'S ALL COMING TOGETHER.
"WE ARE ALMOST READY FOR THE FINAL WEXIAN WAR."

[2]

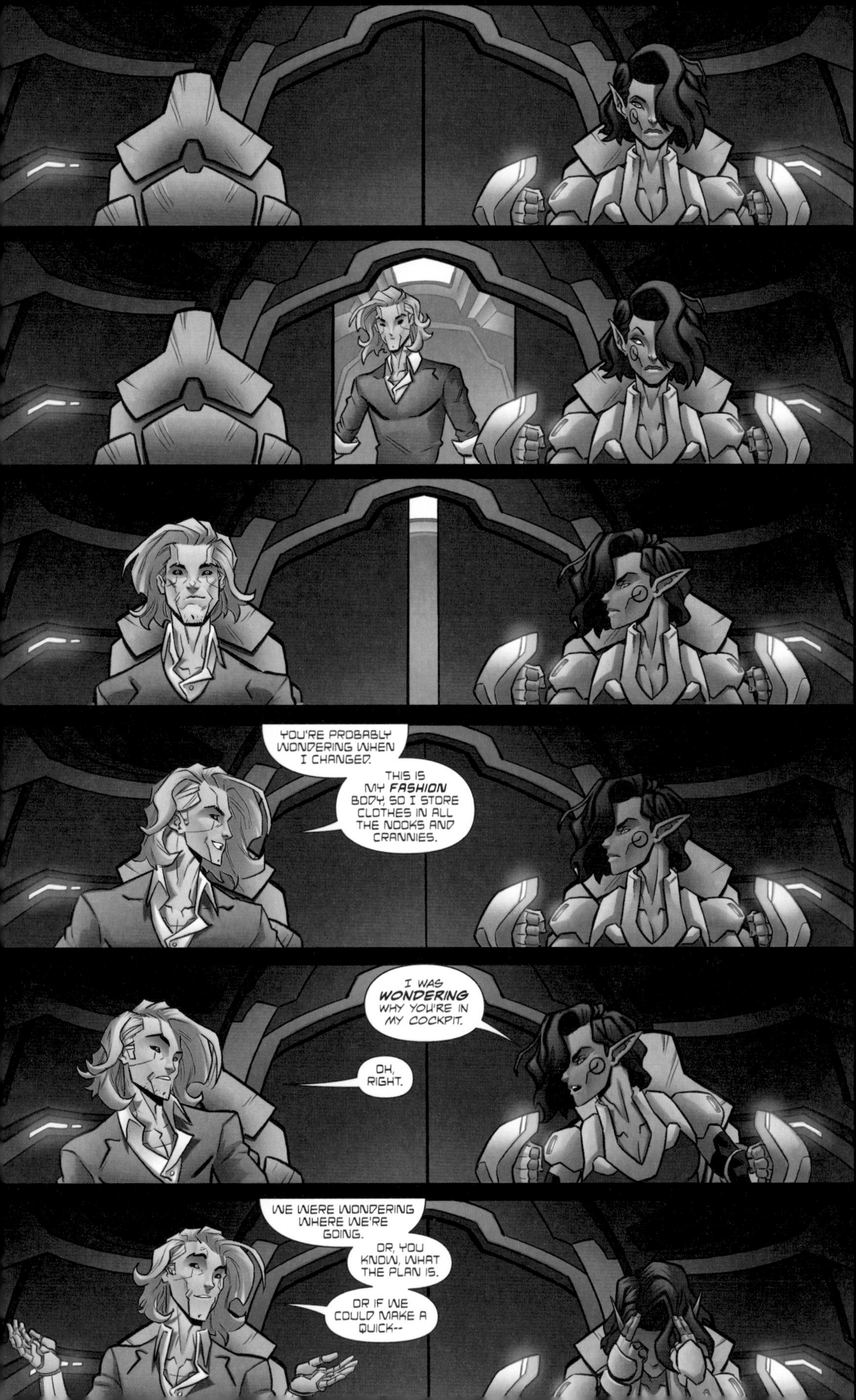
YOU'RE PROBABLY WONDERING WHEN I CHANGED.
THIS IS MY **FASHION** BODY, SO I STORE CLOTHES IN ALL THE NOOKS AND CRANNIES.
I WAS **WONDERING** WHY YOU'RE IN MY COCKPIT.
OH, RIGHT.
WE WERE WONDERING WHERE WE'RE GOING.
OR, YOU KNOW, WHAT THE PLAN IS.
OR IF WE COULD MAKE A QUICK--

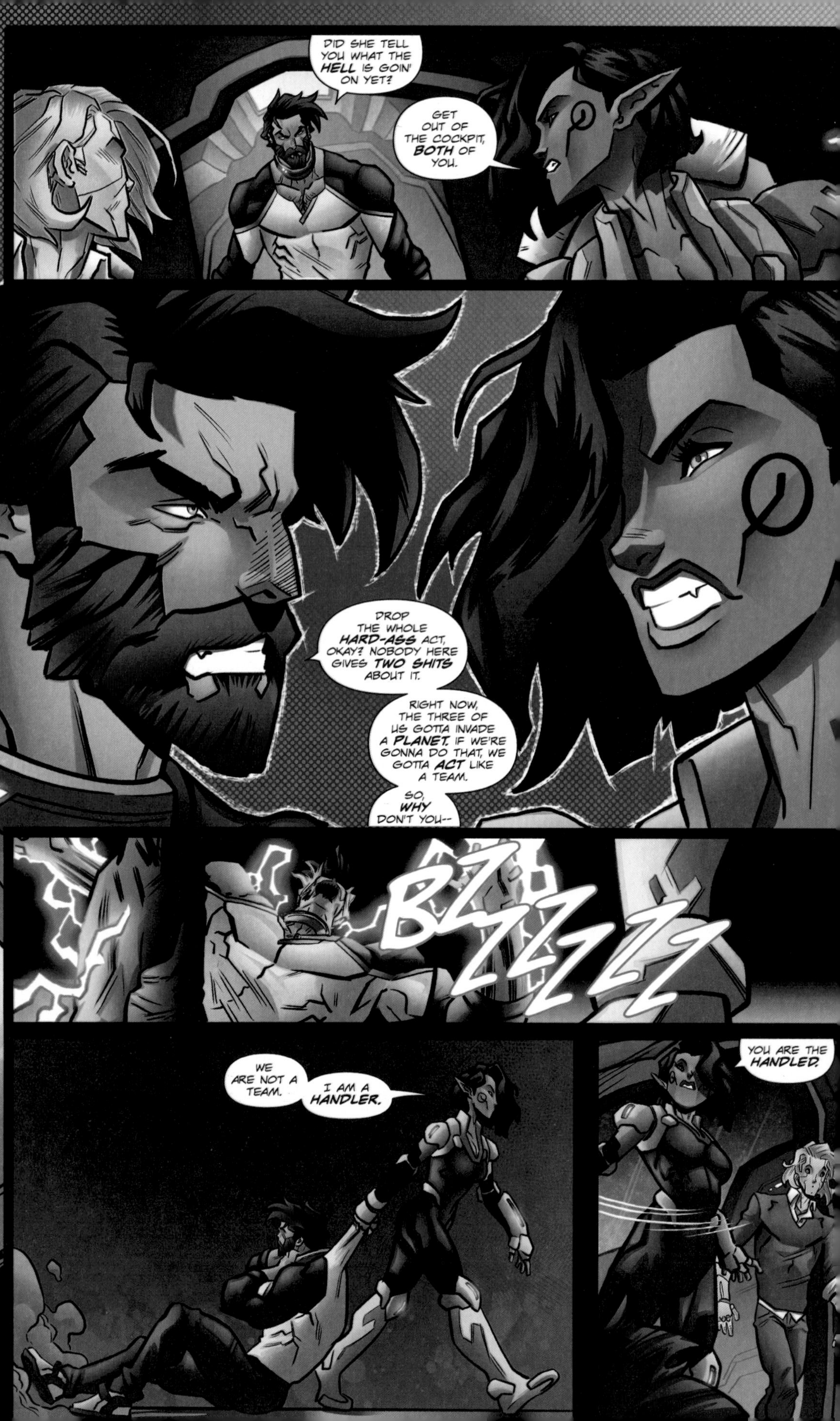
DID SHE TELL YOU WHAT THE HELL IS GOIN' ON YET?
GET OUT OF THE COCKPIT, BOTH OF YOU.
DROP THE WHOLE HARD-ASS ACT, OKAY? NOBODY HERE GIVES TWO SHITS ABOUT IT.
RIGHT NOW, THE THREE OF US GOTTA INVADE A PLANET. IF WE'RE GONNA DO THAT, WE GOTTA ACT LIKE A TEAM.
SO, WHY DON'T YOU--
BZZZZZZ
WE ARE NOT A TEAM.
I AM A HANDLER.
YOU ARE THE HANDLED.

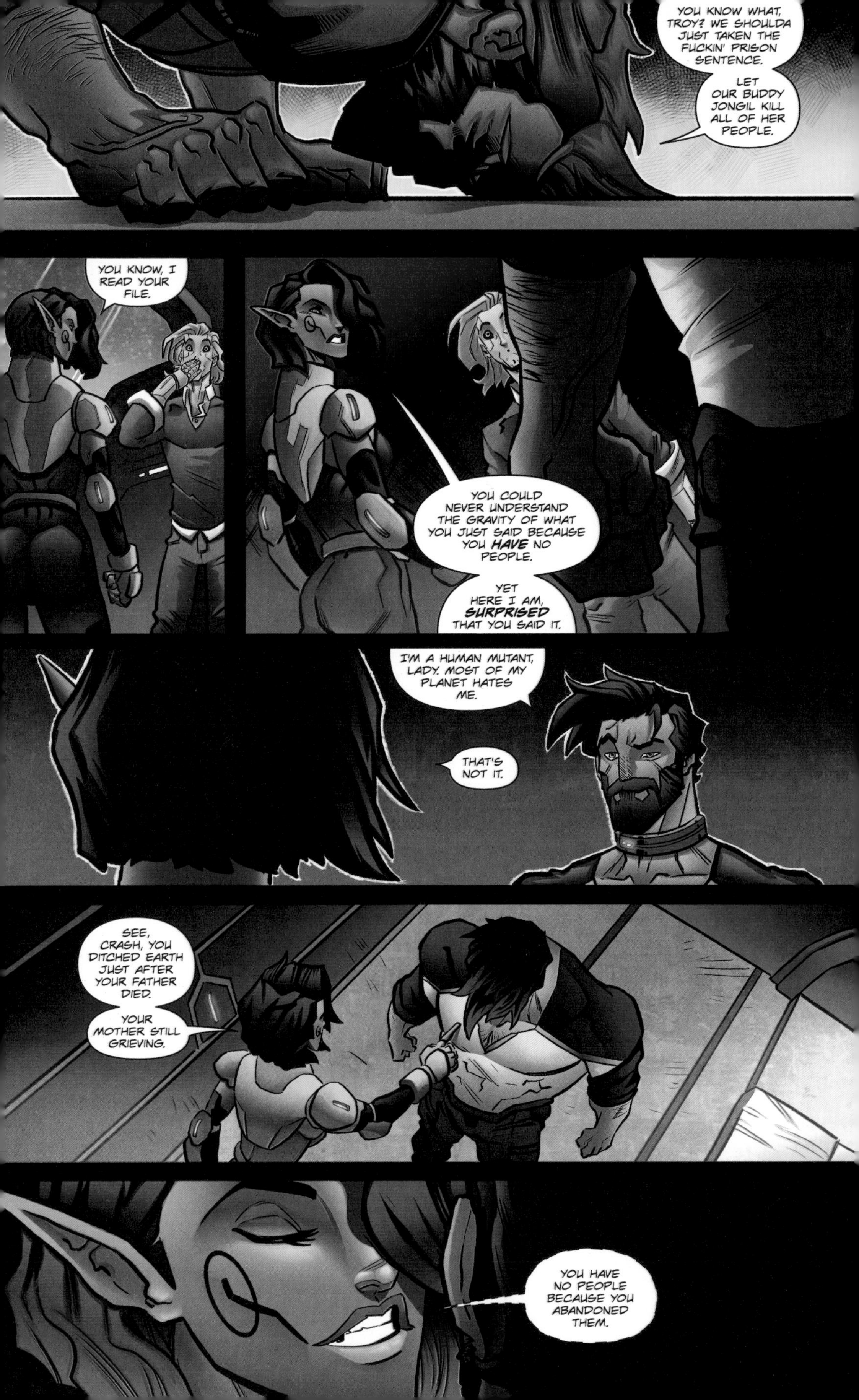

YOU KNOW WHAT, TROY? WE SHOULDA JUST TAKEN THE FUCKIN' PRISON SENTENCE.
LET OUR BUDDY JONGIL KILL ALL OF HER PEOPLE.
YOU KNOW, I READ YOUR FILE.
YOU COULD NEVER UNDERSTAND THE GRAVITY OF WHAT YOU JUST SAID BECAUSE YOU **HAVE** NO PEOPLE.
YET HERE I AM, **SURPRISED** THAT YOU SAID IT.
I'M A HUMAN MUTANT, LADY. MOST OF MY PLANET HATES ME.
THAT'S NOT IT.
SEE, CRASH, YOU DITCHED EARTH JUST AFTER YOUR FATHER DIED.
YOUR MOTHER STILL GRIEVING.
YOU HAVE NO PEOPLE BECAUSE YOU ABANDONED THEM.

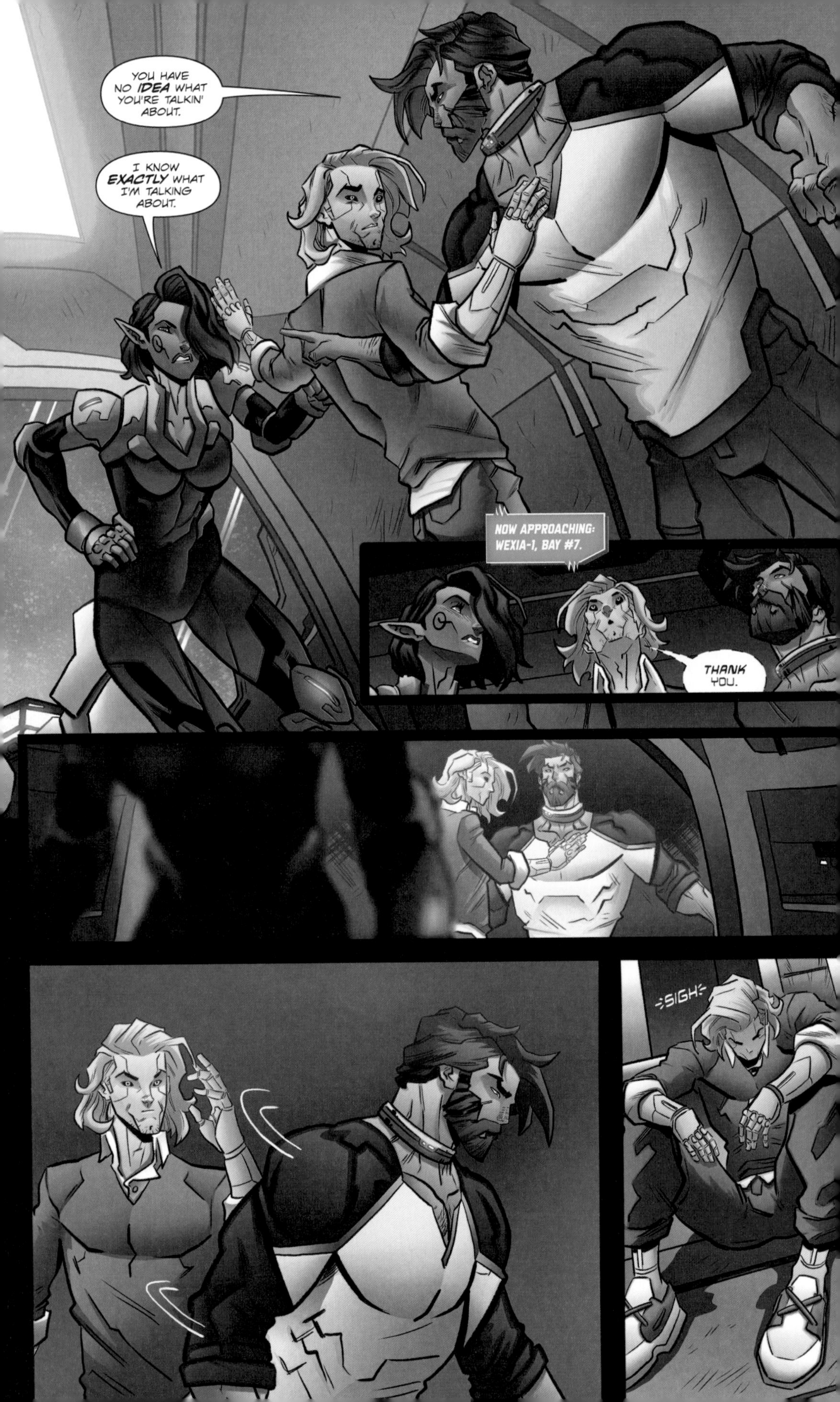
YOU HAVE NO IDEA WHAT YOU'RE TALKIN' ABOUT.
I KNOW EXACTLY WHAT I'M TALKING ABOUT.
NOW APPROACHING: WEXIA-1, BAY #7.
THANK YOU.
SIGH

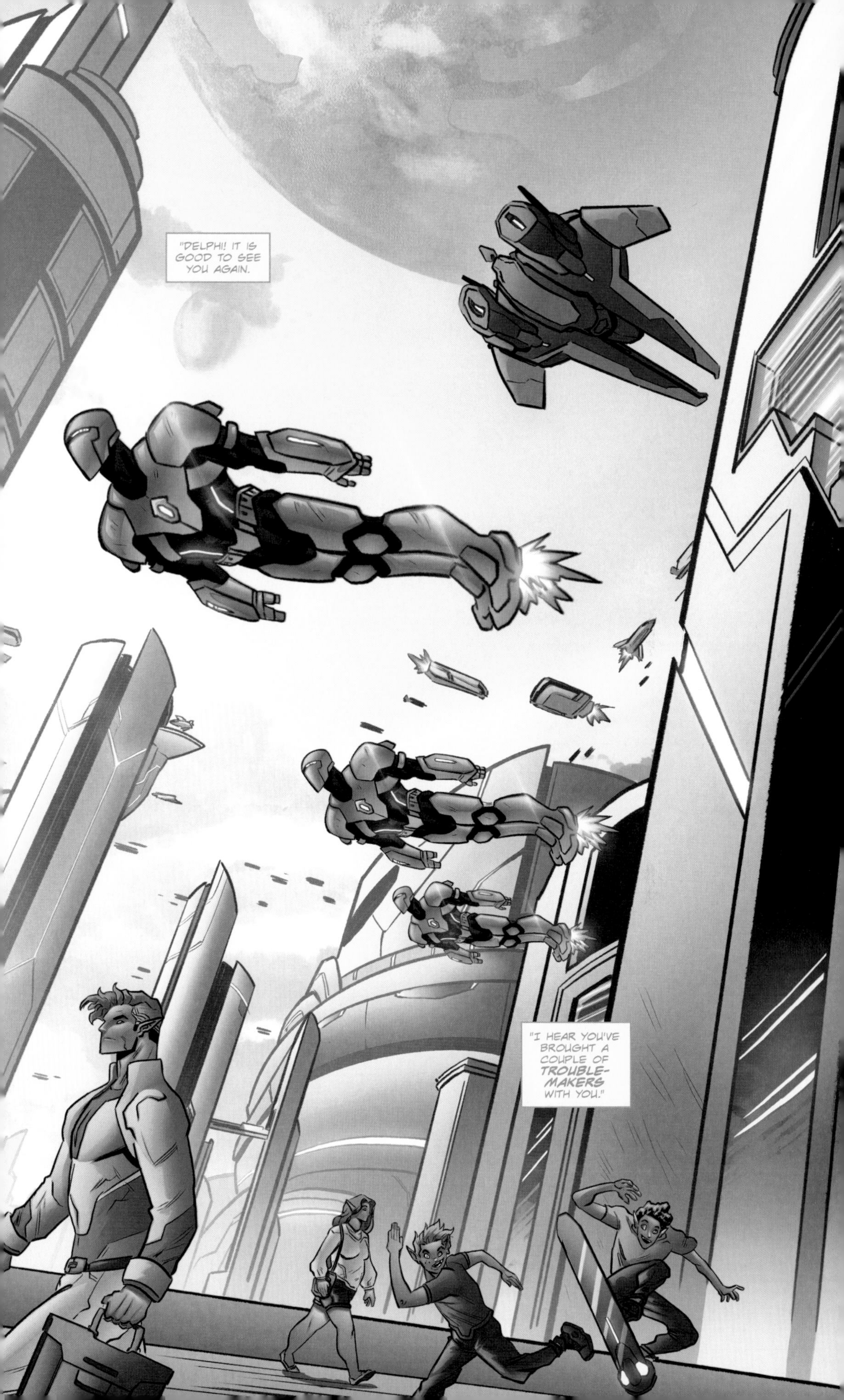
"DELPHI! IT IS GOOD TO SEE YOU AGAIN.
"I HEAR YOU'VE BROUGHT A COUPLE OF TROUBLE-MAKERS WITH YOU."

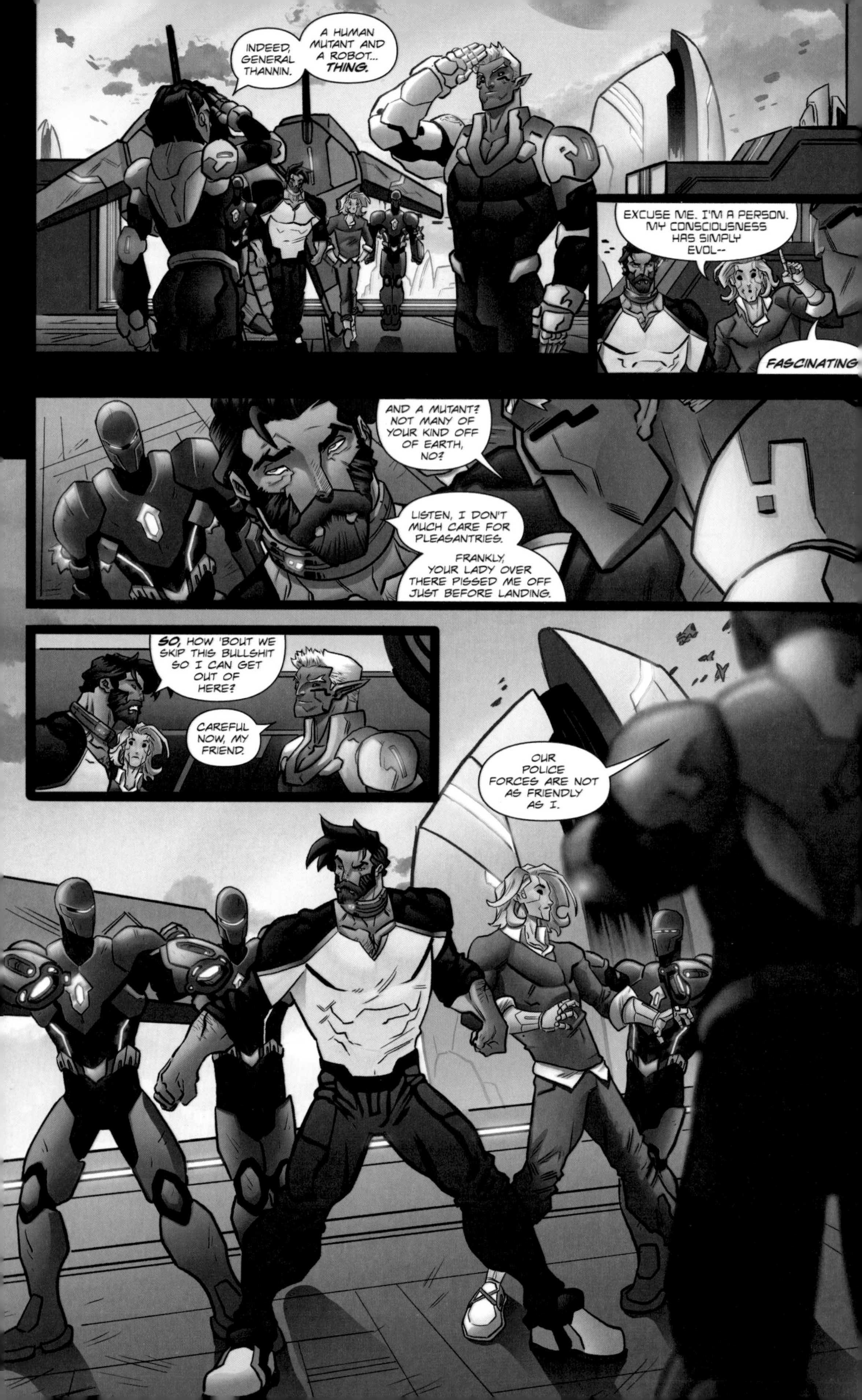
A HUMAN MUTANT AND A ROBOT... THING.
INDEED, GENERAL THANNIN.
EXCUSE ME. I'M A PERSON. MY CONSCIOUSNESS HAS SIMPLY EVOL--
FASCINATING
AND A MUTANT? NOT MANY OF YOUR KIND OFF OF EARTH, NO?
LISTEN, I DON'T MUCH CARE FOR PLEASANTRIES.
FRANKLY, YOUR LADY OVER THERE PISSED ME OFF JUST BEFORE LANDING.
SO, HOW 'BOUT WE SKIP THIS BULLSHIT SO I CAN GET OUT OF HERE?
CAREFUL NOW, MY FRIEND.
OUR POLICE FORCES ARE NOT AS FRIENDLY AS I.

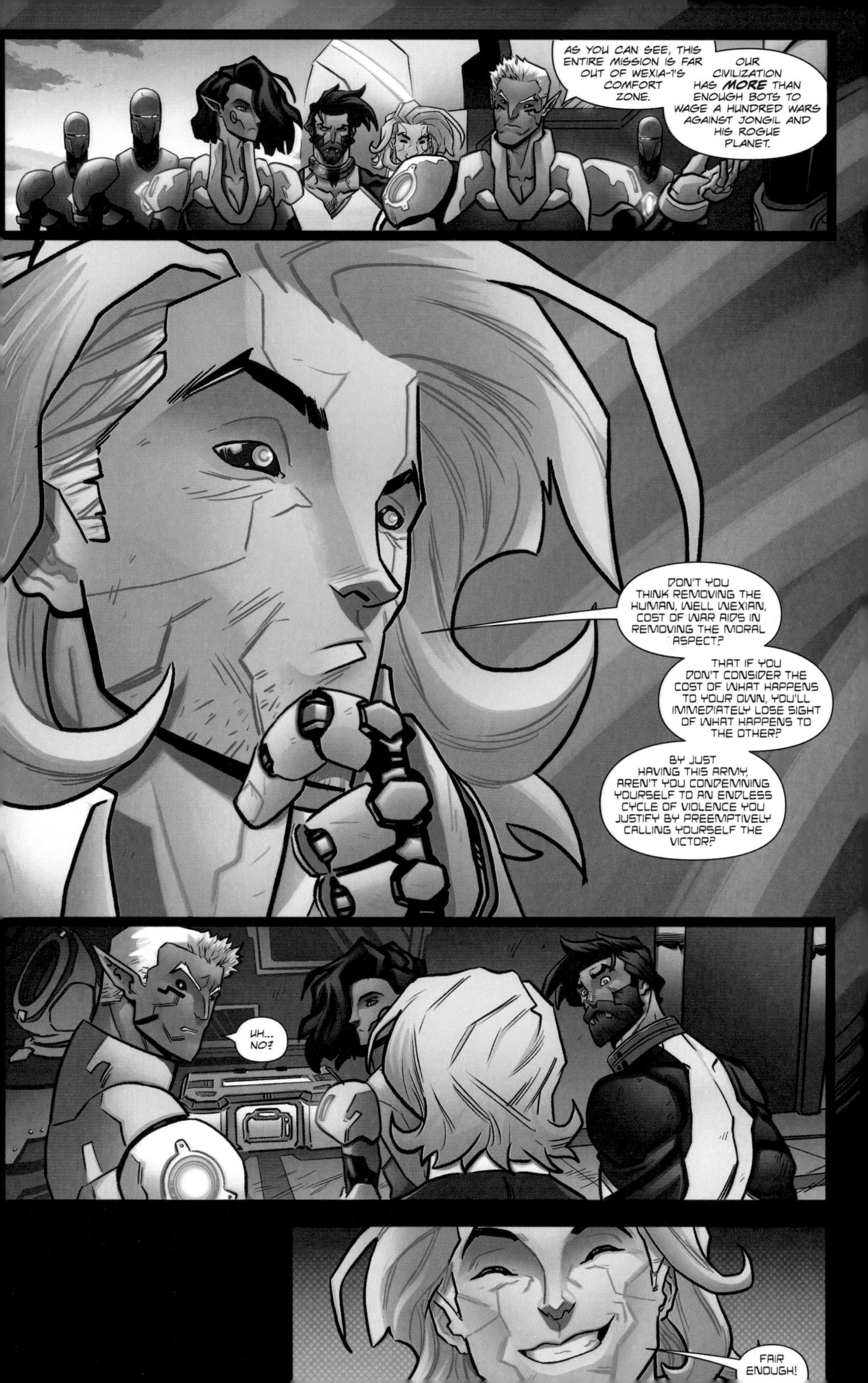
AS YOU CAN SEE, THIS ENTIRE MISSION IS FAR OUT OF WEXIA-1'S COMFORT ZONE.
OUR CIVILIZATION HAS MORE THAN ENOUGH BOTS TO WAGE A HUNDRED WARS AGAINST JONGIL AND HIS ROGUE PLANET.
DON'T YOU THINK REMOVING THE HUMAN, WELL WEXIAN, COST OF WAR AIDS IN REMOVING THE MORAL ASPECT?
THAT IF YOU DON'T CONSIDER THE COST OF WHAT HAPPENS TO YOUR OWN, YOU'LL IMMEDIATELY LOSE SIGHT OF WHAT HAPPENS TO THE OTHER?
BY JUST HAVING THIS ARMY, AREN'T YOU CONDEMNING YOURSELF TO AN ENDLESS CYCLE OF VIOLENCE YOU JUSTIFY BY PREEMPTIVELY CALLING YOURSELF THE VICTOR?
UH... NO?
FAIR ENOUGH!

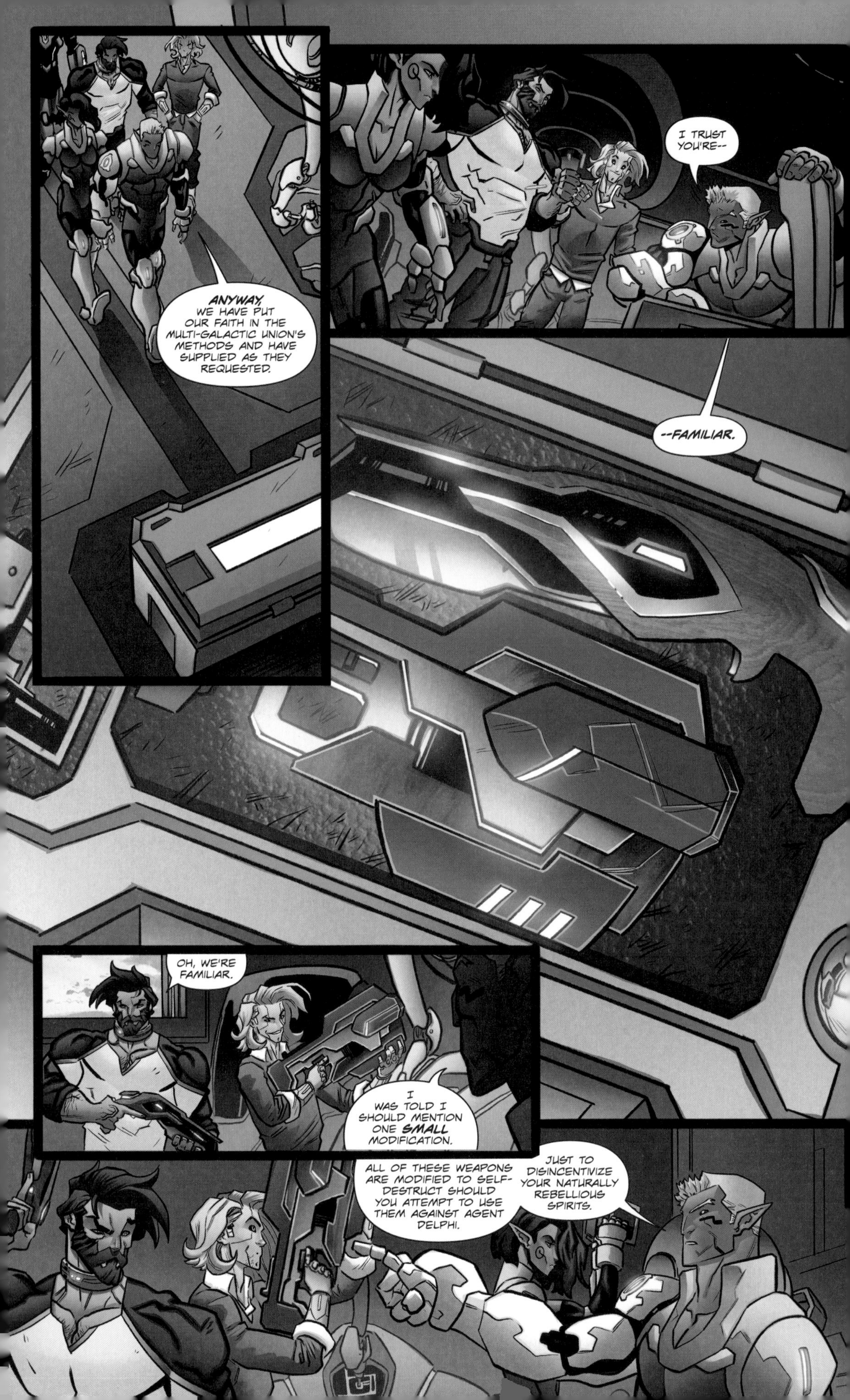
ANYWAY, WE HAVE PUT OUR FAITH IN THE MULTI-GALACTIC UNION'S METHODS AND HAVE SUPPLIED AS THEY REQUESTED.
I TRUST YOU'RE--
--FAMILIAR.
OH, WE'RE FAMILIAR.
I WAS TOLD I SHOULD MENTION ONE SMALL MODIFICATION.
ALL OF THESE WEAPONS ARE MODIFIED TO SELF-DESTRUCT SHOULD YOU ATTEMPT TO USE THEM AGAINST AGENT DELPHI.
JUST TO DISINCENTIVIZE YOUR NATURALLY REBELLIOUS SPIRITS.

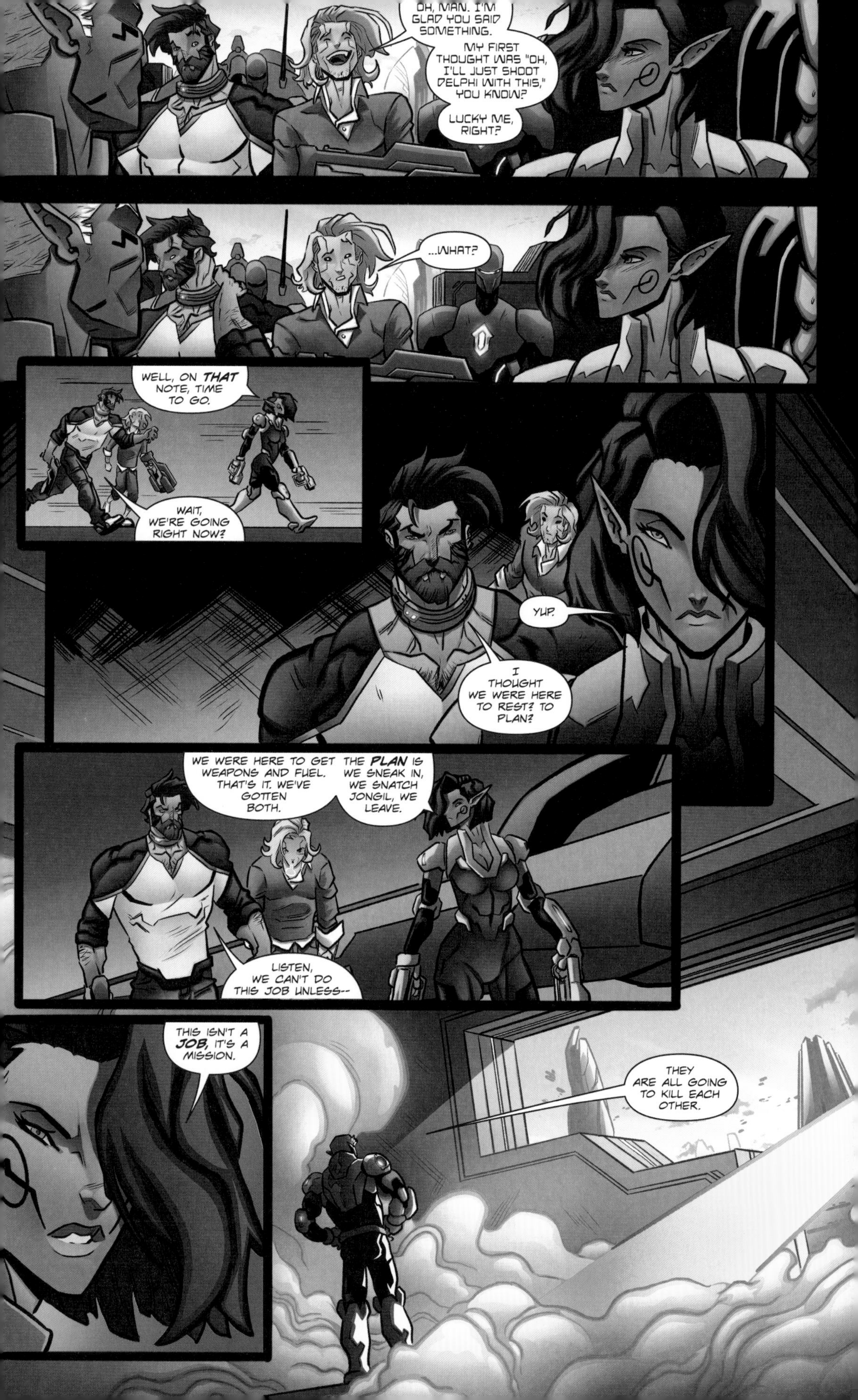
OH, MAN. I'M GLAD YOU SAID SOMETHING.
MY FIRST THOUGHT WAS "OH, I'LL JUST SHOOT DELPHI WITH THIS," YOU KNOW?
LUCKY ME, RIGHT?
...WHAT?
WELL, ON THAT NOTE, TIME TO GO.
WAIT, WE'RE GOING RIGHT NOW?
YUP.
I THOUGHT WE WERE HERE TO REST? TO PLAN?
WE WERE HERE TO GET WEAPONS AND FUEL. THAT'S IT. WE'VE GOTTEN BOTH.
THE PLAN IS WE SNEAK IN, WE SNATCH JONGIL, WE LEAVE.
LISTEN, WE CAN'T DO THIS JOB UNLESS--
THIS ISN'T A JOB, IT'S A MISSION.
THEY ARE ALL GOING TO KILL EACH OTHER.

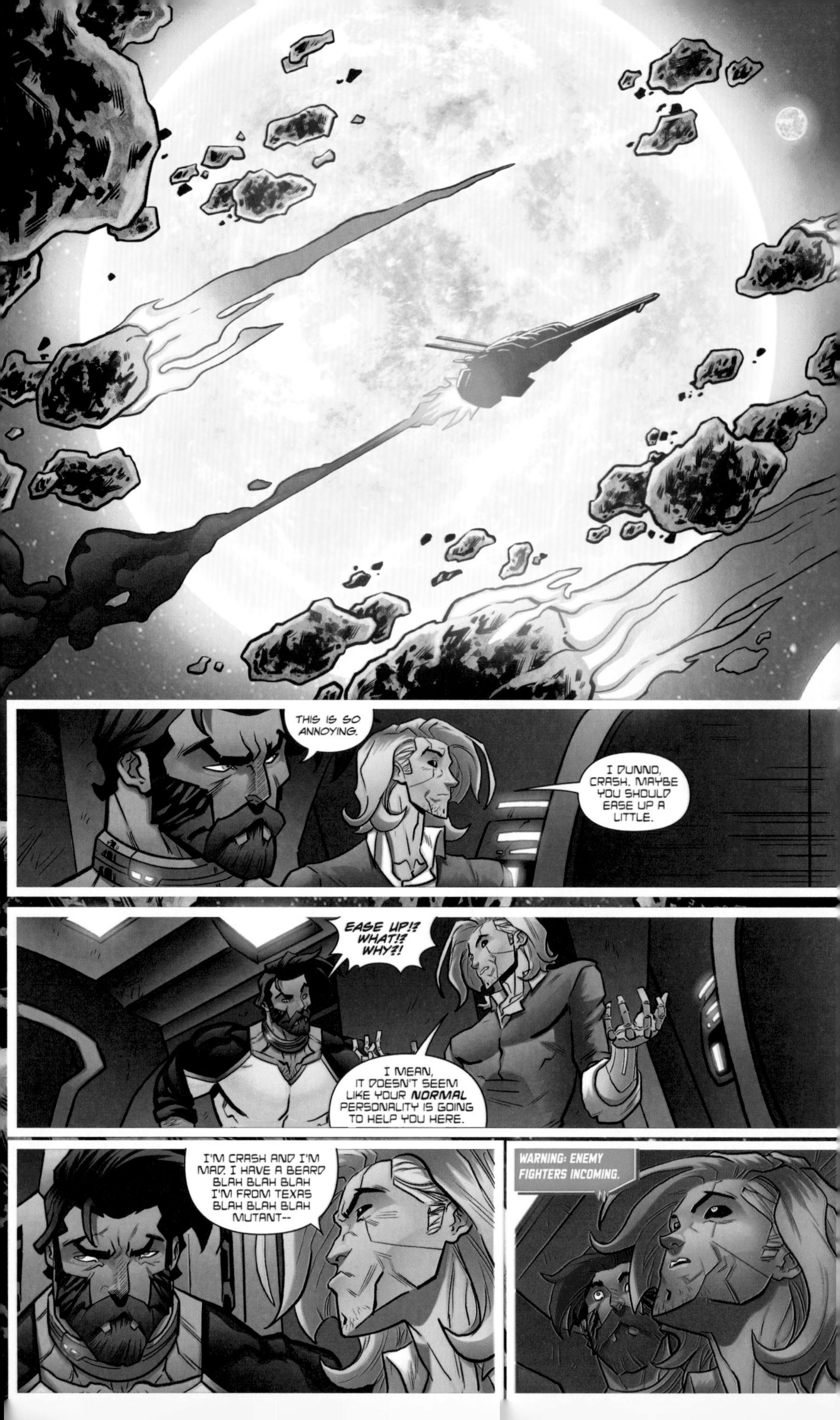
THIS IS SO ANNOYING.
I DUNNO, CRASH. MAYBE YOU SHOULD EASE UP A LITTLE.
EASE UP!? WHAT!? WHY?!
I MEAN, IT DOESN'T SEEM LIKE YOUR NORMAL PERSONALITY IS GOING TO HELP YOU HERE.
I'M CRASH AND I'M MAD. I HAVE A BEARD BLAH BLAH BLAH I'M FROM TEXAS BLAH BLAH BLAH MUTANT--
WARNING: ENEMY FIGHTERS INCOMING.

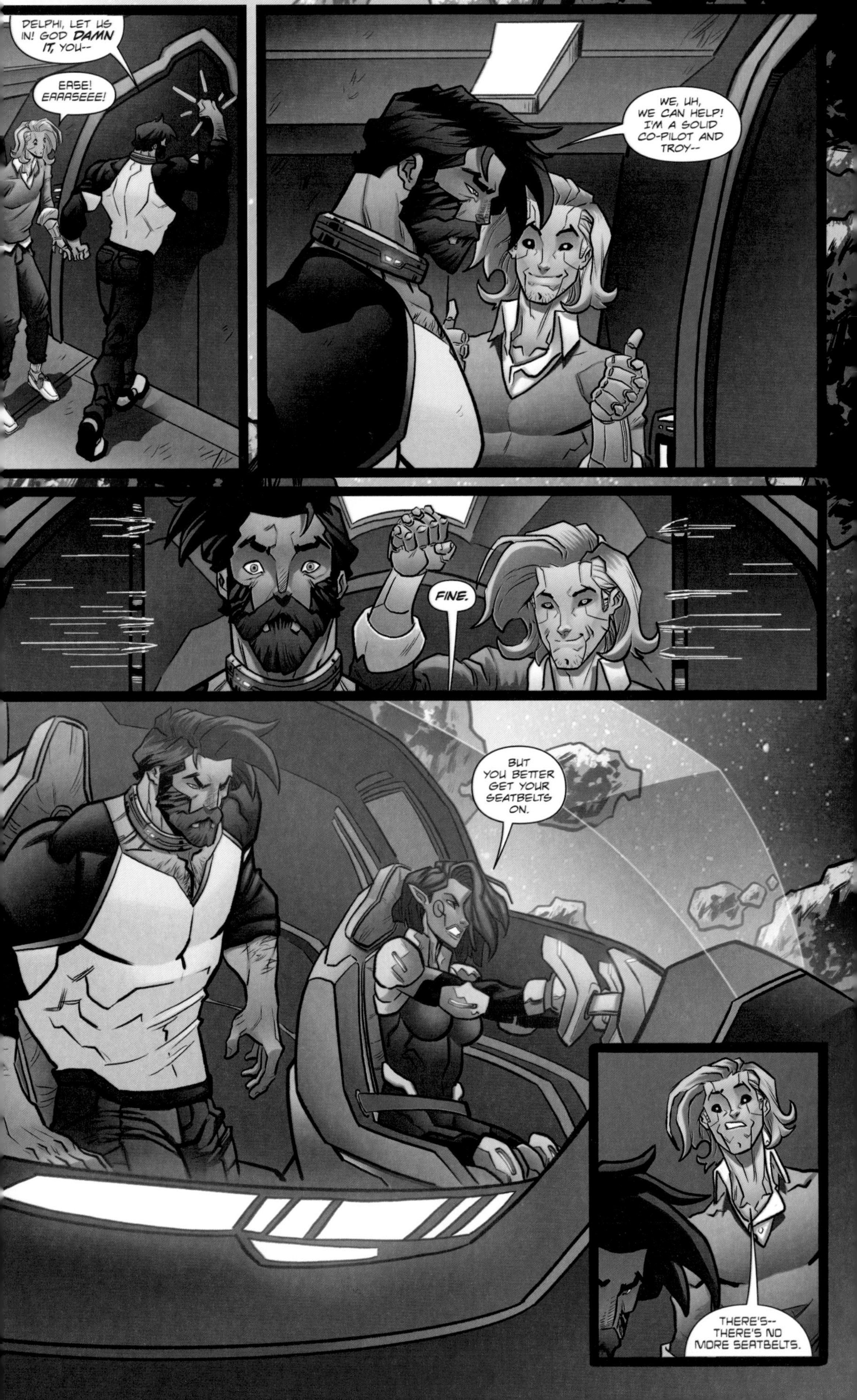

DELPHI, LET US IN! GOD DAMN IT, YOU--
EASE! EAAAASEEE!
WE, UH, WE CAN HELP! I'M A SOLID CO-PILOT AND TROY--
FINE.
BUT YOU BETTER GET YOUR SEATBELTS ON.
THERE'S-- THERE'S NO MORE SEATBELTS.

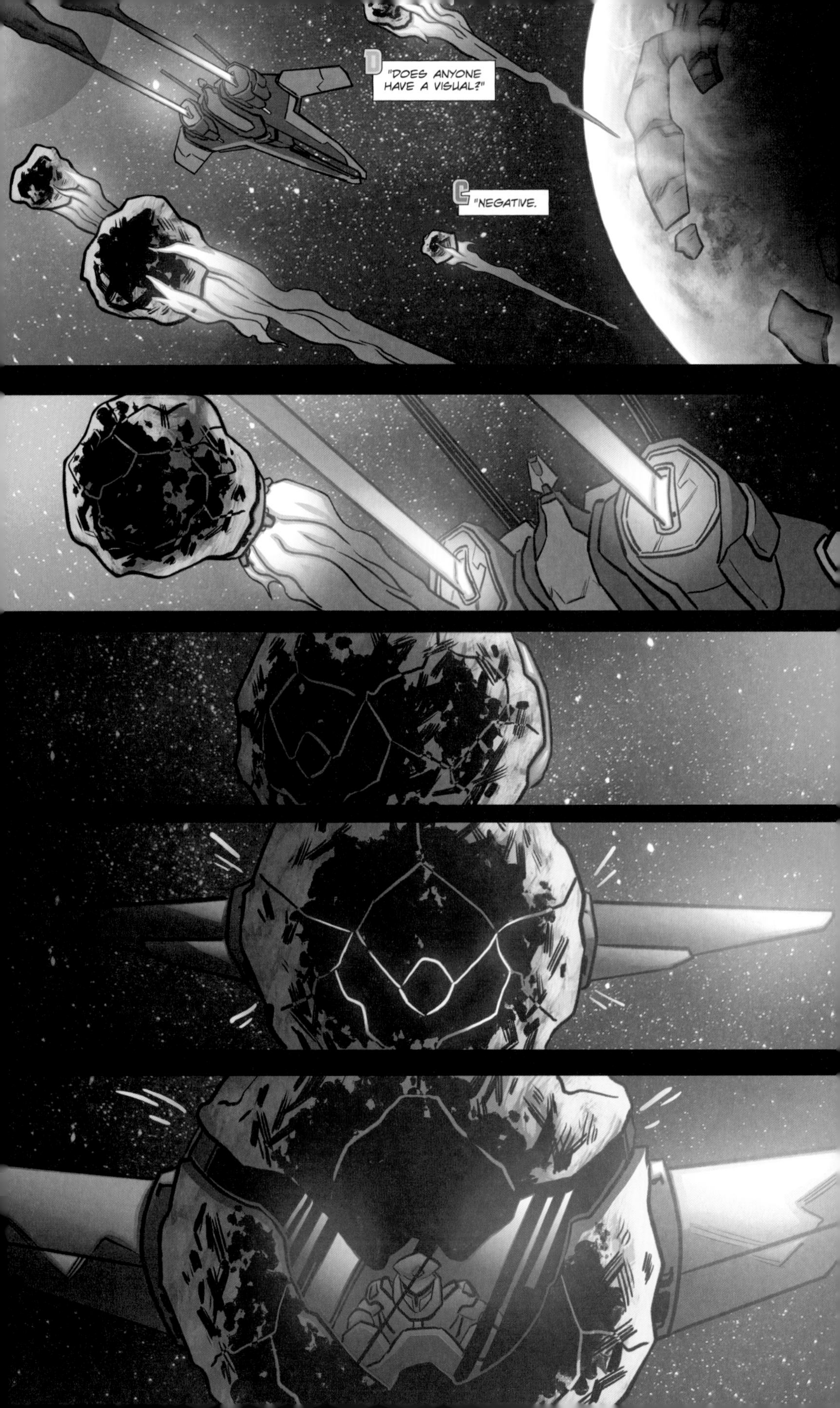
"DOES ANYONE HAVE A VISUAL?"
"NEGATIVE.

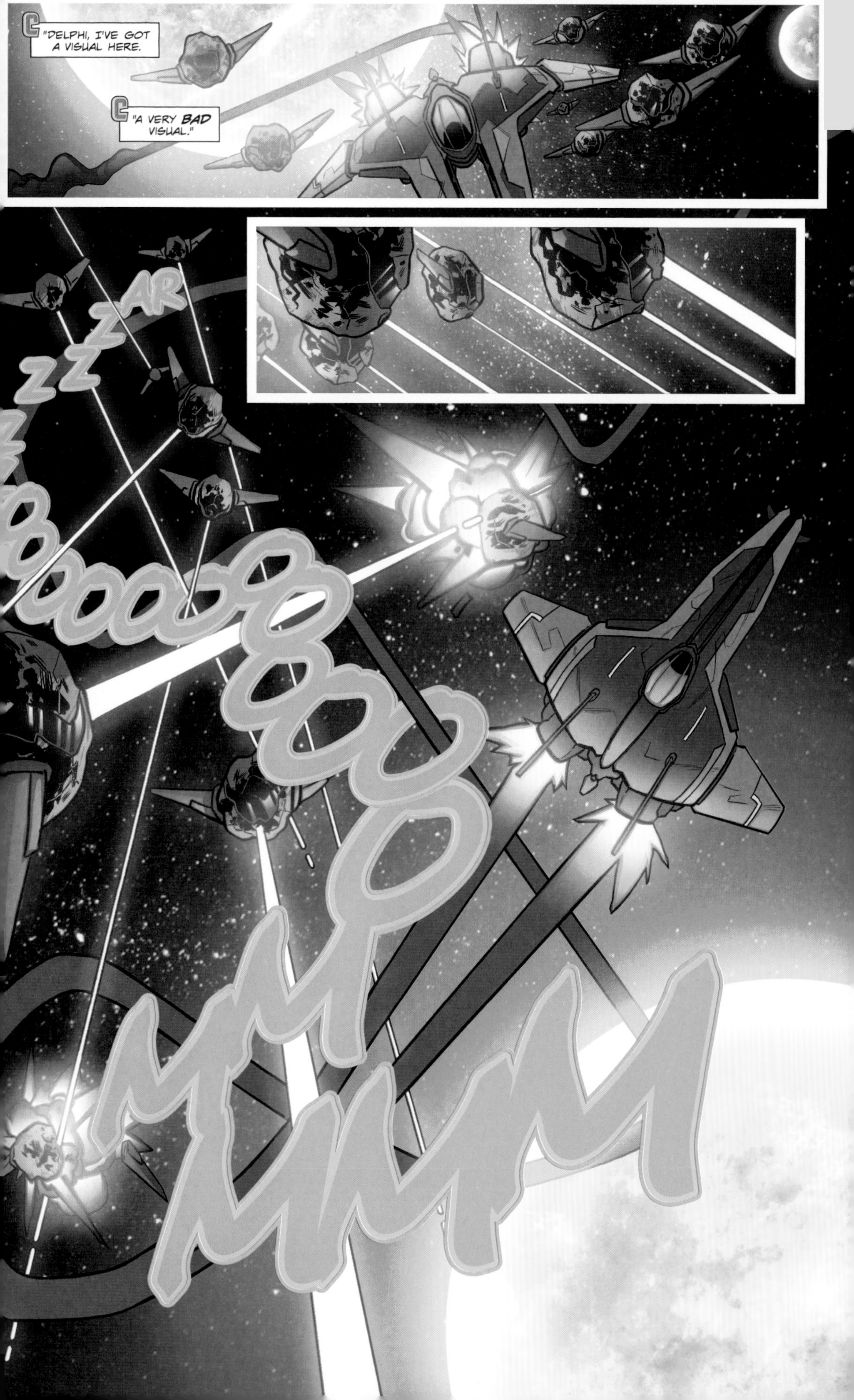
"DELPHI, I'VE GOT A VISUAL HERE.
"A VERY BAD VISUAL."

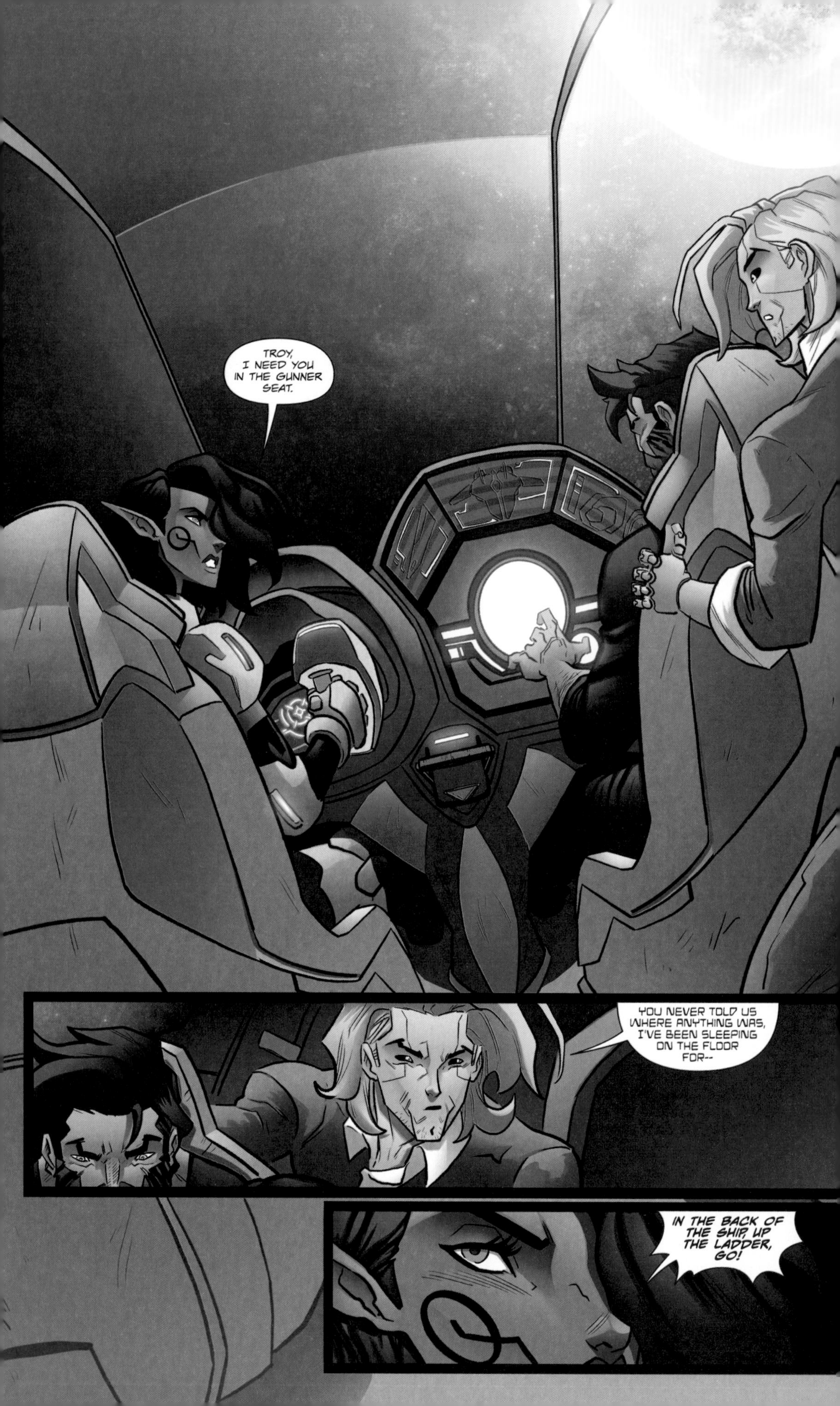
TROY, I NEED YOU IN THE GUNNER SEAT.
YOU NEVER TOLD US WHERE ANYTHING WAS, I'VE BEEN SLEEPING ON THE FLOOR FOR--
IN THE BACK OF THE SHIP, UP THE LADDER, GO!

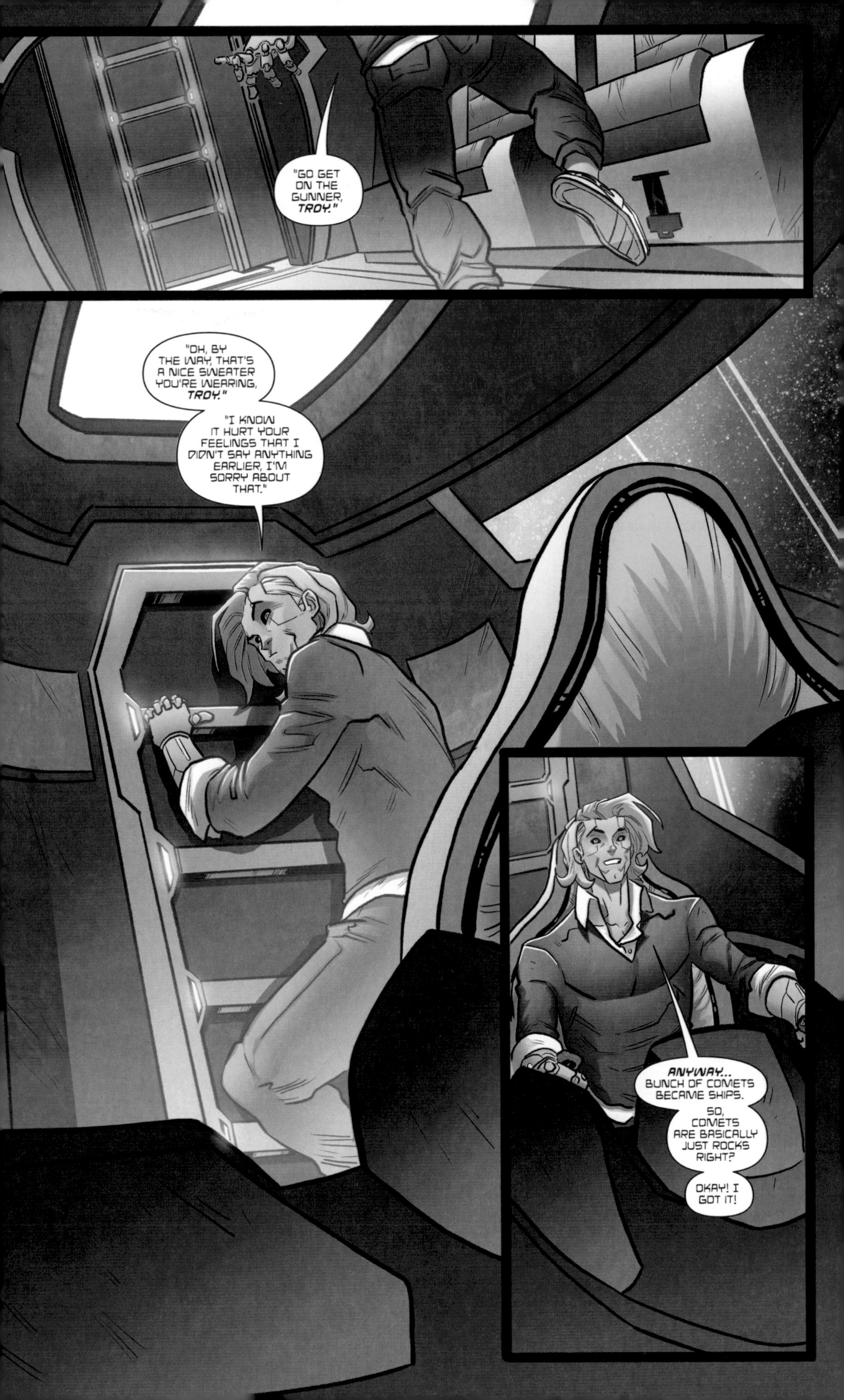
"GO GET ON THE GUNNER, TROY."
"OH, BY THE WAY, THAT'S A NICE SWEATER YOU'RE WEARING, TROY."
"I KNOW IT HURT YOUR FEELINGS THAT I DIDN'T SAY ANYTHING EARLIER, I'M SORRY ABOUT THAT."
ANYWAY... BUNCH OF COMETS BECAME SHIPS.
SO, COMETS ARE BASICALLY JUST ROCKS RIGHT?
OKAY! I GOT IT!

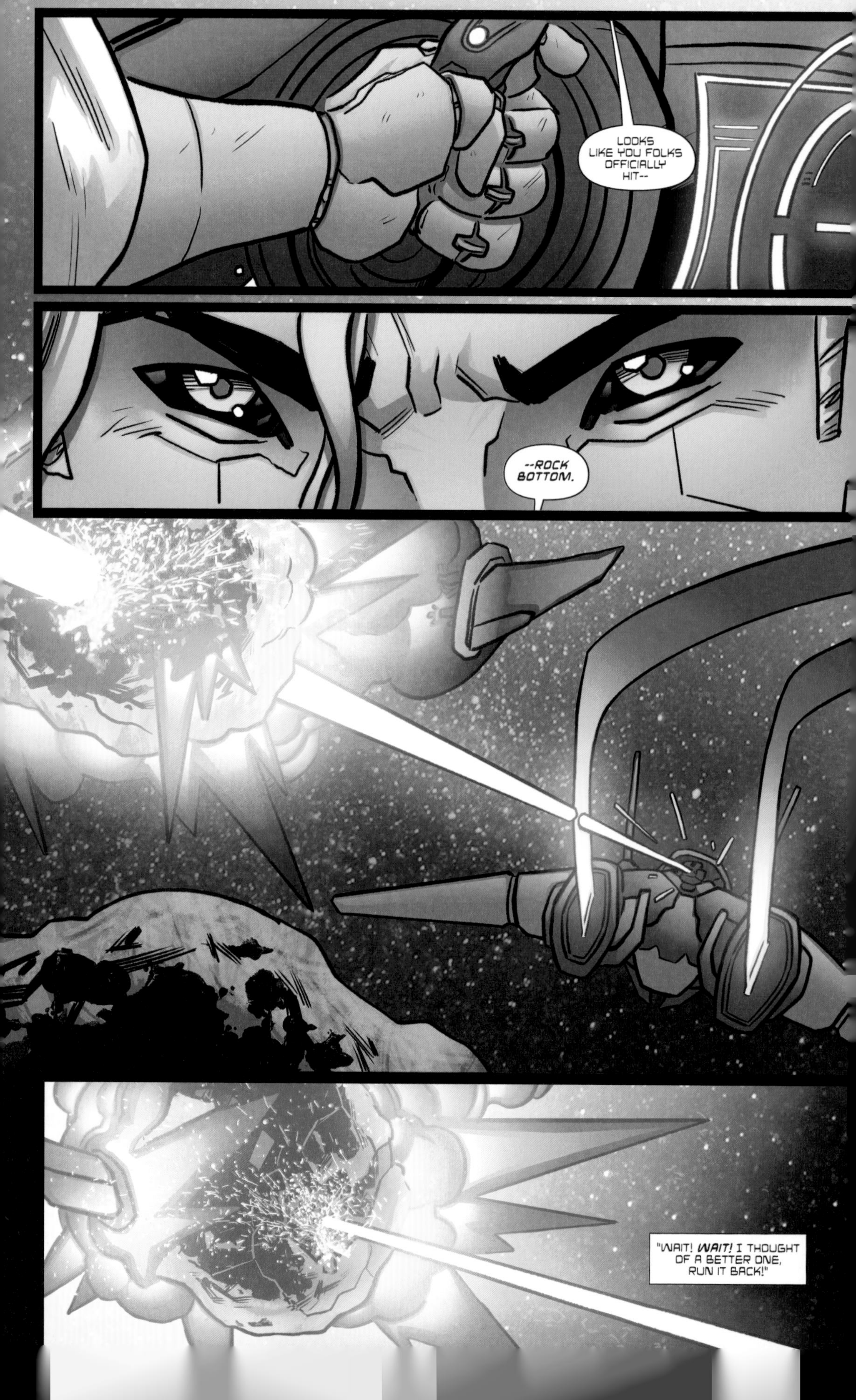
LOOKS LIKE YOU FOLKS OFFICIALLY HIT--
--ROCK BOTTOM.
"WAIT! *WAIT!* I THOUGHT OF A BETTER ONE, RUN IT BACK!"

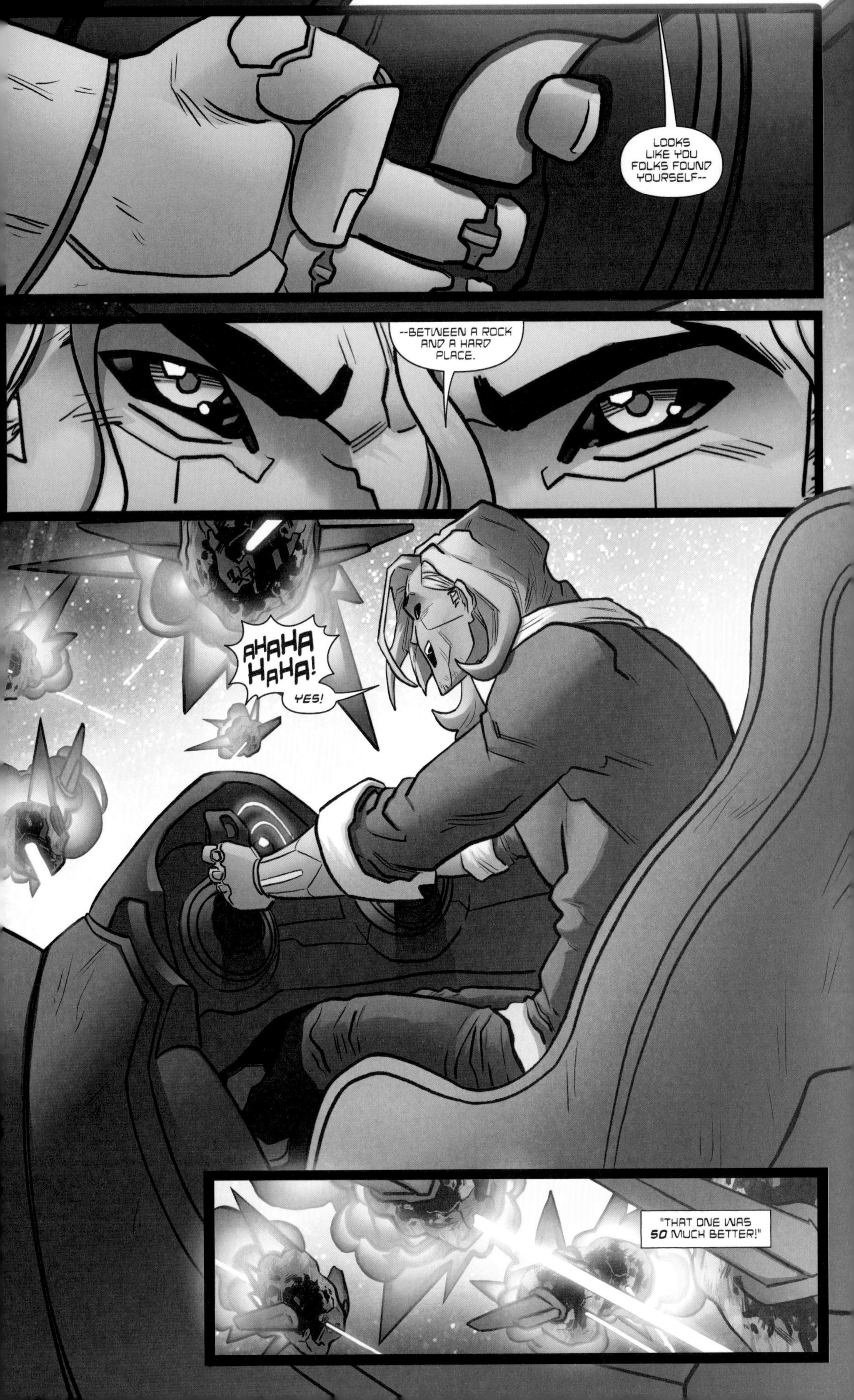
LOOKS LIKE YOU FOLKS FOUND YOURSELF--
--BETWEEN A ROCK AND A HARD PLACE.
AHAHA HAHA!
YES!
"THAT ONE WAS SO MUCH BETTER!"

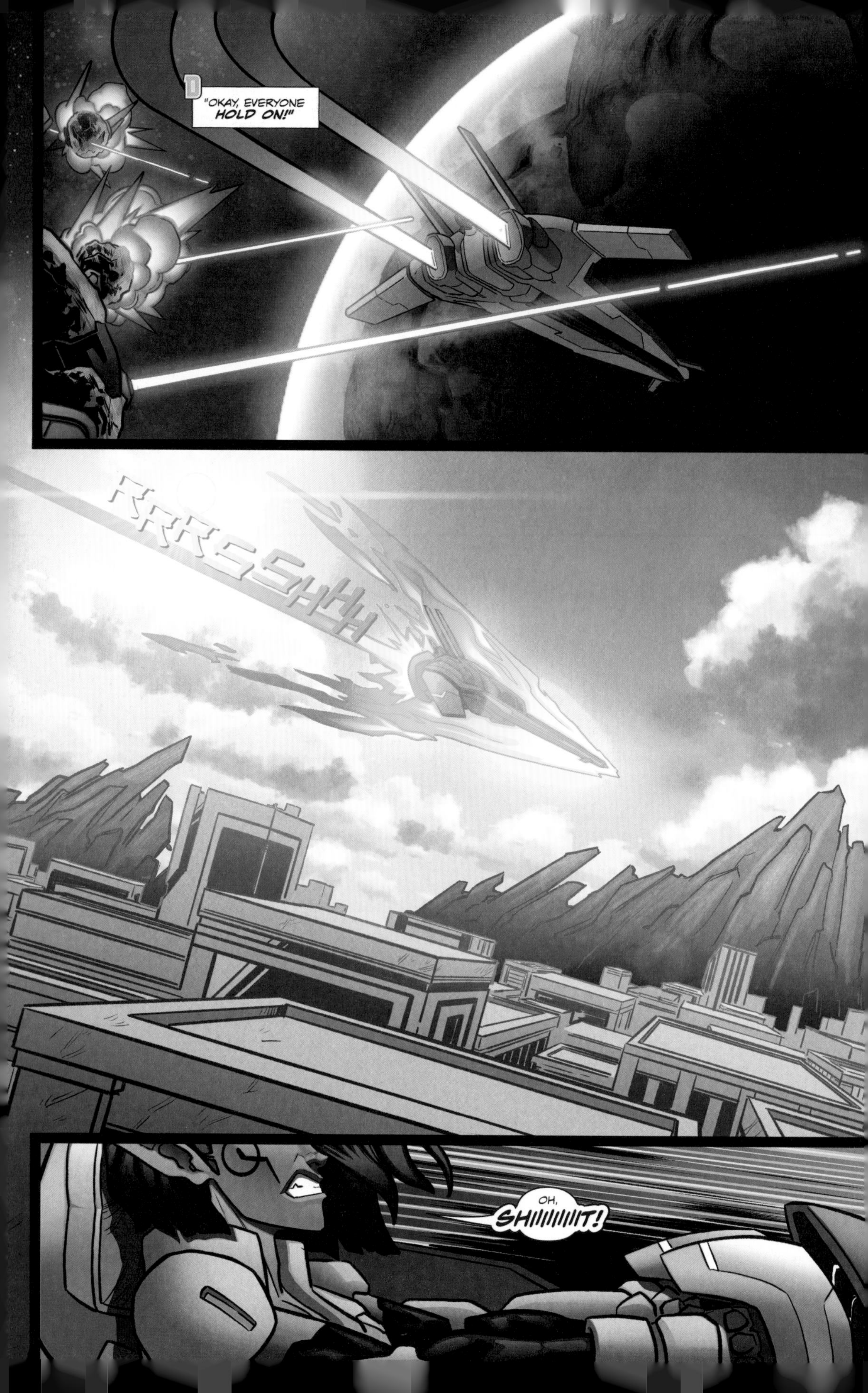

"OKAY, EVERYONE HOLD ON!"
RRRSSHHH
OH, SHIIIIIIIT!

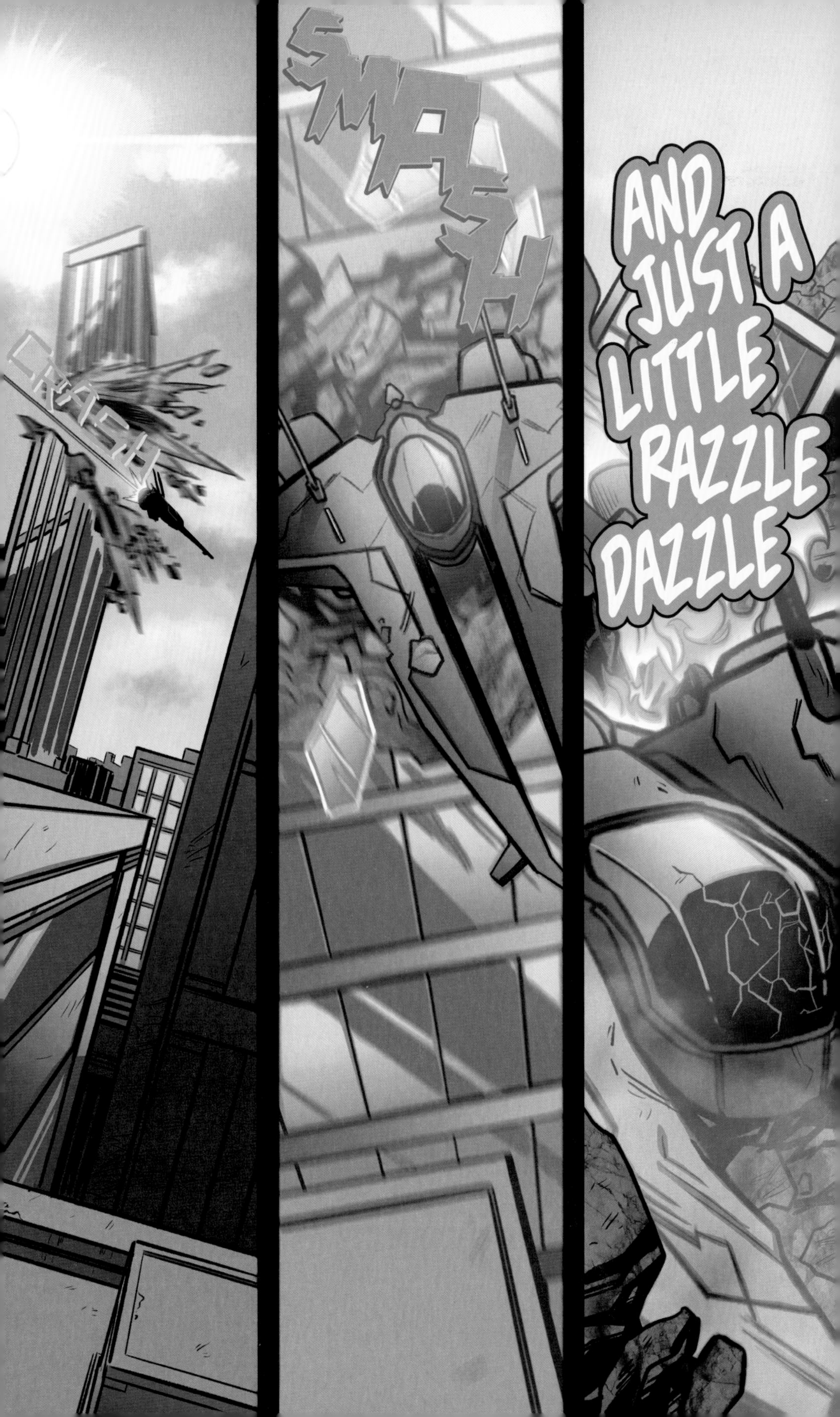
CRASH
SMASH
AND JUST A LITTLE RAZZLE DAZZLE

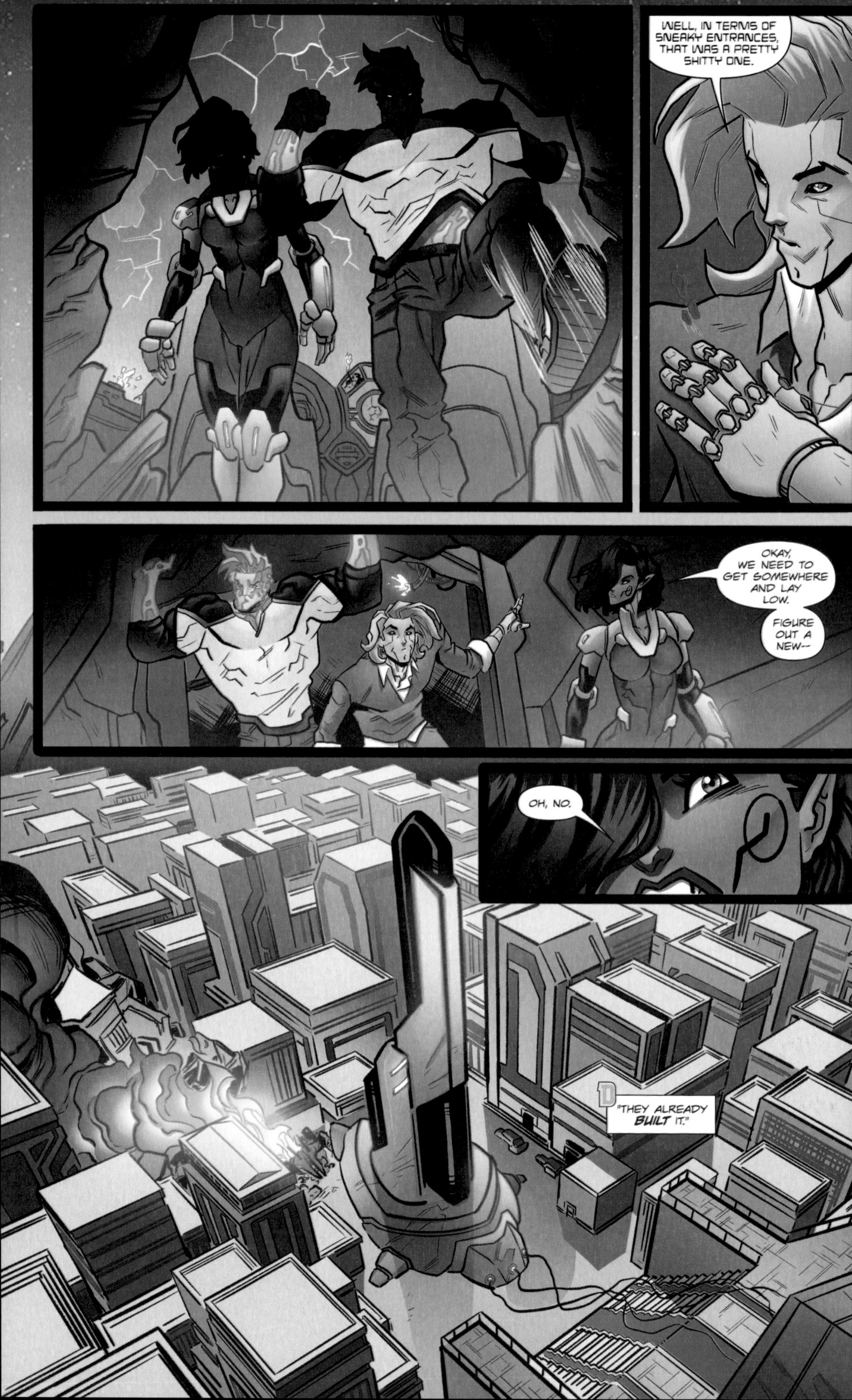
WELL, IN TERMS OF SNEAKY ENTRANCES, THAT WAS A PRETTY SHITTY ONE.
OKAY, WE NEED TO GET SOMEWHERE AND LAY LOW.
FIGURE OUT A NEW--
OH, NO.
"THEY ALREADY BUILT IT."

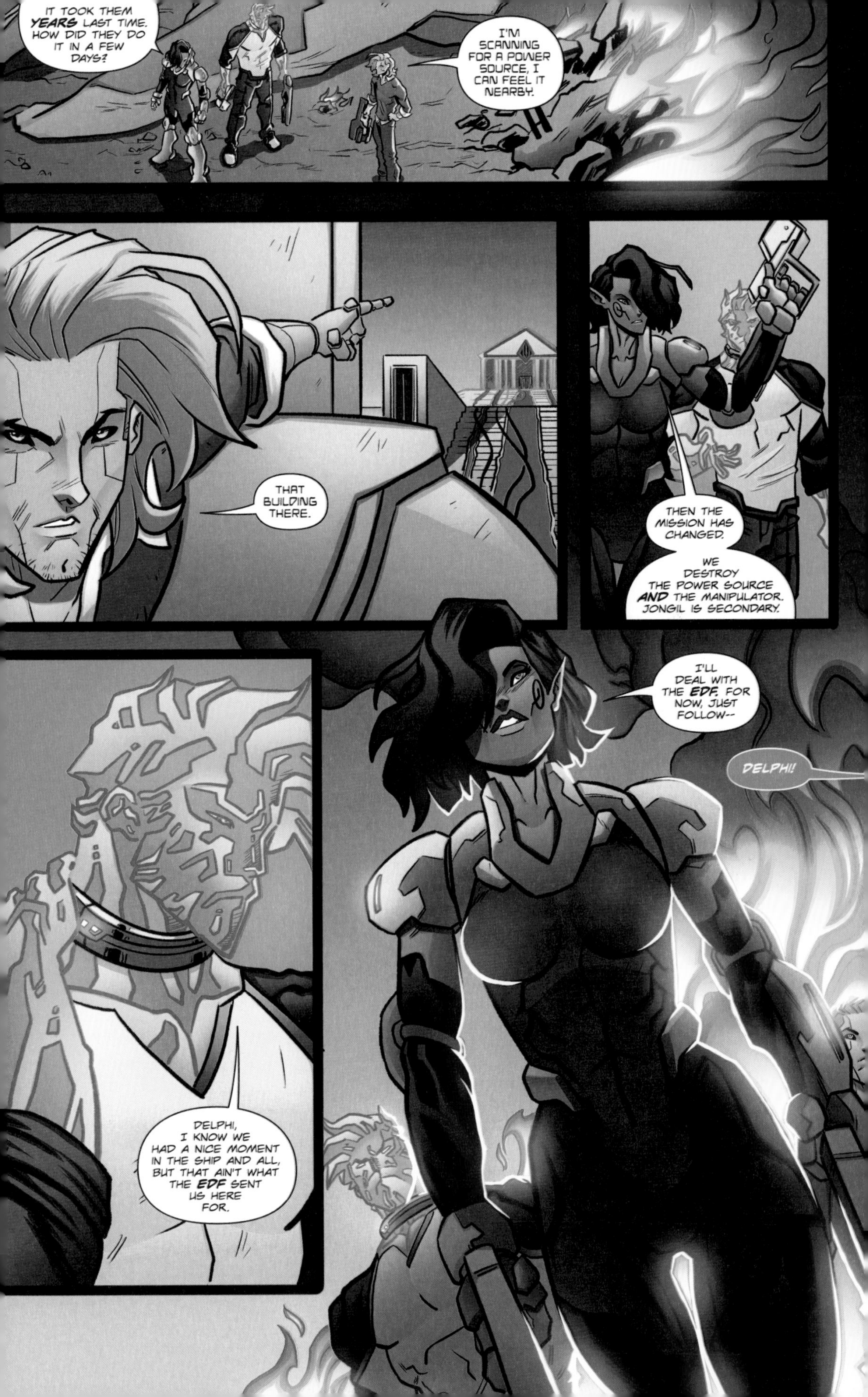

IT TOOK THEM YEARS LAST TIME. HOW DID THEY DO IT IN A FEW DAYS?
I'M SCANNING FOR A POWER SOURCE, I CAN FEEL IT NEARBY.
THAT BUILDING THERE.
THEN THE MISSION HAS CHANGED.
WE DESTROY THE POWER SOURCE AND THE MANIPULATOR. JONGIL IS SECONDARY.
I'LL DEAL WITH THE EDF. FOR NOW, JUST FOLLOW--
DELPHI!
DELPHI, I KNOW WE HAD A NICE MOMENT IN THE SHIP AND ALL, BUT THAT AIN'T WHAT THE EDF SENT US HERE FOR.

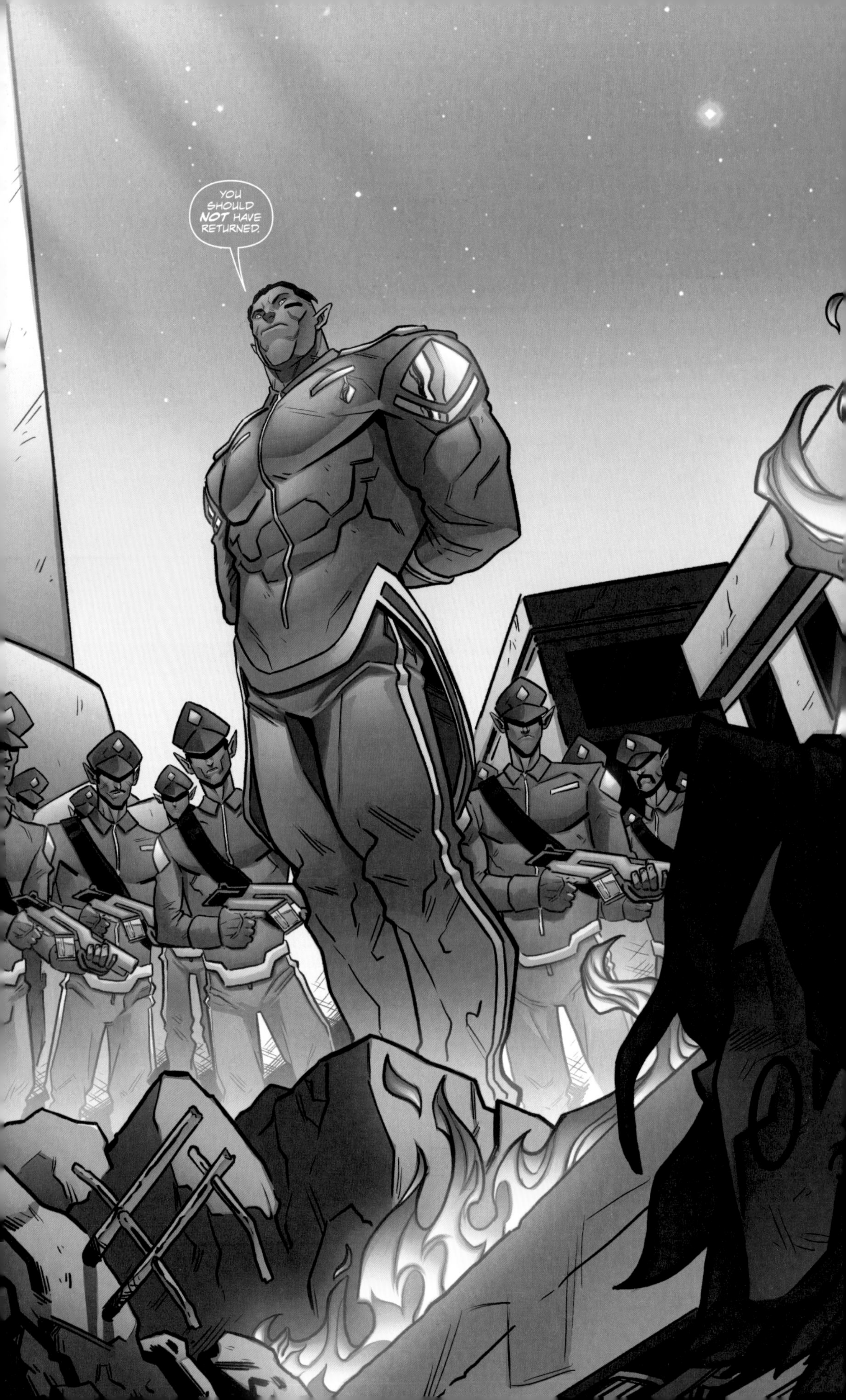
YOU SHOULD NOT HAVE RETURNED.

[3]

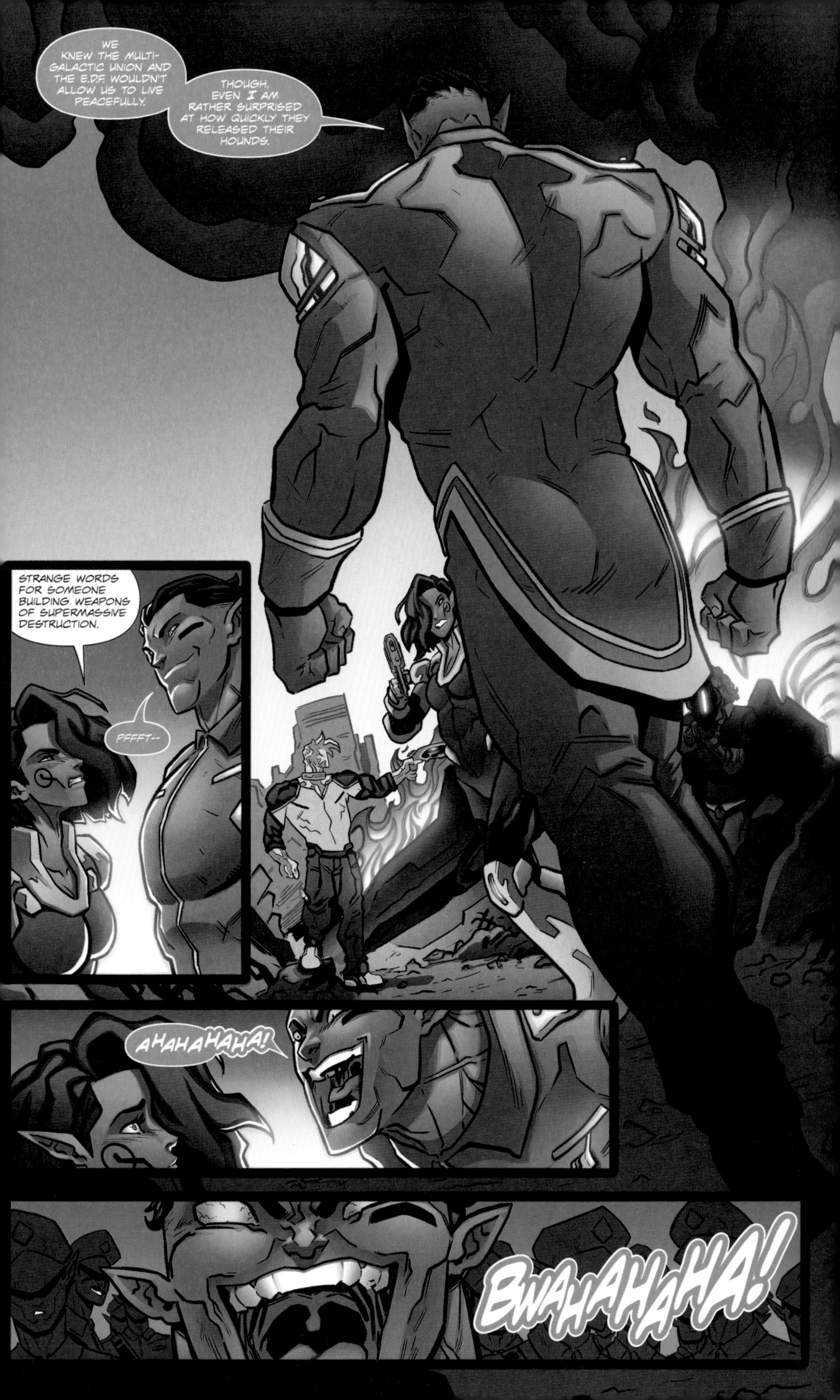
WE KNEW THE MULTI-GALACTIC UNION AND THE E.D.F. WOULDN'T ALLOW US TO LIVE PEACEFULLY.
THOUGH, EVEN I AM RATHER SURPRISED AT HOW QUICKLY THEY RELEASED THEIR HOUNDS.
STRANGE WORDS FOR SOMEONE BUILDING WEAPONS OF SUPERMASSIVE DESTRUCTION.
PFFFT--
AHAHAHAHA!
BWAHAHAHAHA!

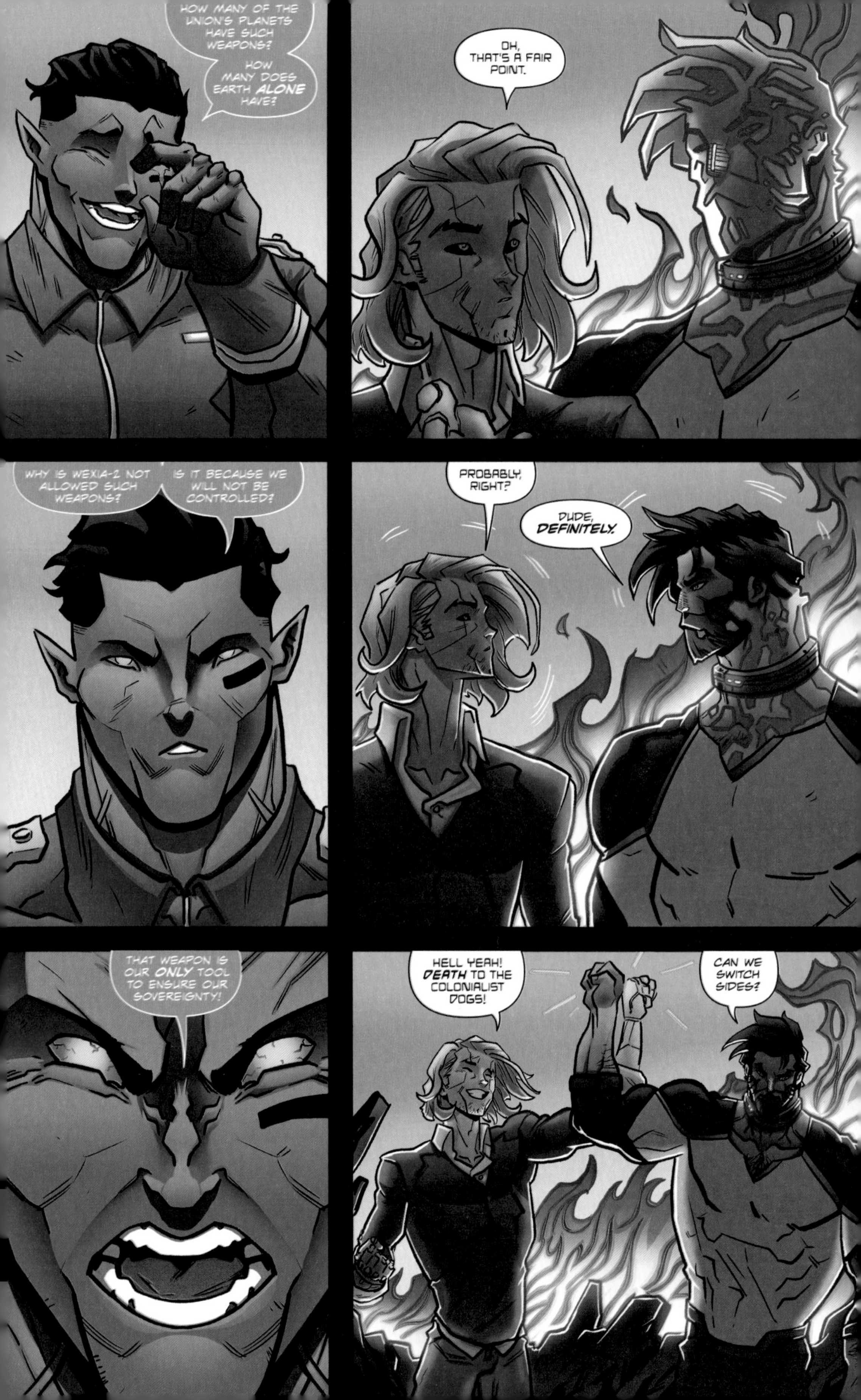
HOW MANY OF THE UNION'S PLANETS HAVE SUCH WEAPONS?
HOW MANY DOES EARTH ALONE HAVE?
OH, THAT'S A FAIR POINT.
WHY IS WEXIA-2 NOT ALLOWED SUCH WEAPONS?
IS IT BECAUSE WE WILL NOT BE CONTROLLED?
PROBABLY, RIGHT?
DUDE, DEFINITELY.
THAT WEAPON IS OUR ONLY TOOL TO ENSURE OUR SOVEREIGNTY!
HELL YEAH! DEATH TO THE COLONIALIST DOGS!
CAN WE SWITCH SIDES?

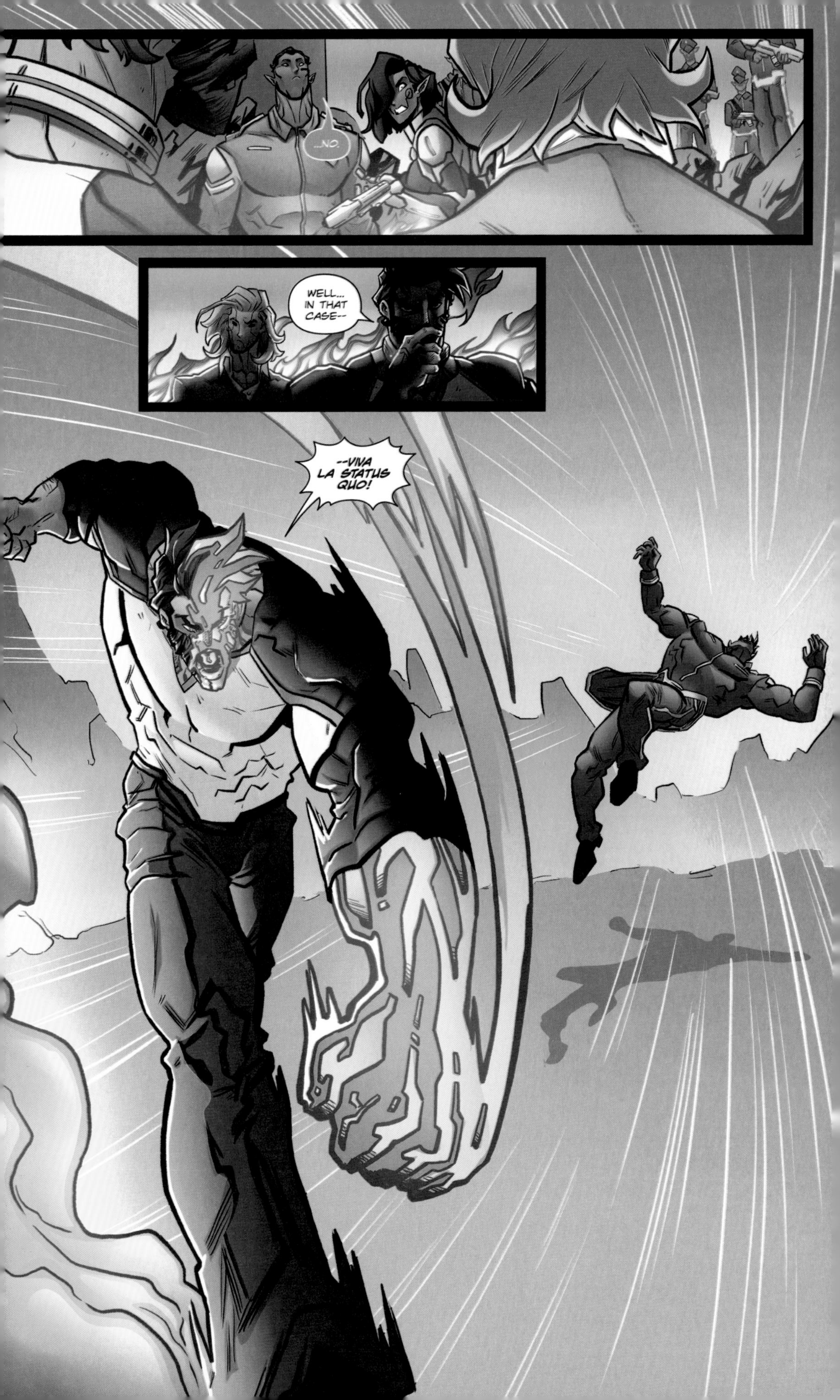
...NO.
WELL... IN THAT CASE--
--VIVA LA STATUS QUO!

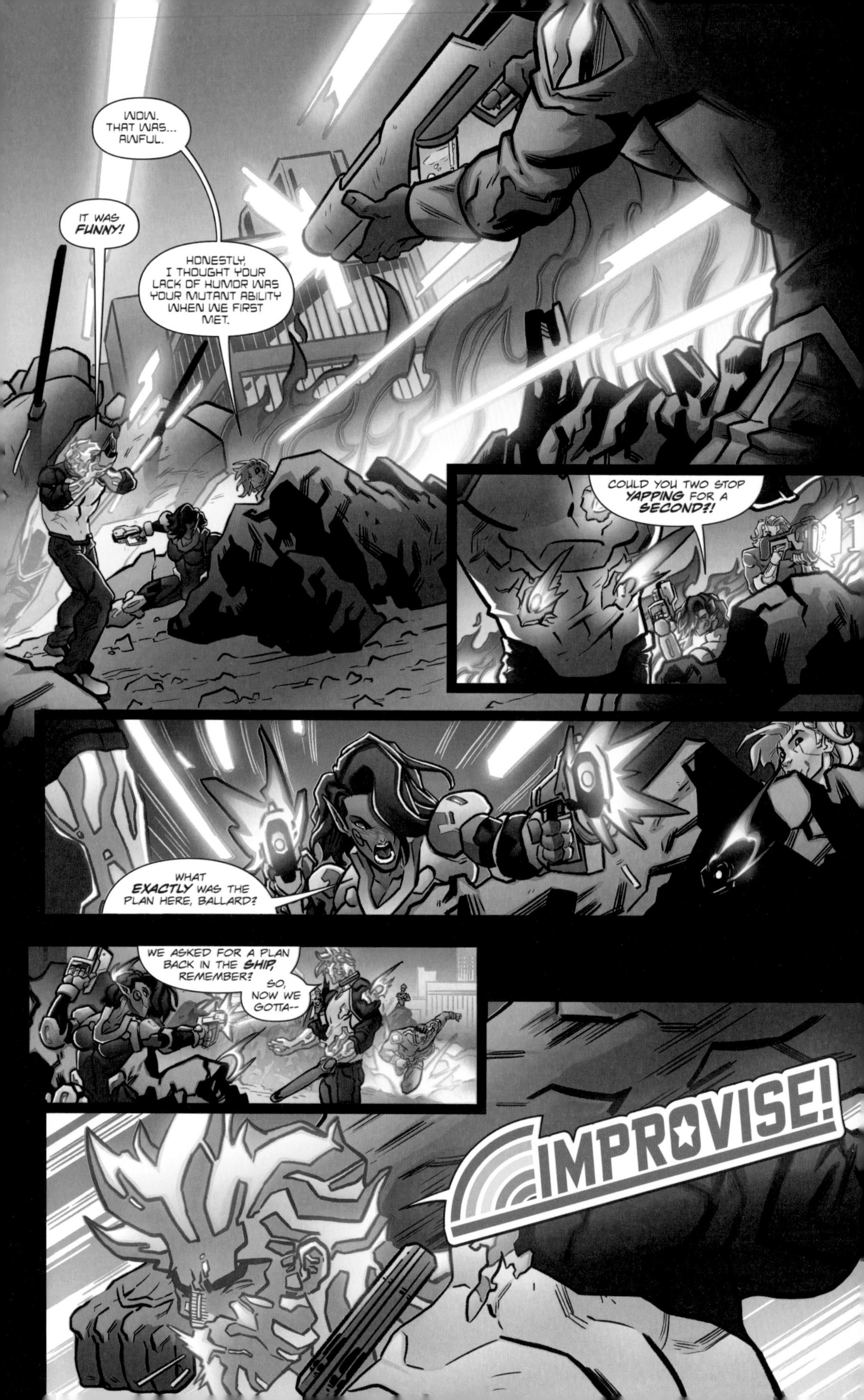
WOW. THAT WAS... AWFUL.
IT WAS FUNNY!
HONESTLY, I THOUGHT YOUR LACK OF HUMOR WAS YOUR MUTANT ABILITY WHEN WE FIRST MET.
COULD YOU TWO STOP YAPPING FOR A SECOND?!
WHAT EXACTLY WAS THE PLAN HERE, BALLARD?
WE ASKED FOR A PLAN BACK IN THE SHIP, REMEMBER?
SO, NOW WE GOTTA--
IMPROVISE!

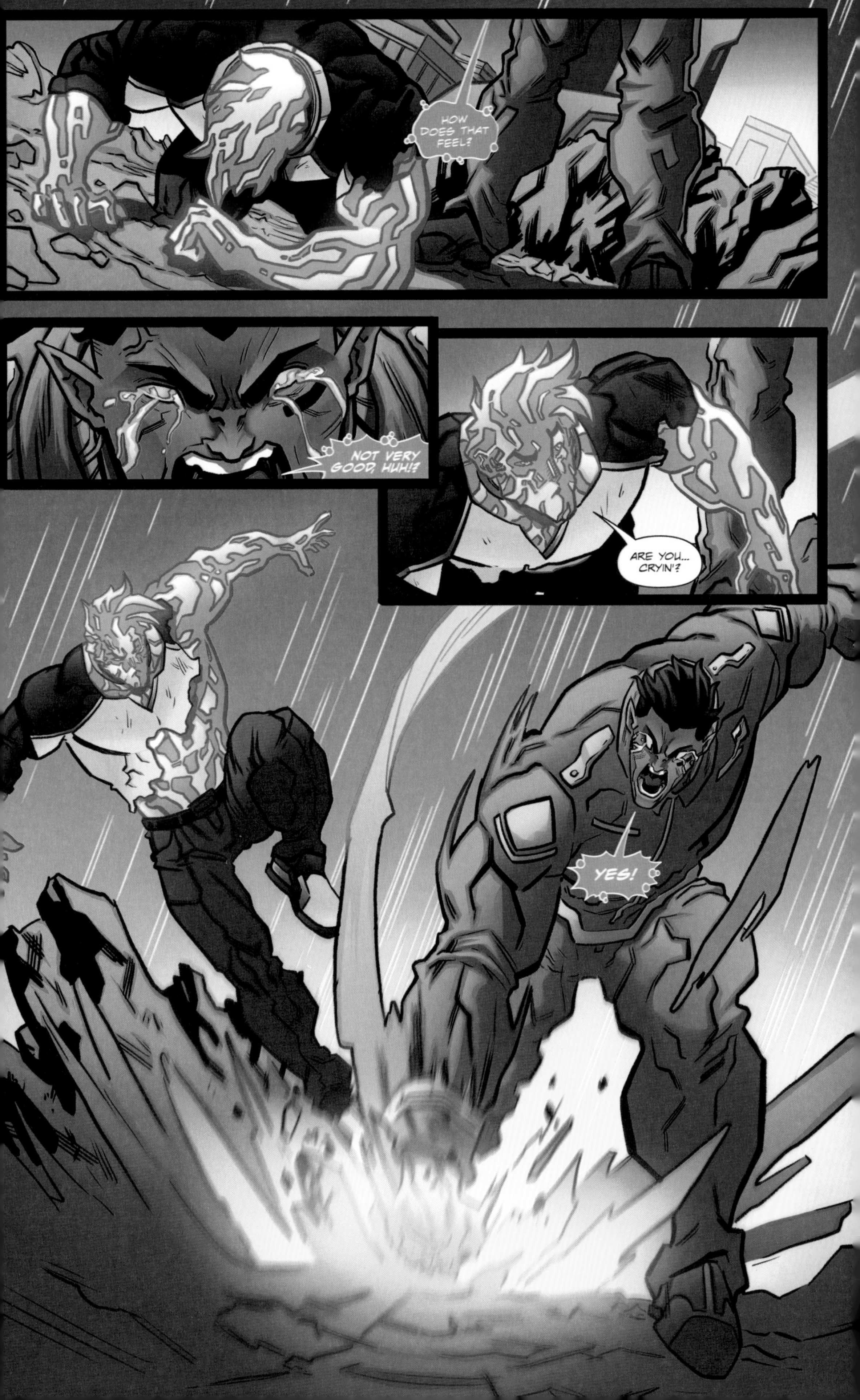
HOW DOES THAT FEEL?
NOT VERY GOOD, HUH!?
ARE YOU... CRYIN'?
YES!

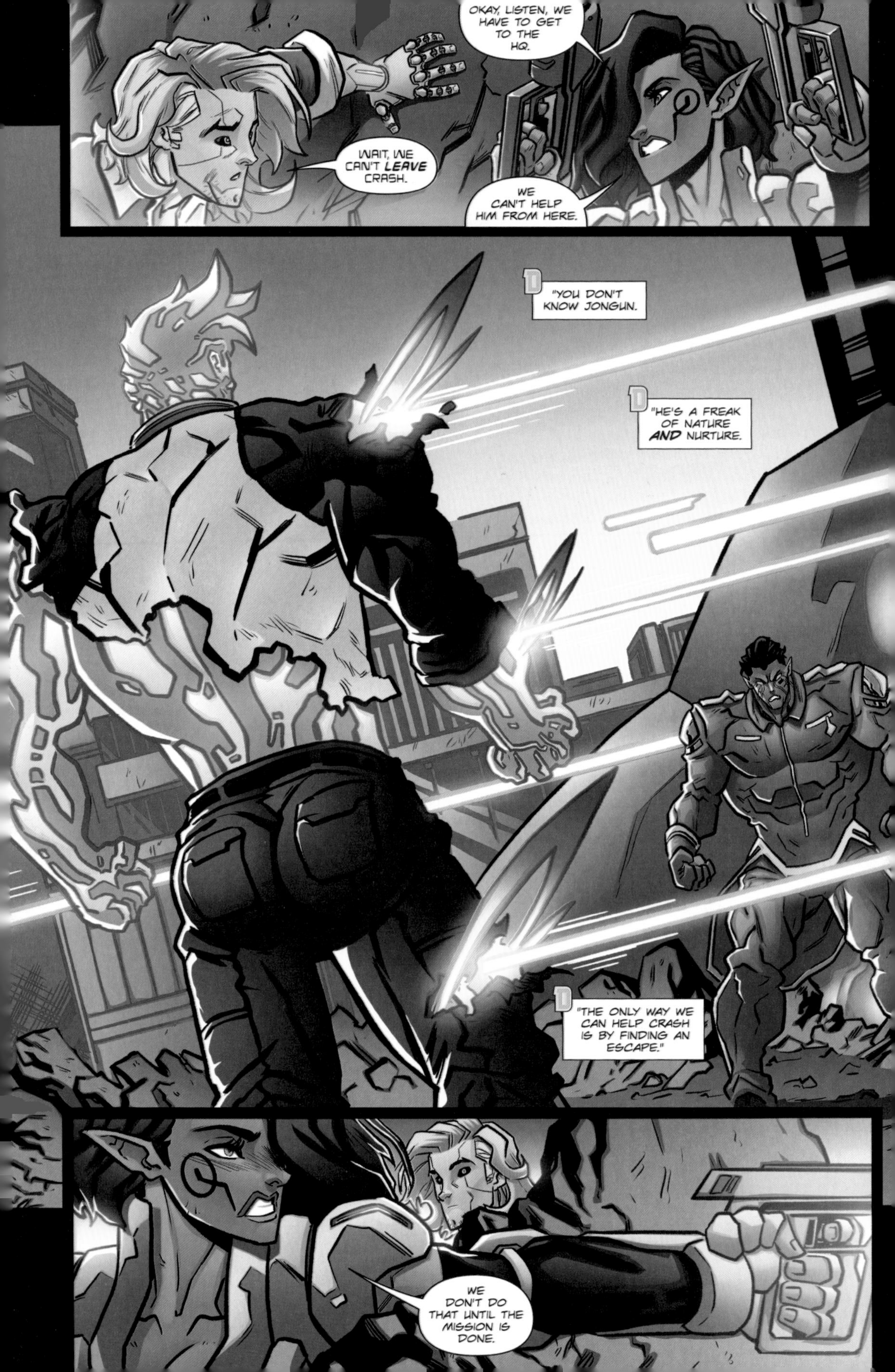
OKAY, LISTEN, WE HAVE TO GET TO THE HQ.
WAIT, WE CAN'T **LEAVE** CRASH.
WE CAN'T HELP HIM FROM HERE.
"YOU DON'T KNOW JONGUN.
"HE'S A FREAK OF NATURE **AND** NURTURE.
"THE ONLY WAY WE CAN HELP CRASH IS BY FINDING AN ESCAPE."
WE DON'T DO THAT UNTIL THE MISSION IS DONE.

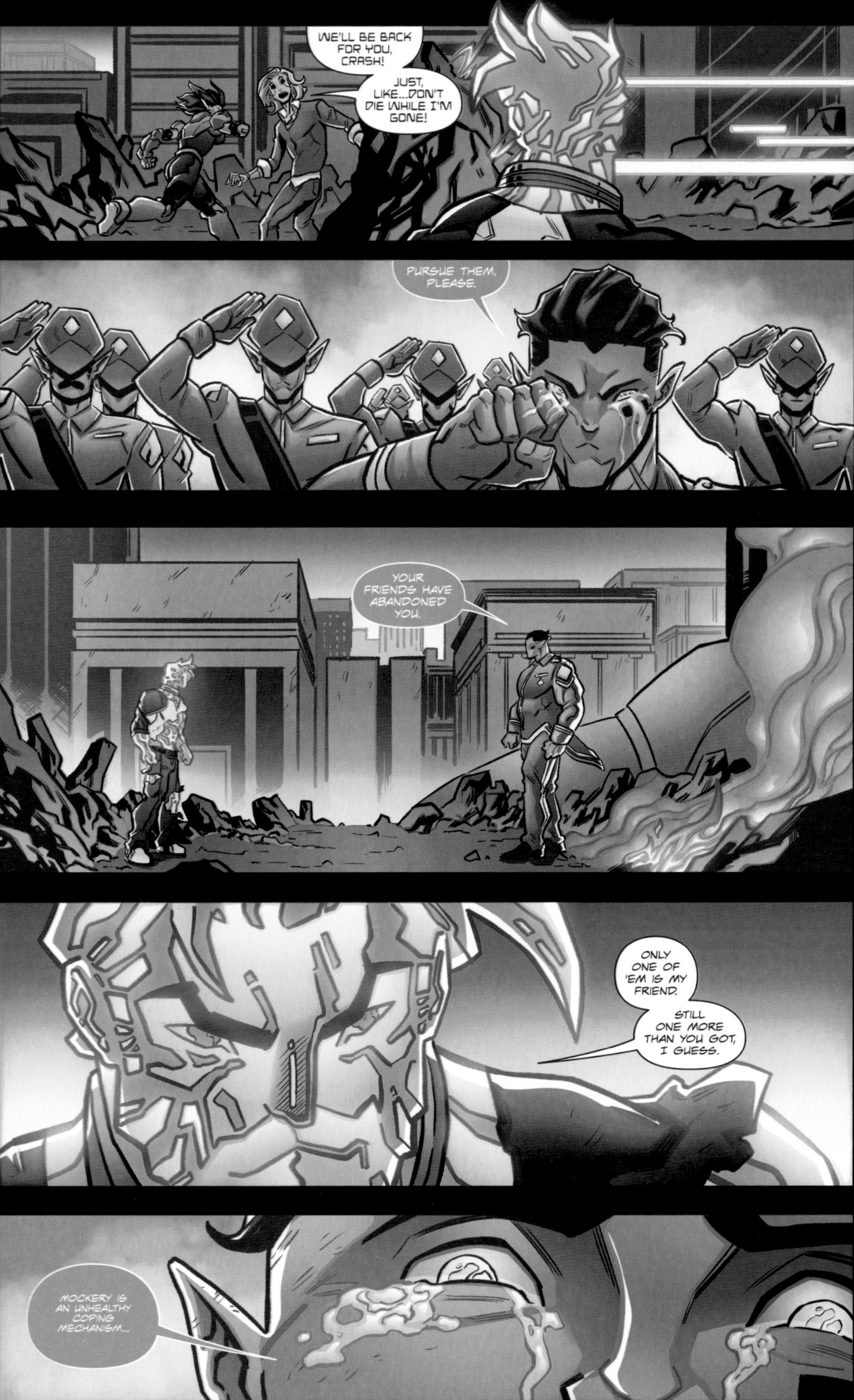
WE'LL BE BACK FOR YOU, CRASH!
JUST, LIKE...DON'T DIE WHILE I'M GONE!
PURSUE THEM, PLEASE.
YOUR FRIENDS HAVE ABANDONED YOU.
ONLY ONE OF 'EM IS MY FRIEND.
STILL ONE MORE THAN YOU GOT, I GUESS.
MOCKERY IS AN UNHEALTHY COPING MECHANISM...

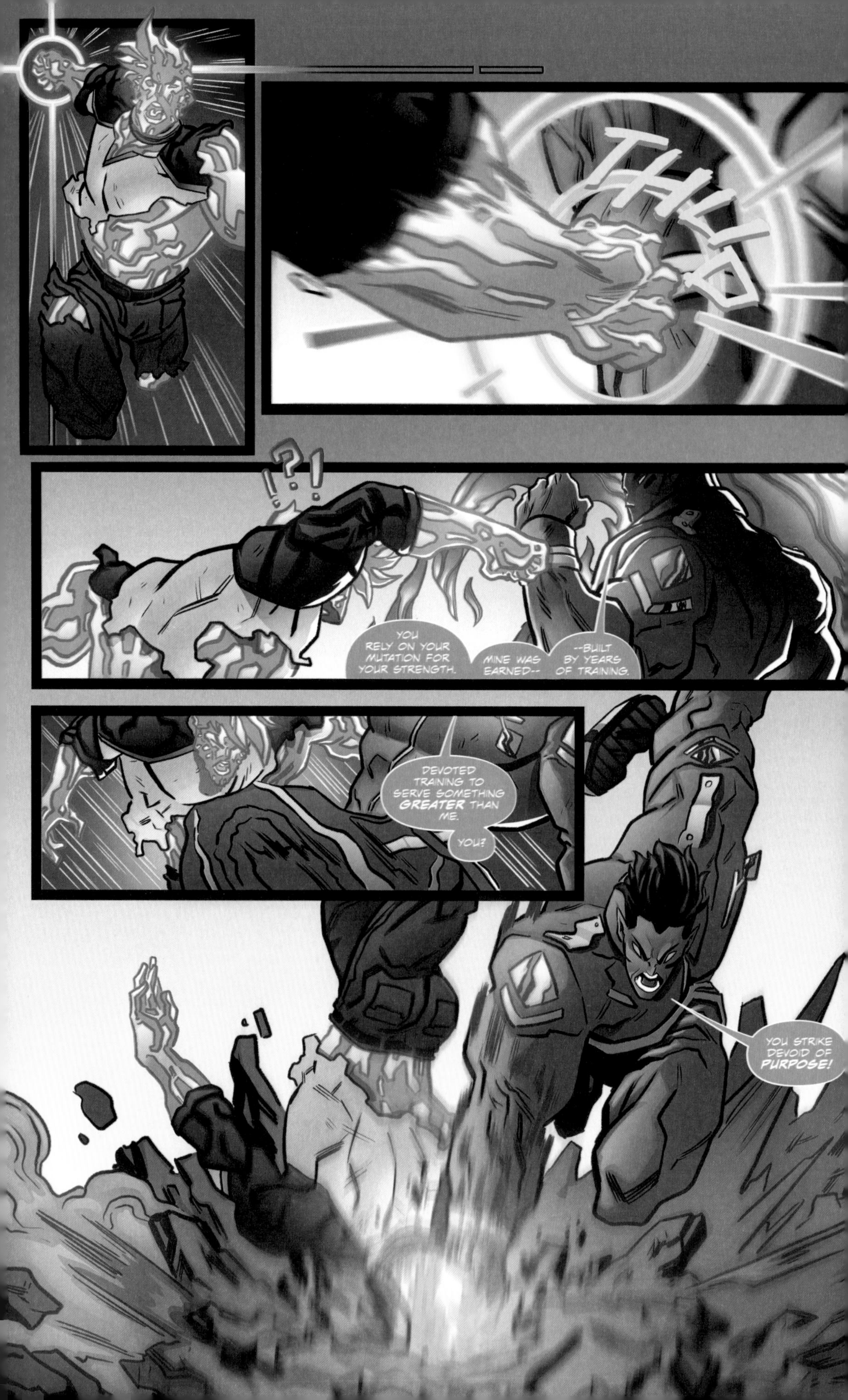
THUD
!?!
YOU RELY ON YOUR MUTATION FOR YOUR STRENGTH.
MINE WAS EARNED--
--BUILT BY YEARS OF TRAINING.
DEVOTED TRAINING TO SERVE SOMETHING GREATER THAN ME.
YOU?
YOU STRIKE DEVOID OF PURPOSE!

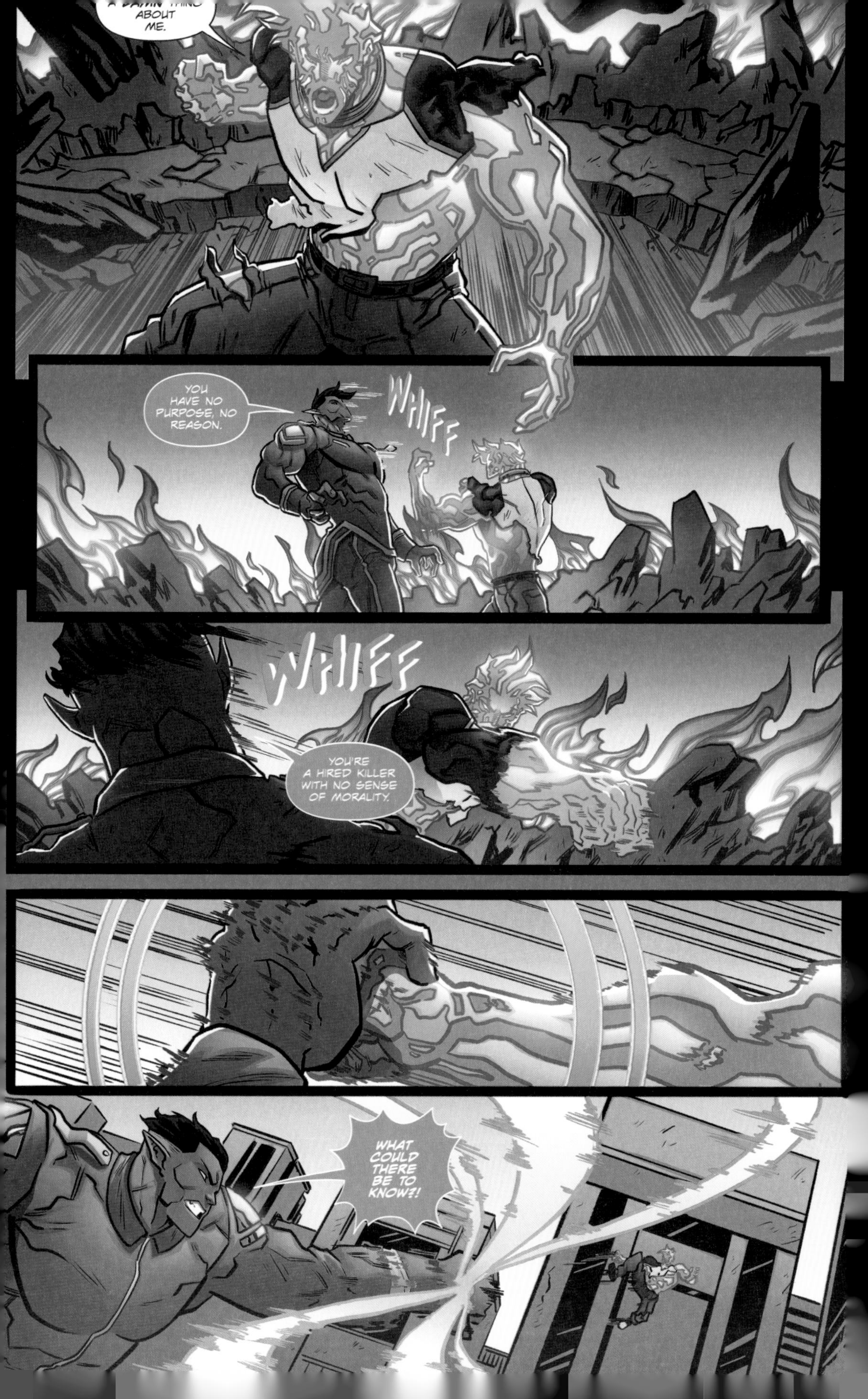
ABOUT ME.
YOU HAVE NO PURPOSE, NO REASON.
WHIFF
WHIFF
YOU'RE A HIRED KILLER WITH NO SENSE OF MORALITY.
WHAT COULD THERE BE TO KNOW?!

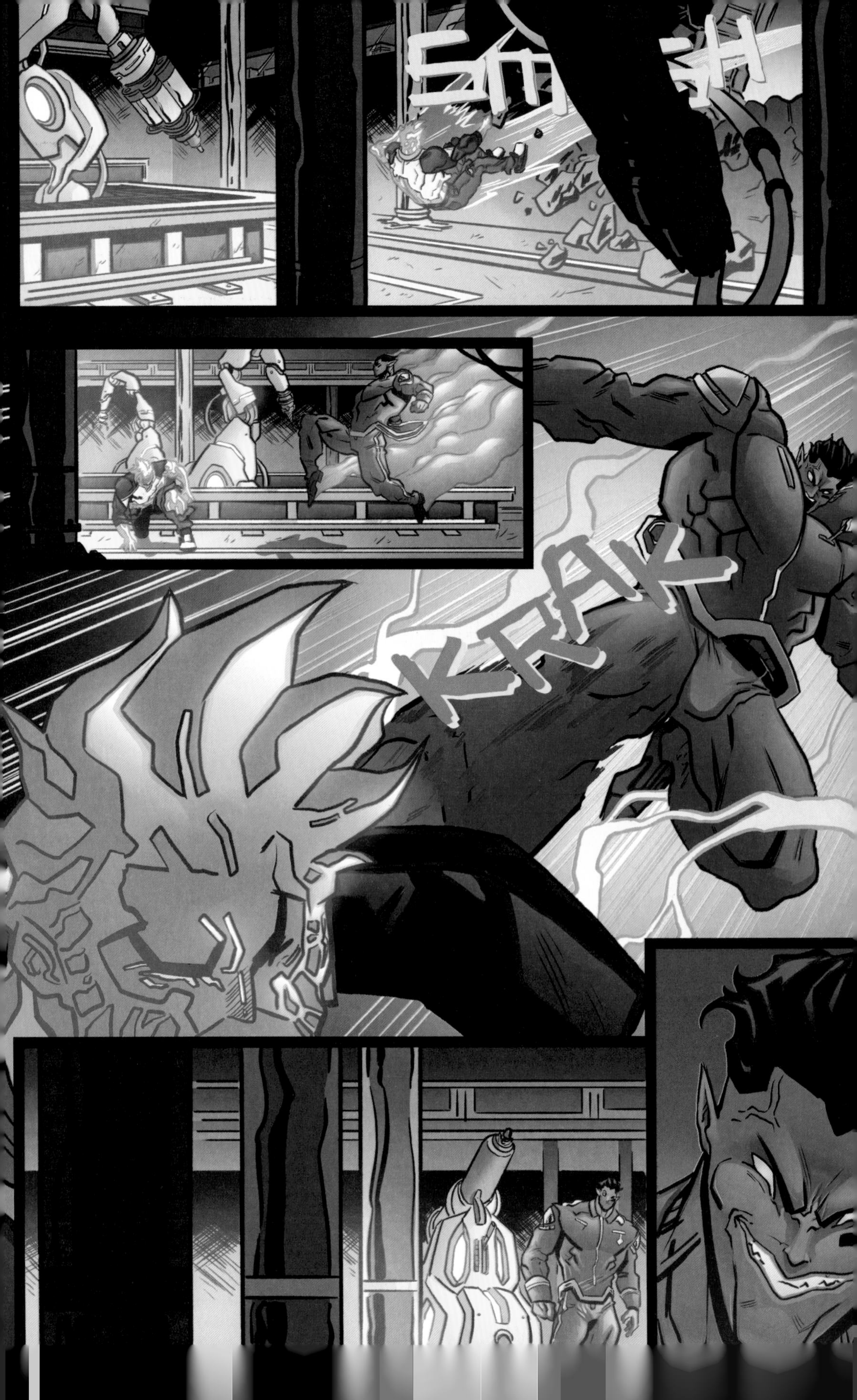
KRAK

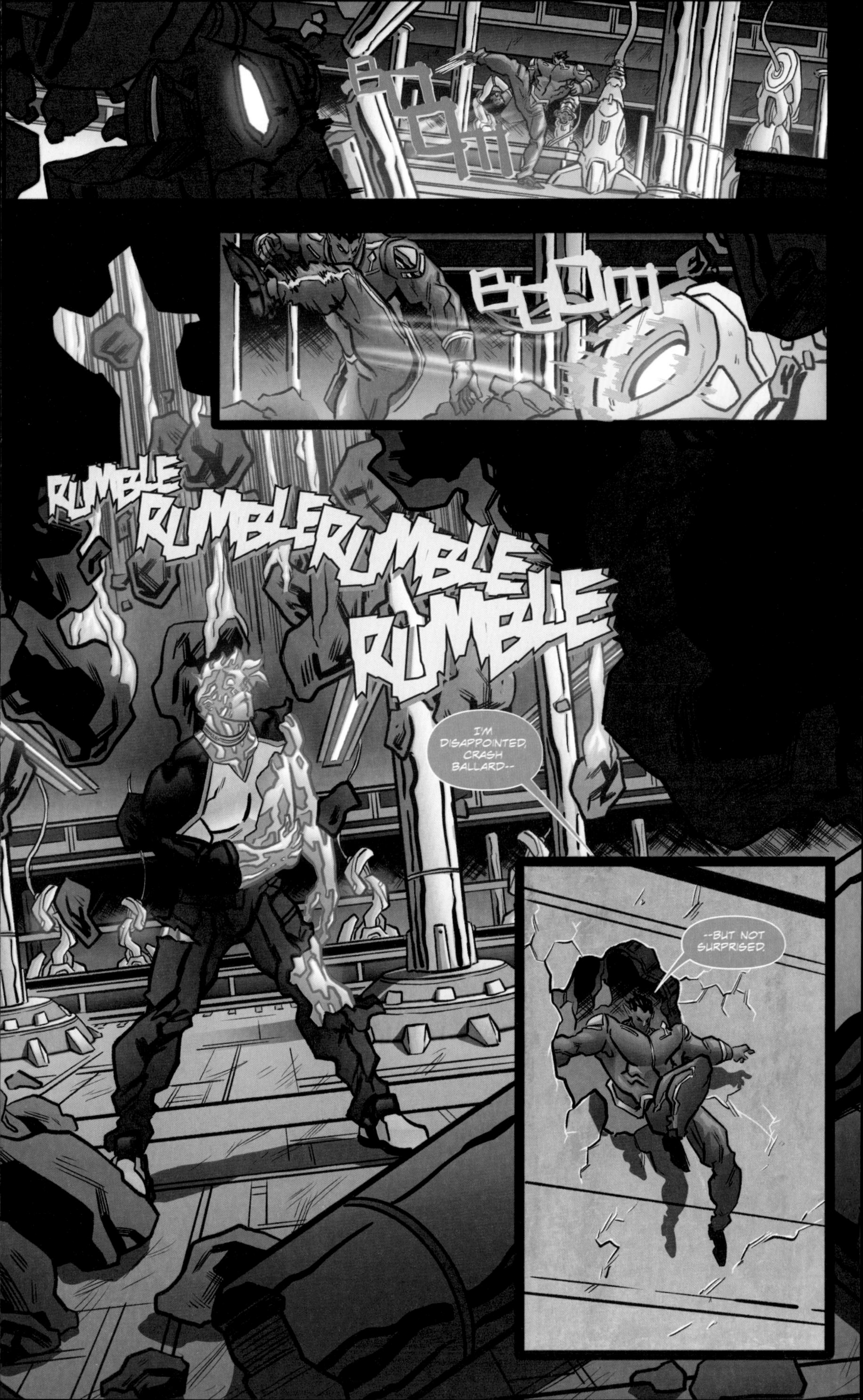

BOOOM
BOOM
RUMBLE RUMBLE RUMBLE RUMBLE
I'M DISAPPOINTED, CRASH BALLARD--
--BUT NOT SURPRISED.

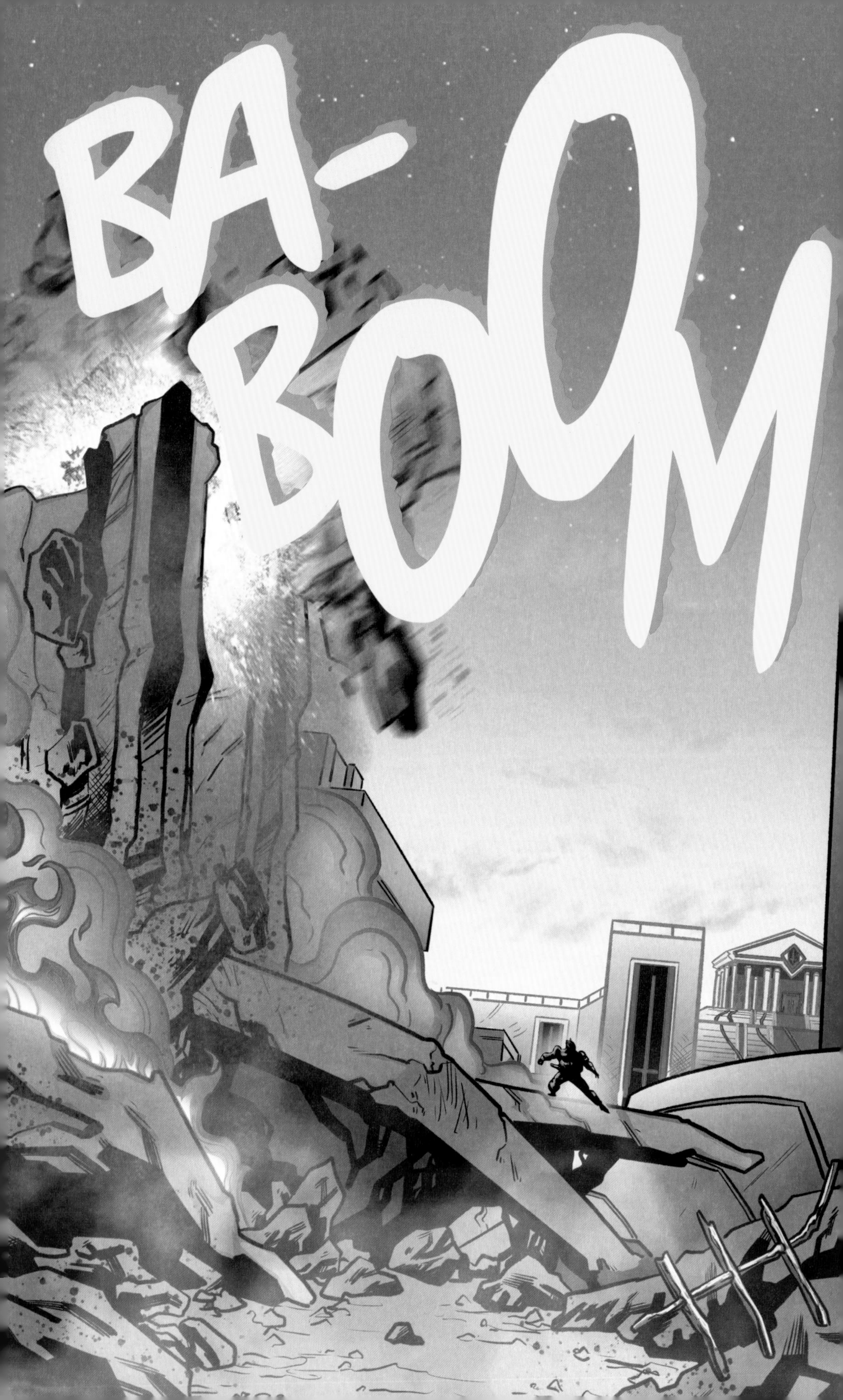
BA-BOOM

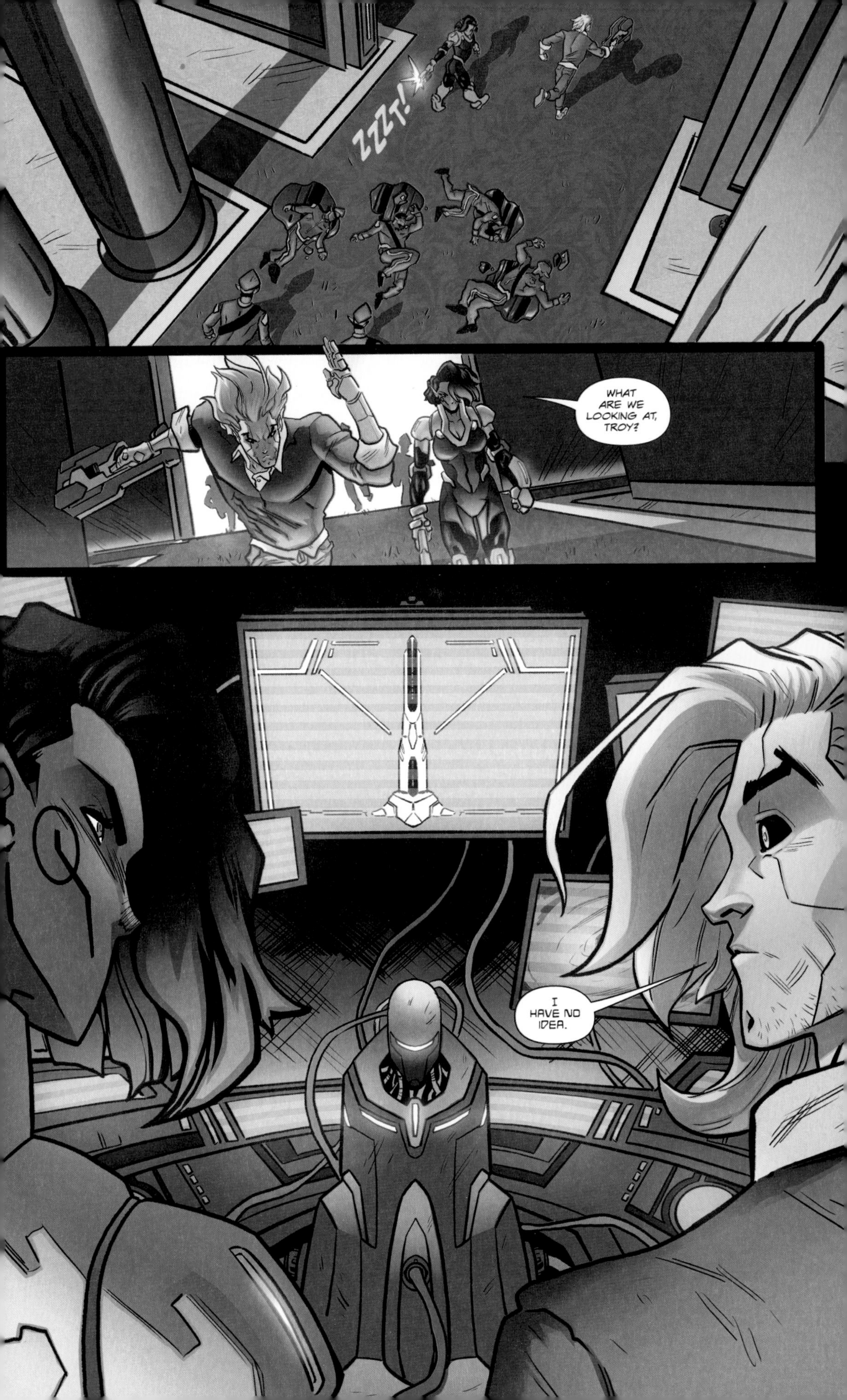
ZZZT!
WHAT ARE WE LOOKING AT, TROY?
I HAVE NO IDEA.

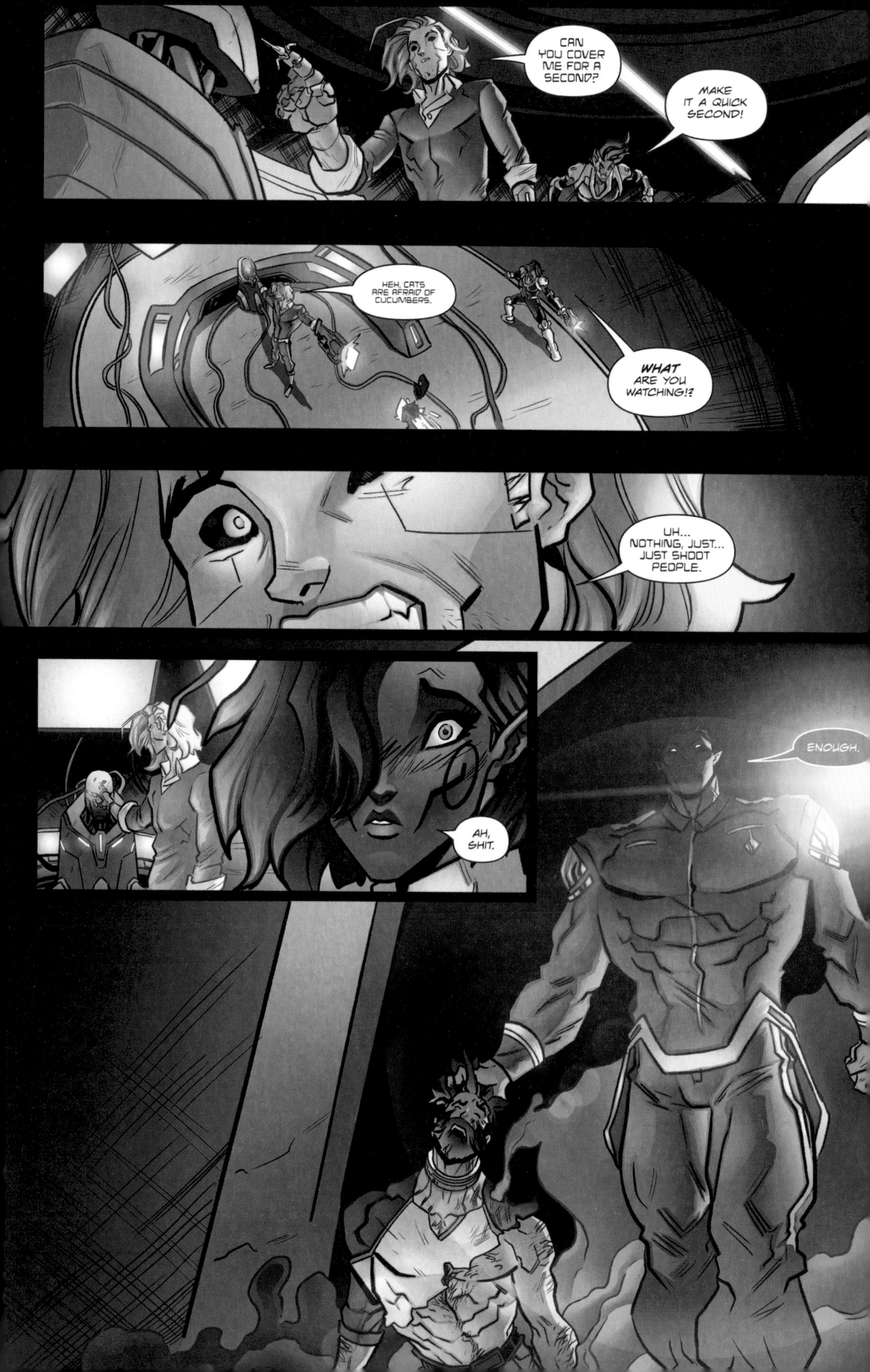
CAN YOU COVER ME FOR A SECOND?
MAKE IT A QUICK SECOND!
HEH, CATS ARE AFRAID OF CUCUMBERS.
WHAT ARE YOU WATCHING!?
UH... NOTHING, JUST... JUST SHOOT PEOPLE.
AH, SHIT.
ENOUGH.

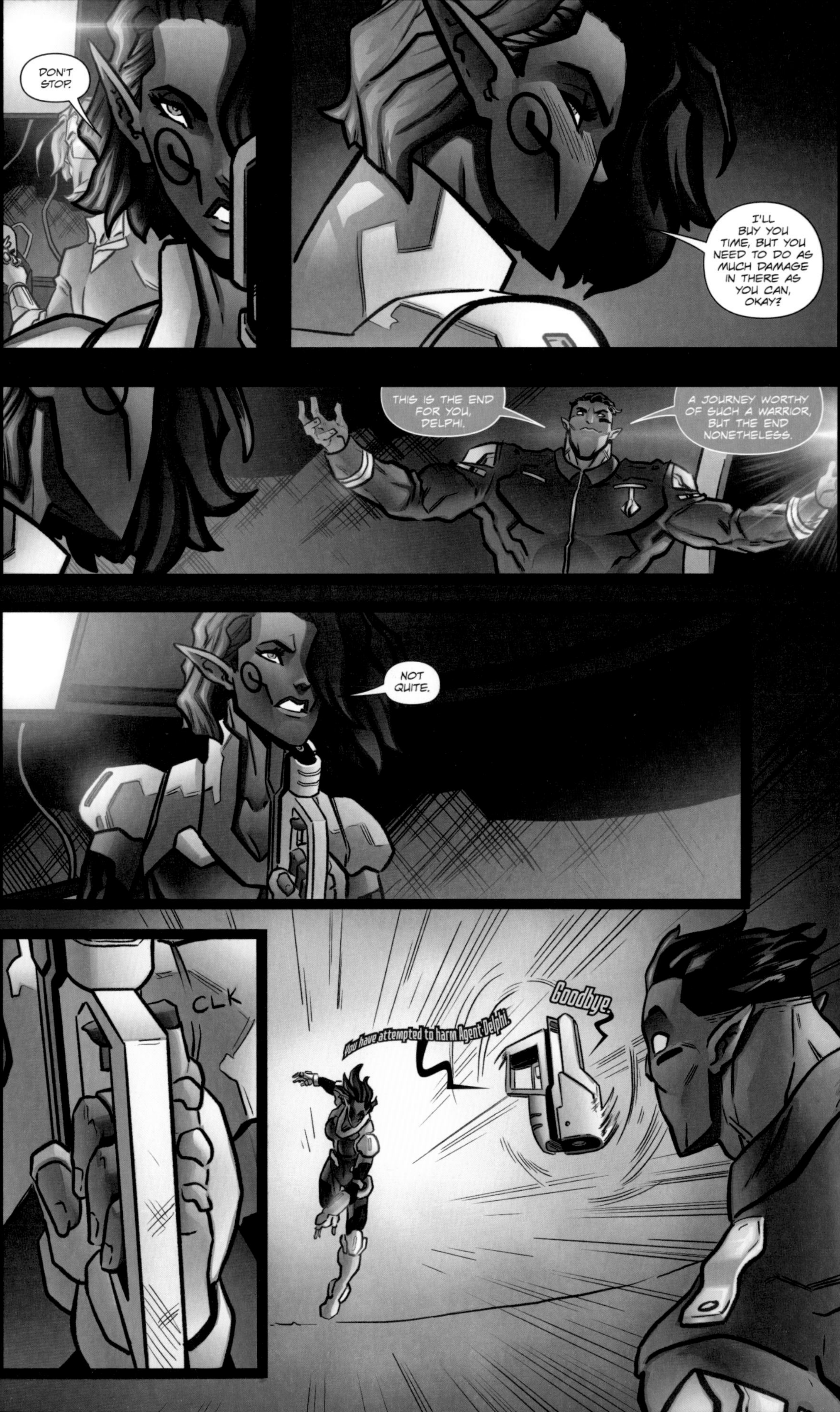
DON'T STOP.
I'LL BUY YOU TIME, BUT YOU NEED TO DO AS MUCH DAMAGE IN THERE AS YOU CAN, OKAY?
THIS IS THE END FOR YOU, DELPHI.
A JOURNEY WORTHY OF SUCH A WARRIOR, BUT THE END NONETHELESS.
NOT QUITE.
CLK
You have attempted to harm Agent Delphi.
Goodbye.

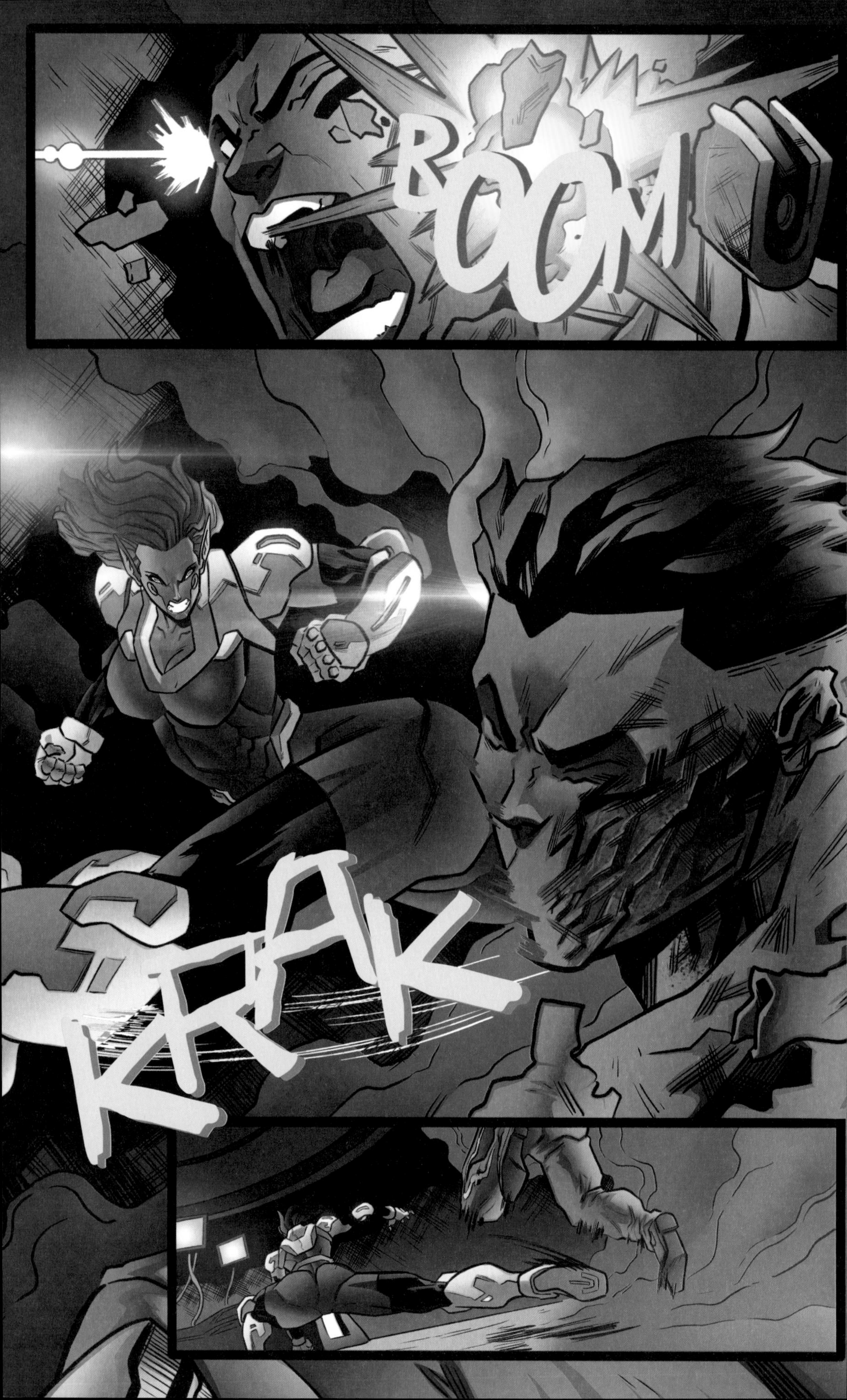
BOOM
KRAK

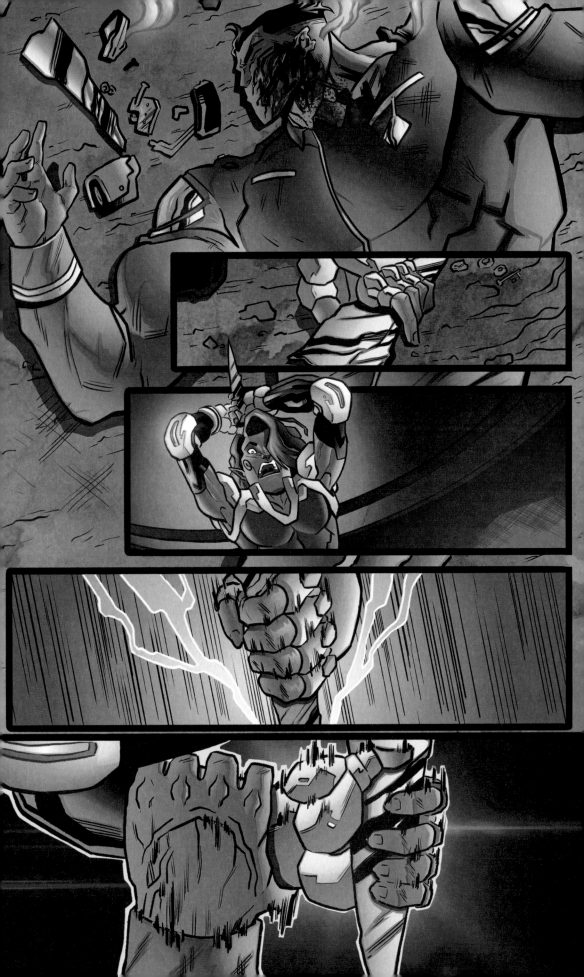

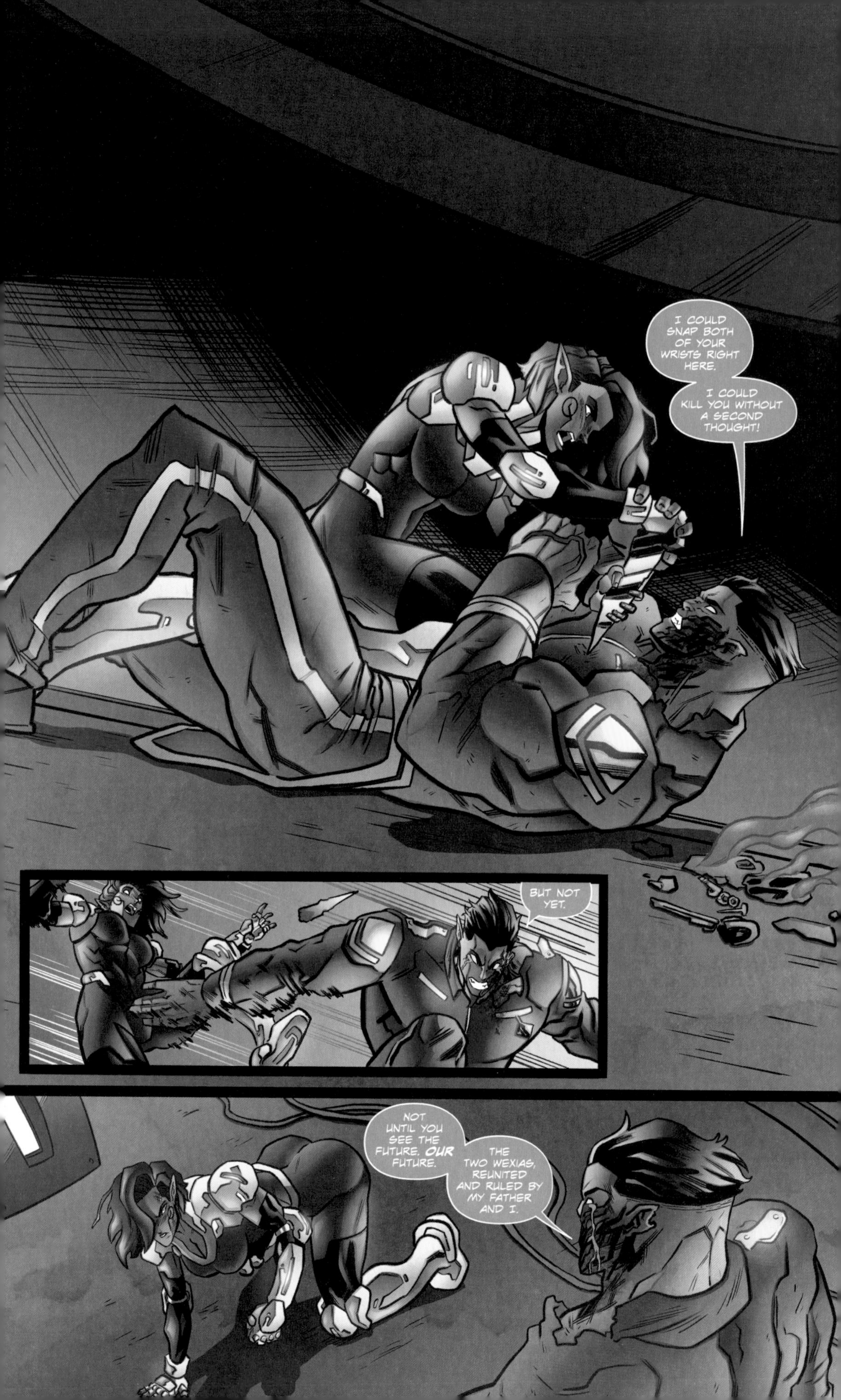
I COULD SNAP BOTH OF YOUR WRISTS RIGHT HERE.
I COULD KILL YOU WITHOUT A SECOND THOUGHT!
BUT NOT YET.
NOT UNTIL YOU SEE THE FUTURE. *OUR* FUTURE.
THE TWO WEXIAS, REUNITED AND RULED BY MY FATHER AND I.

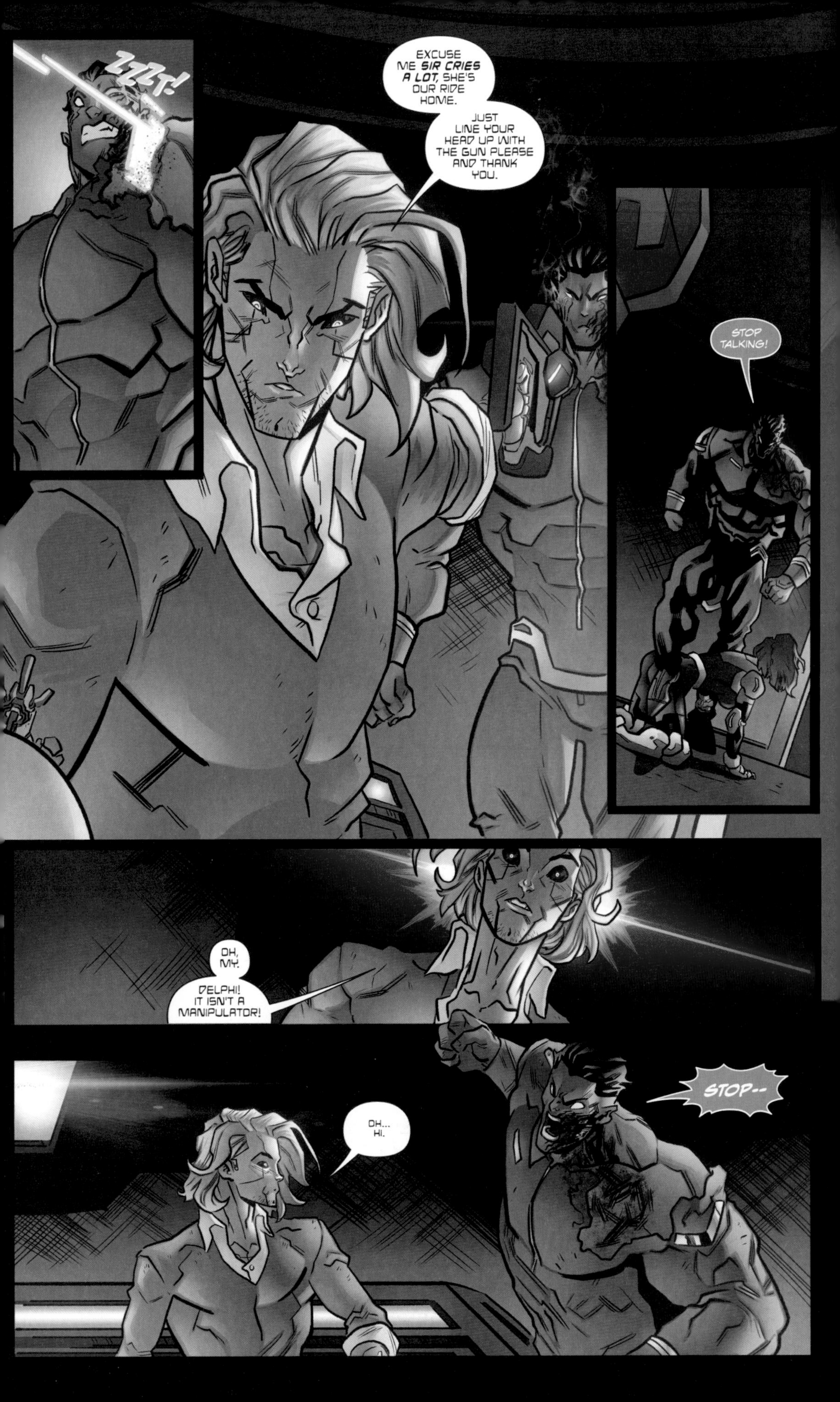
ZZZT!
EXCUSE ME **SIR CRIES A LOT**, SHE'S OUR RIDE HOME.
JUST LINE YOUR HEAD UP WITH THE GUN PLEASE AND THANK YOU.
STOP TALKING!
OH, MY.
DELPHI! IT ISN'T A MANIPULATOR!
OH... HI.
STOP--

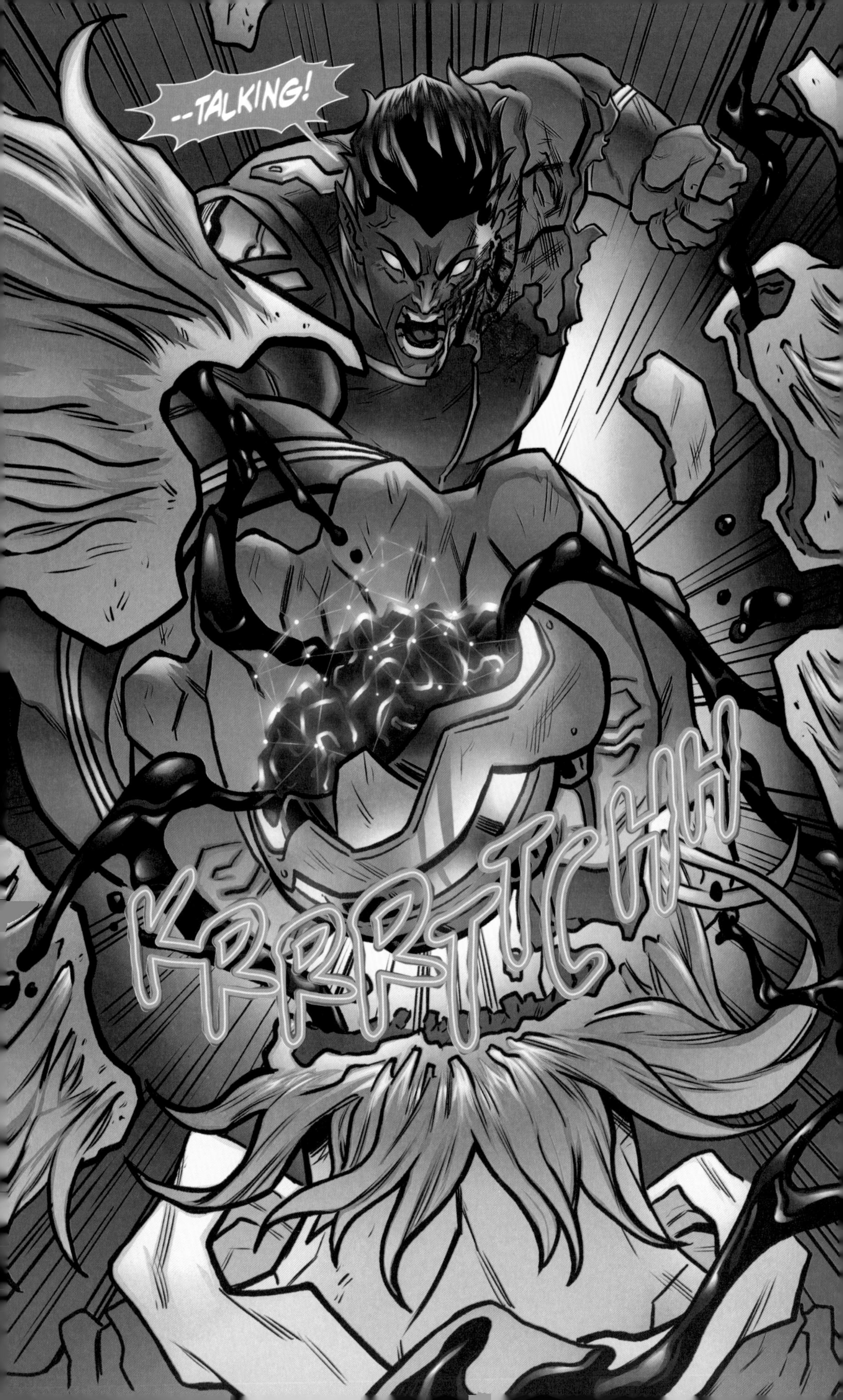
--TALKING!
KRRRTCHH

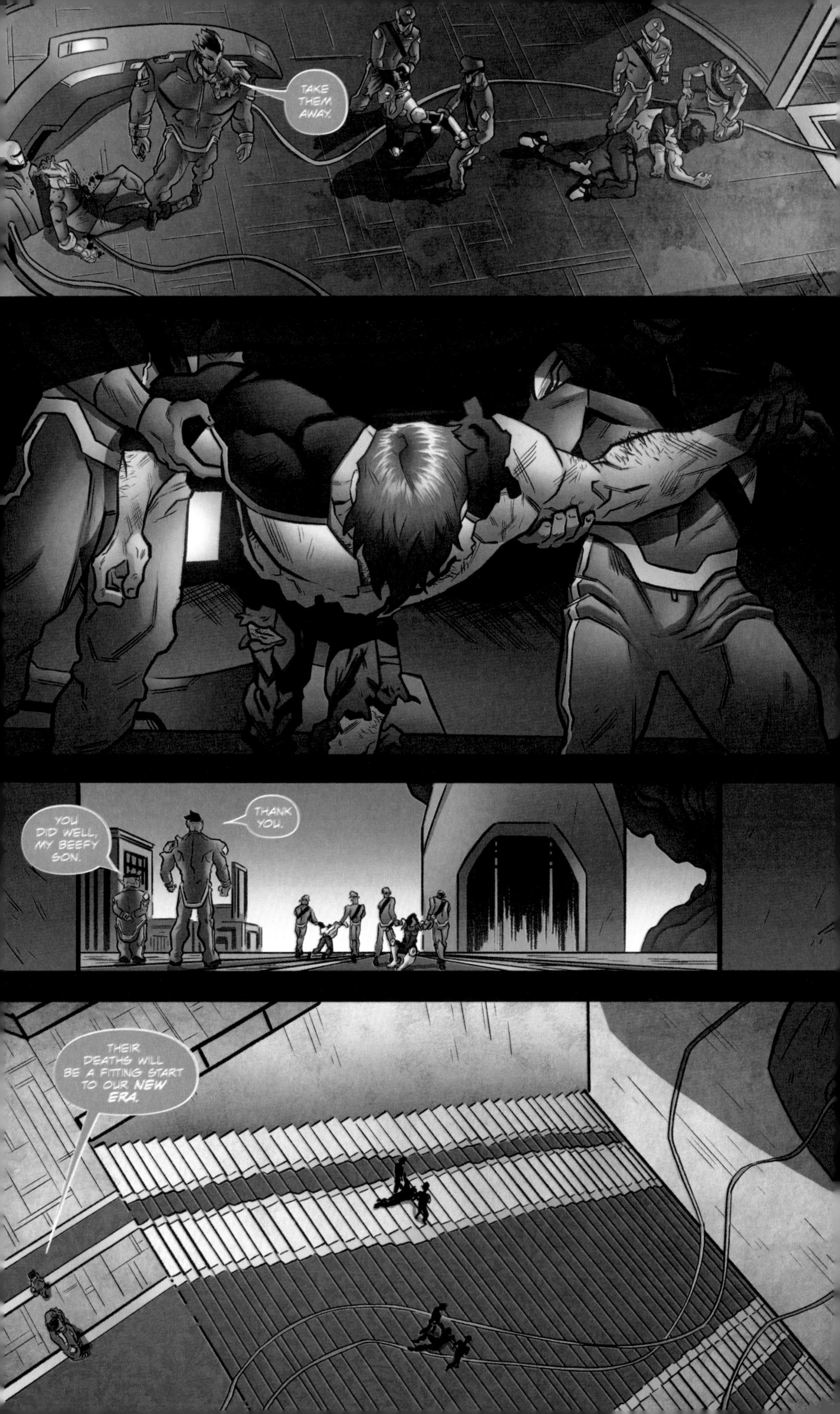
TAKE THEM AWAY.
YOU DID WELL, MY BEEFY SON.
THANK YOU.
THEIR DEATHS WILL BE A FITTING START TO OUR NEW ERA.

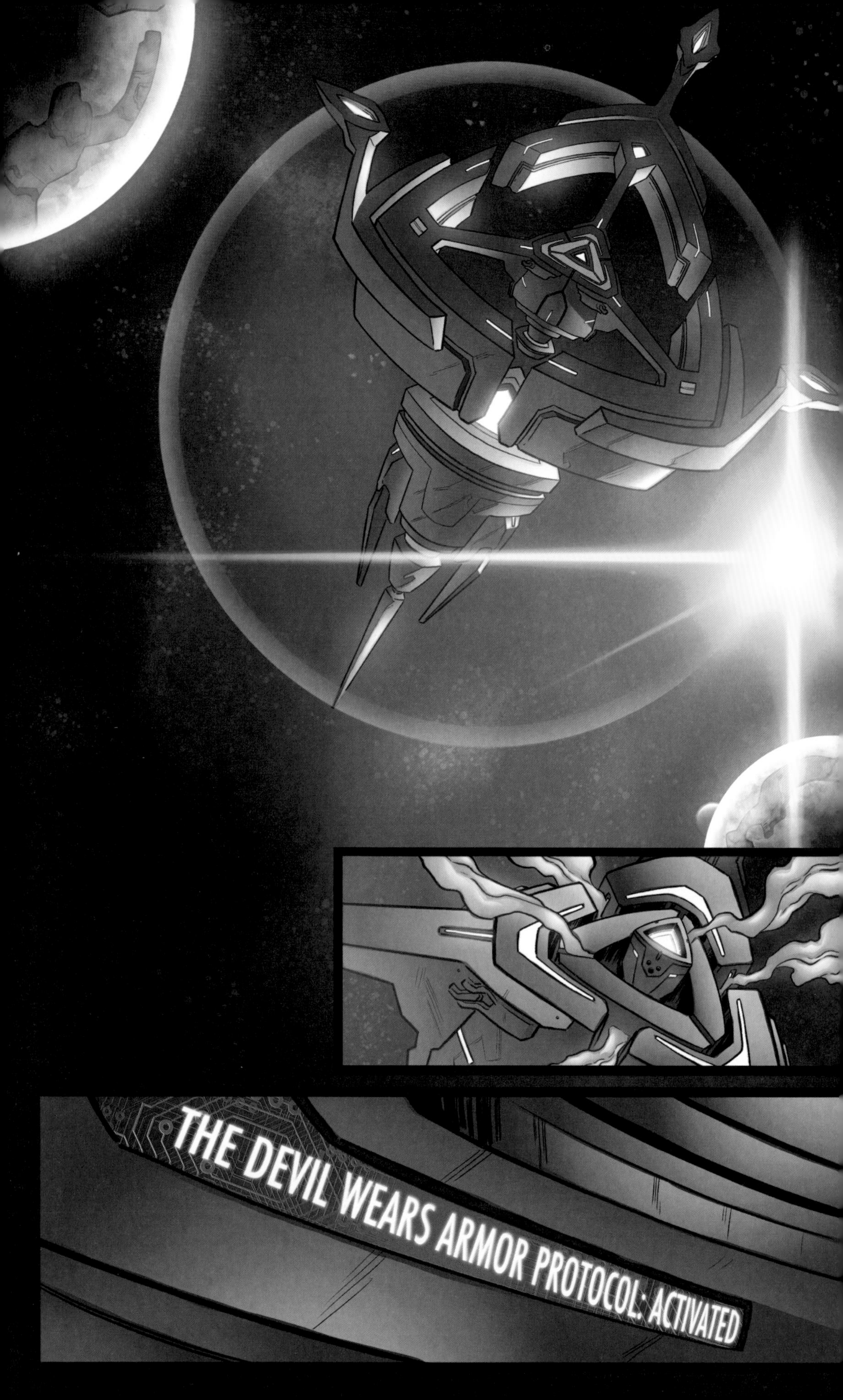
THE DEVIL WEARS ARMOR PROTOCOL: ACTIVATED

[4]

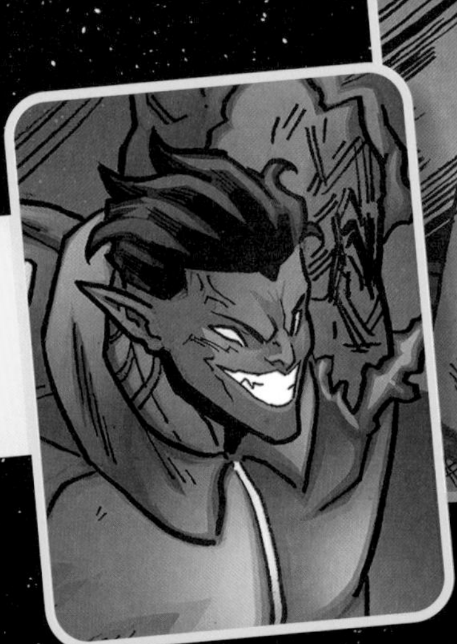

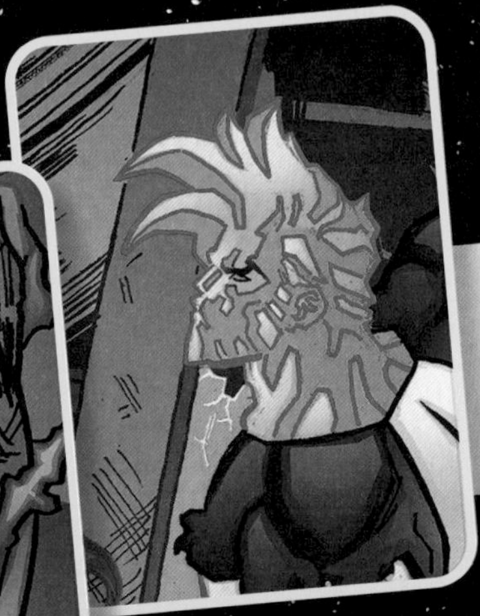

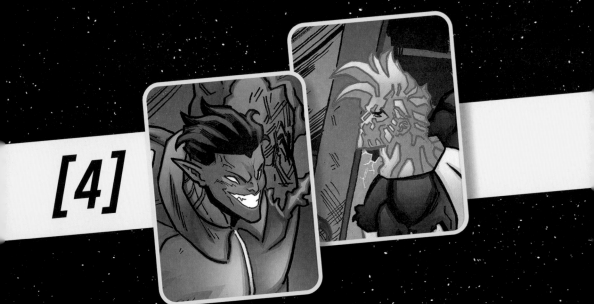

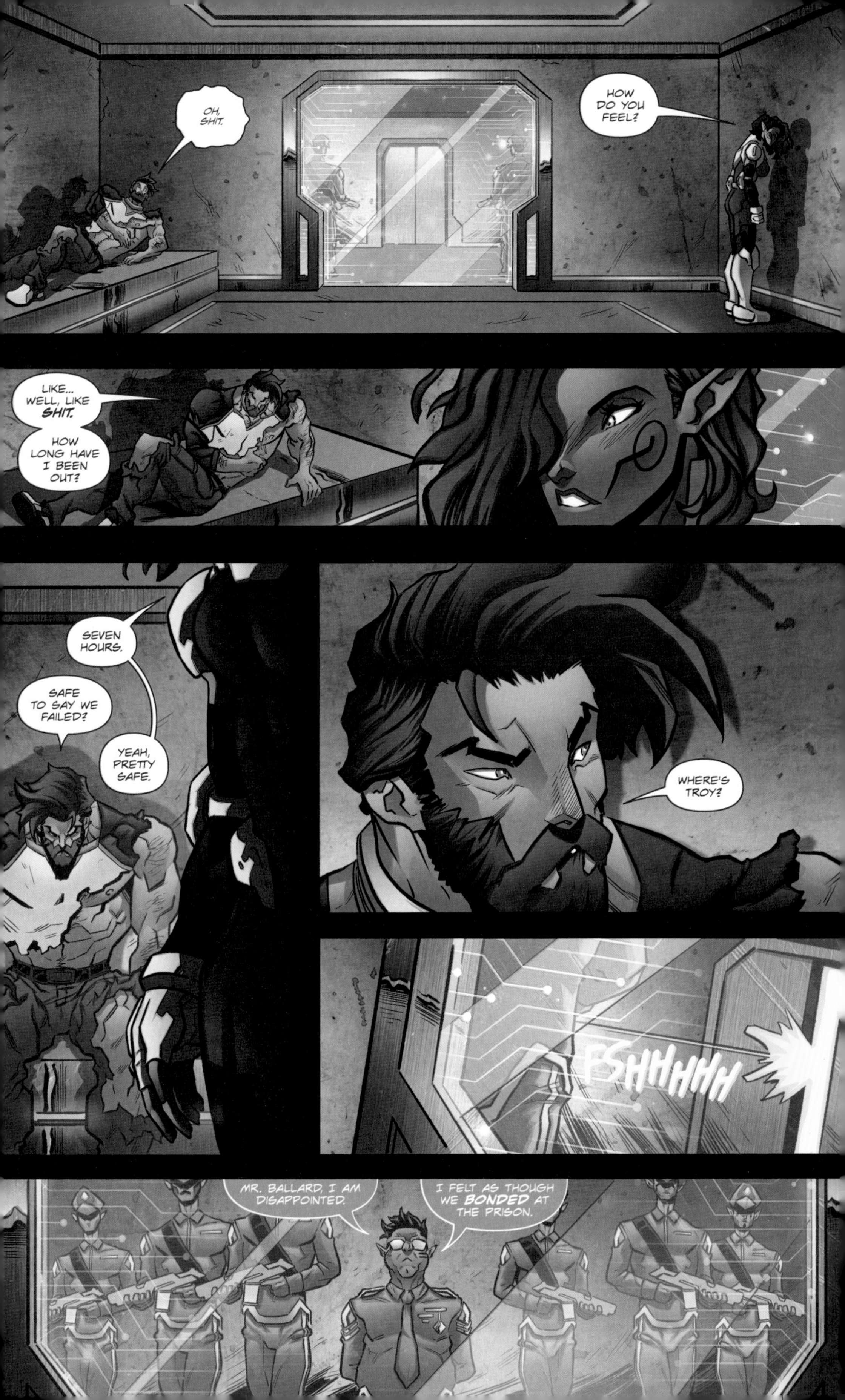

OH, SHIT.
HOW DO YOU FEEL?
LIKE... WELL, LIKE SHIT.
HOW LONG HAVE I BEEN OUT?
SEVEN HOURS.
SAFE TO SAY WE FAILED?
YEAH, PRETTY SAFE.
WHERE'S TROY?
FSHHHHHH
MR. BALLARD, I AM DISAPPOINTED.
I FELT AS THOUGH WE BONDED AT THE PRISON.

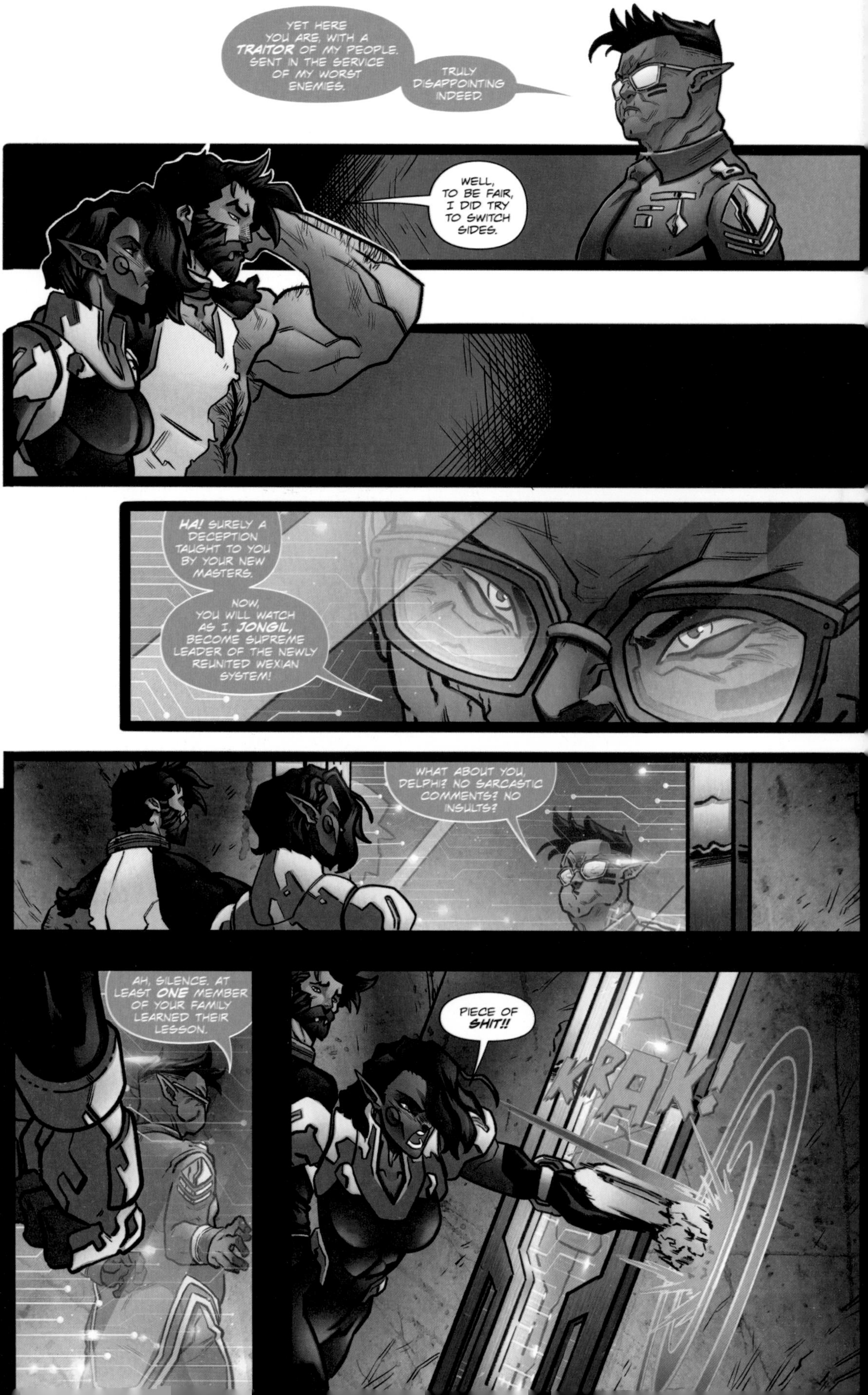
YET HERE YOU ARE, WITH A TRAITOR OF MY PEOPLE. SENT IN THE SERVICE OF MY WORST ENEMIES.
TRULY DISAPPOINTING INDEED.
WELL, TO BE FAIR, I DID TRY TO SWITCH SIDES.
HA! SURELY A DECEPTION TAUGHT TO YOU BY YOUR NEW MASTERS.
NOW, YOU WILL WATCH AS I, JONGIL, BECOME SUPREME LEADER OF THE NEWLY REUNITED WEXIAN SYSTEM!
WHAT ABOUT YOU, DELPHI? NO SARCASTIC COMMENTS? NO INSULTS?
AH, SILENCE. AT LEAST ONE MEMBER OF YOUR FAMILY LEARNED THEIR LESSON.
PIECE OF SHIT!!
KRAK!

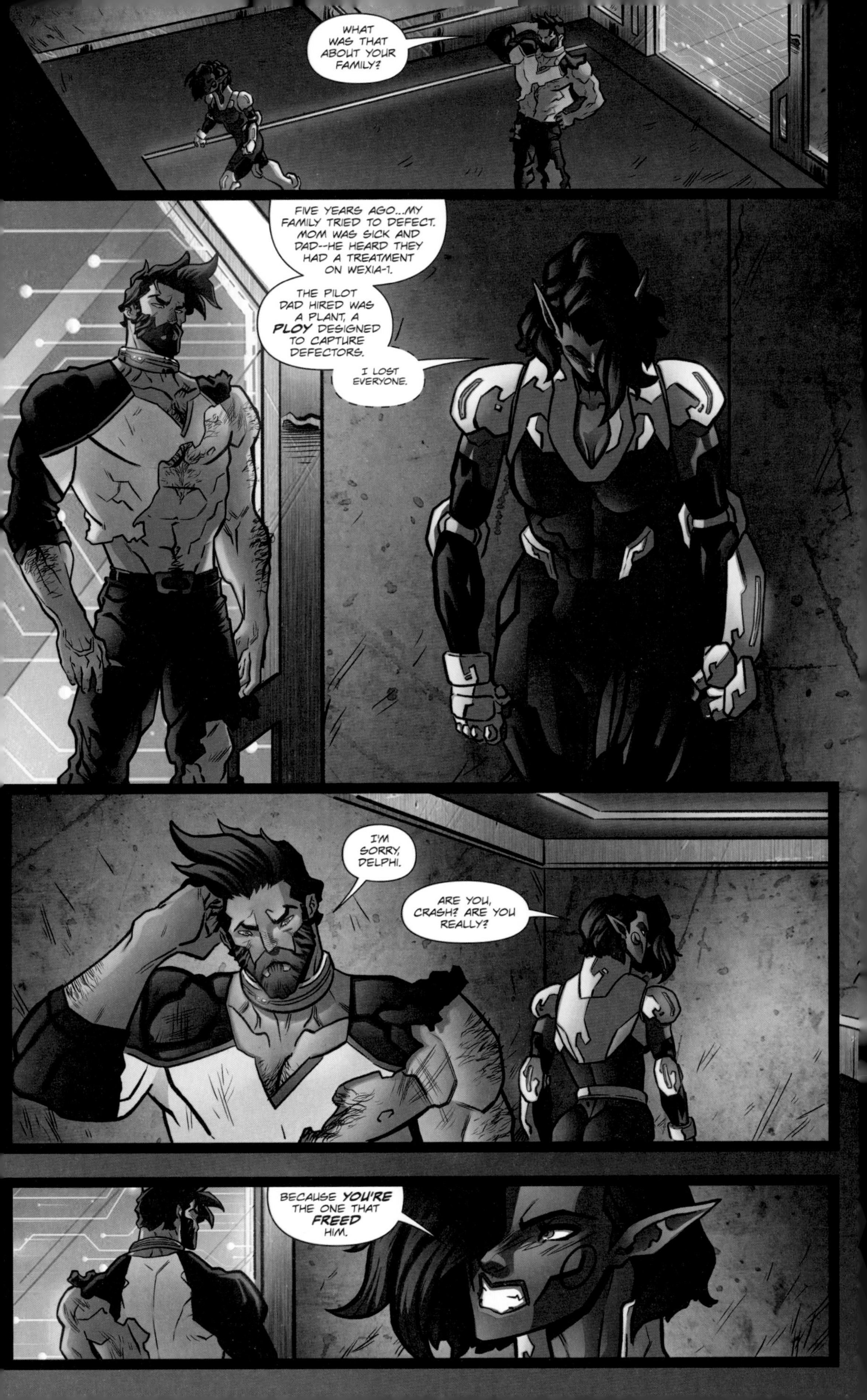
WHAT WAS THAT ABOUT YOUR FAMILY?
FIVE YEARS AGO...MY FAMILY TRIED TO DEFECT. MOM WAS SICK AND DAD--HE HEARD THEY HAD A TREATMENT ON WEXIA-1.
THE PILOT DAD HIRED WAS A PLANT, A PLOY DESIGNED TO CAPTURE DEFECTORS.
I LOST EVERYONE.
I'M SORRY, DELPHI.
ARE YOU, CRASH? ARE YOU REALLY?
BECAUSE YOU'RE THE ONE THAT FREED HIM.

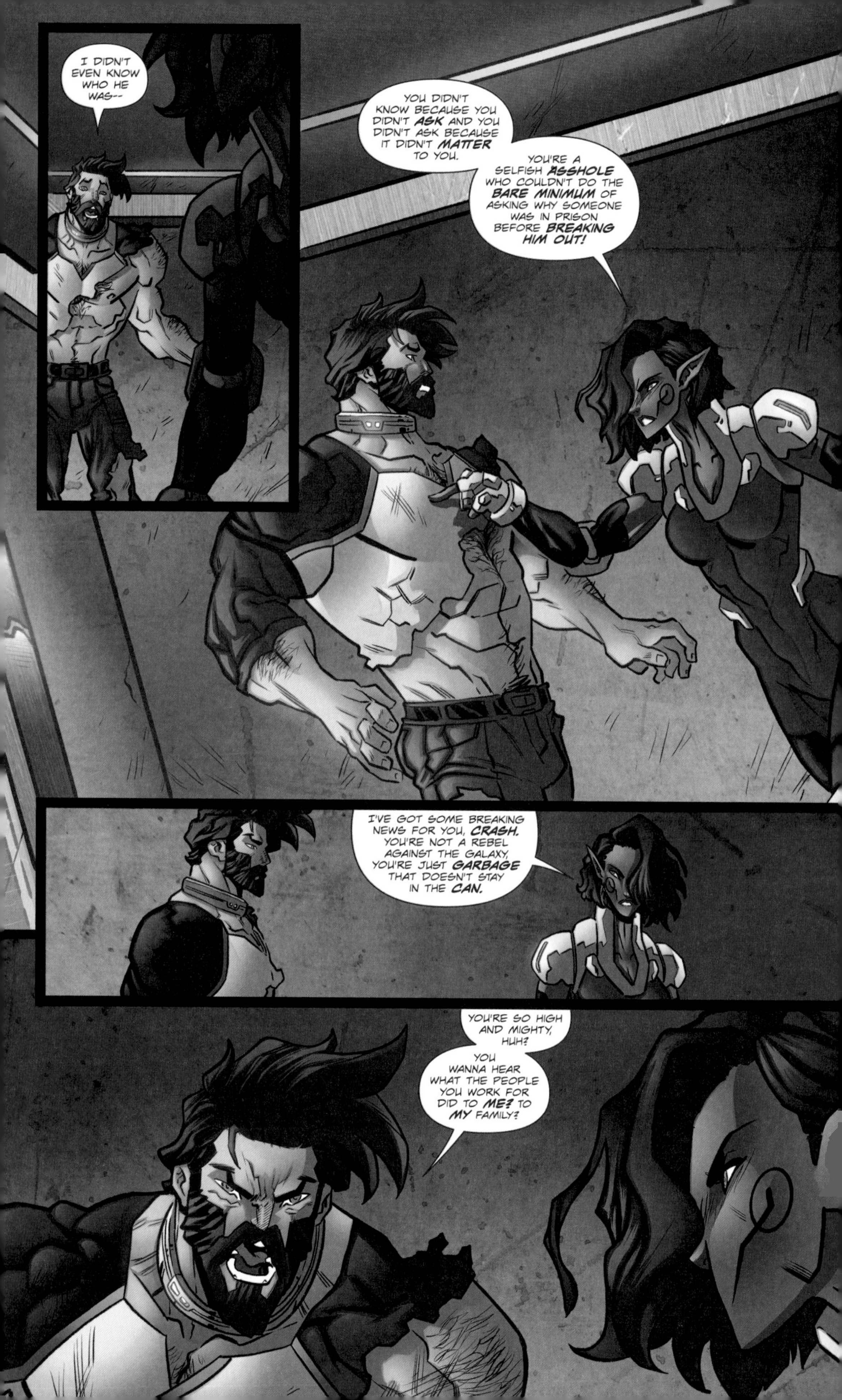
I DIDN'T EVEN KNOW WHO HE WAS--
YOU DIDN'T KNOW BECAUSE YOU DIDN'T ASK AND YOU DIDN'T ASK BECAUSE IT DIDN'T MATTER TO YOU.
YOU'RE A SELFISH ASSHOLE WHO COULDN'T DO THE BARE MINIMUM OF ASKING WHY SOMEONE WAS IN PRISON BEFORE BREAKING HIM OUT!
I'VE GOT SOME BREAKING NEWS FOR YOU, CRASH. YOU'RE NOT A REBEL AGAINST THE GALAXY, YOU'RE JUST GARBAGE THAT DOESN'T STAY IN THE CAN.
YOU'RE SO HIGH AND MIGHTY, HUH?
YOU WANNA HEAR WHAT THE PEOPLE YOU WORK FOR DID TO ME? TO MY FAMILY?

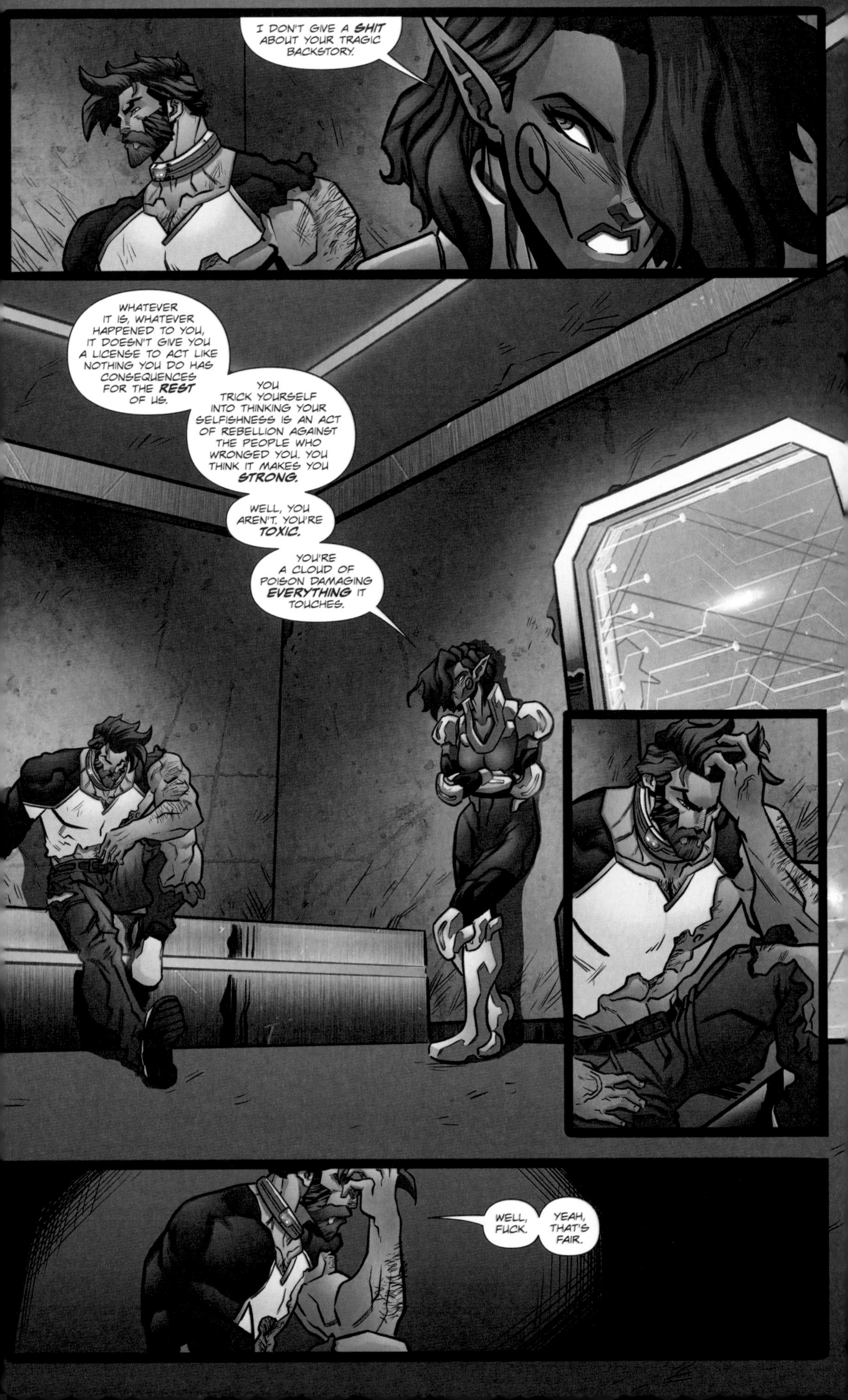
I DON'T GIVE A SHIT ABOUT YOUR TRAGIC BACKSTORY.
WHATEVER IT IS, WHATEVER HAPPENED TO YOU, IT DOESN'T GIVE YOU A LICENSE TO ACT LIKE NOTHING YOU DO HAS CONSEQUENCES FOR THE REST OF US.
YOU TRICK YOURSELF INTO THINKING YOUR SELFISHNESS IS AN ACT OF REBELLION AGAINST THE PEOPLE WHO WRONGED YOU. YOU THINK IT MAKES YOU STRONG.
WELL, YOU AREN'T. YOU'RE TOXIC.
YOU'RE A CLOUD OF POISON DAMAGING EVERYTHING IT TOUCHES.
WELL, FUCK.
YEAH, THAT'S FAIR.

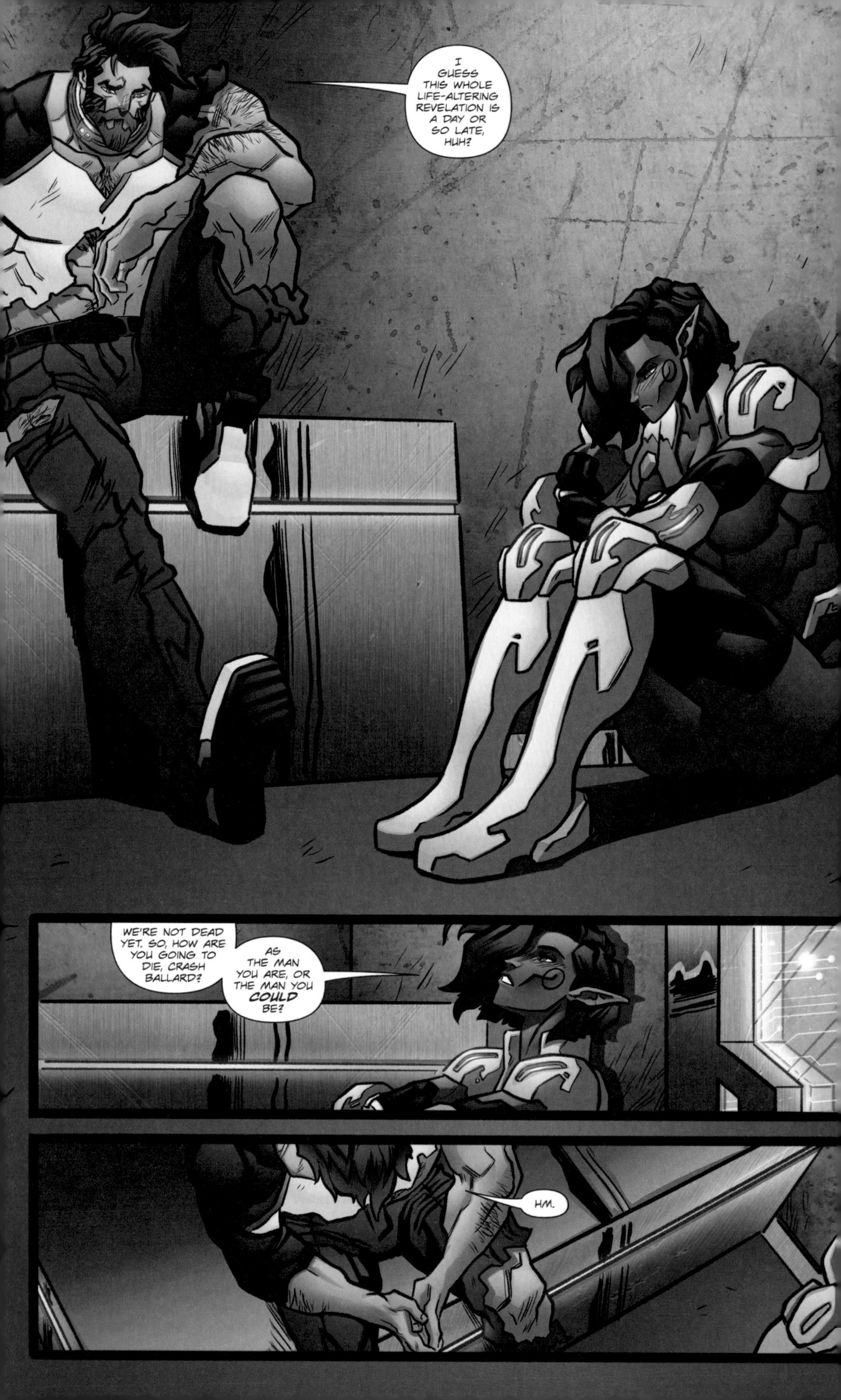
I GUESS THIS WHOLE LIFE-ALTERING REVELATION IS A DAY OR SO LATE, HUH?
WE'RE NOT DEAD YET. SO, HOW ARE YOU GOING TO DIE, CRASH BALLARD?
AS THE MAN YOU ARE, OR THE MAN YOU *COULD* BE?
HM.

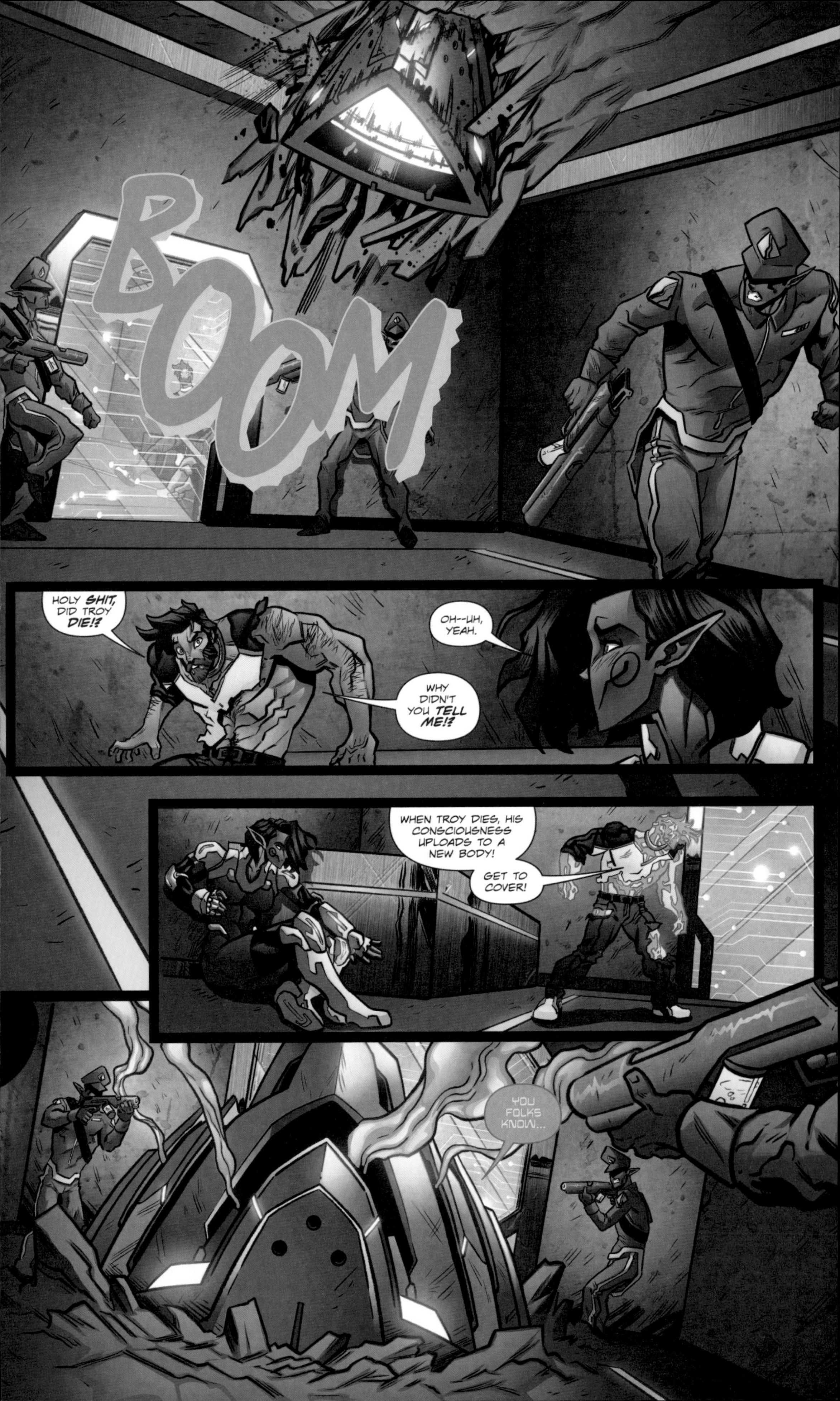
BOOM
HOLY SHIT, DID TROY DIE!?
OH--UH, YEAH.
WHY DIDN'T YOU TELL ME!?
WHEN TROY DIES, HIS CONSCIOUSNESS UPLOADS TO A NEW BODY!
GET TO COVER!
YOU FOLKS KNOW...

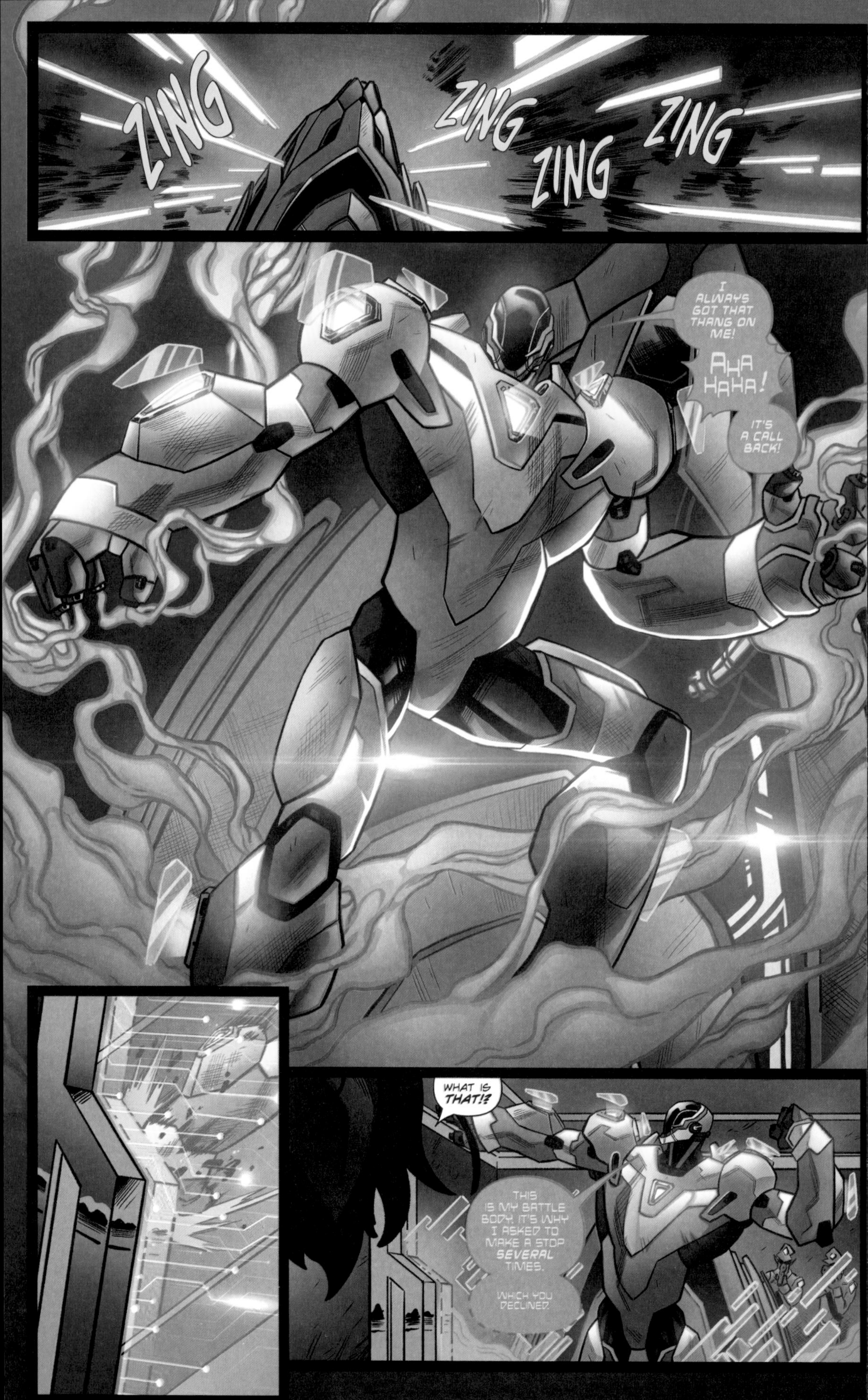
ZING
ZING
ZING
ZING
I ALWAYS GOT THAT THANG ON ME!
AHA HAHA!
IT'S A CALL BACK!
WHAT IS THAT!?
THIS IS MY BATTLE BODY. IT'S WHY I ASKED TO MAKE A STOP SEVERAL TIMES.
WHICH YOU DECLINED.

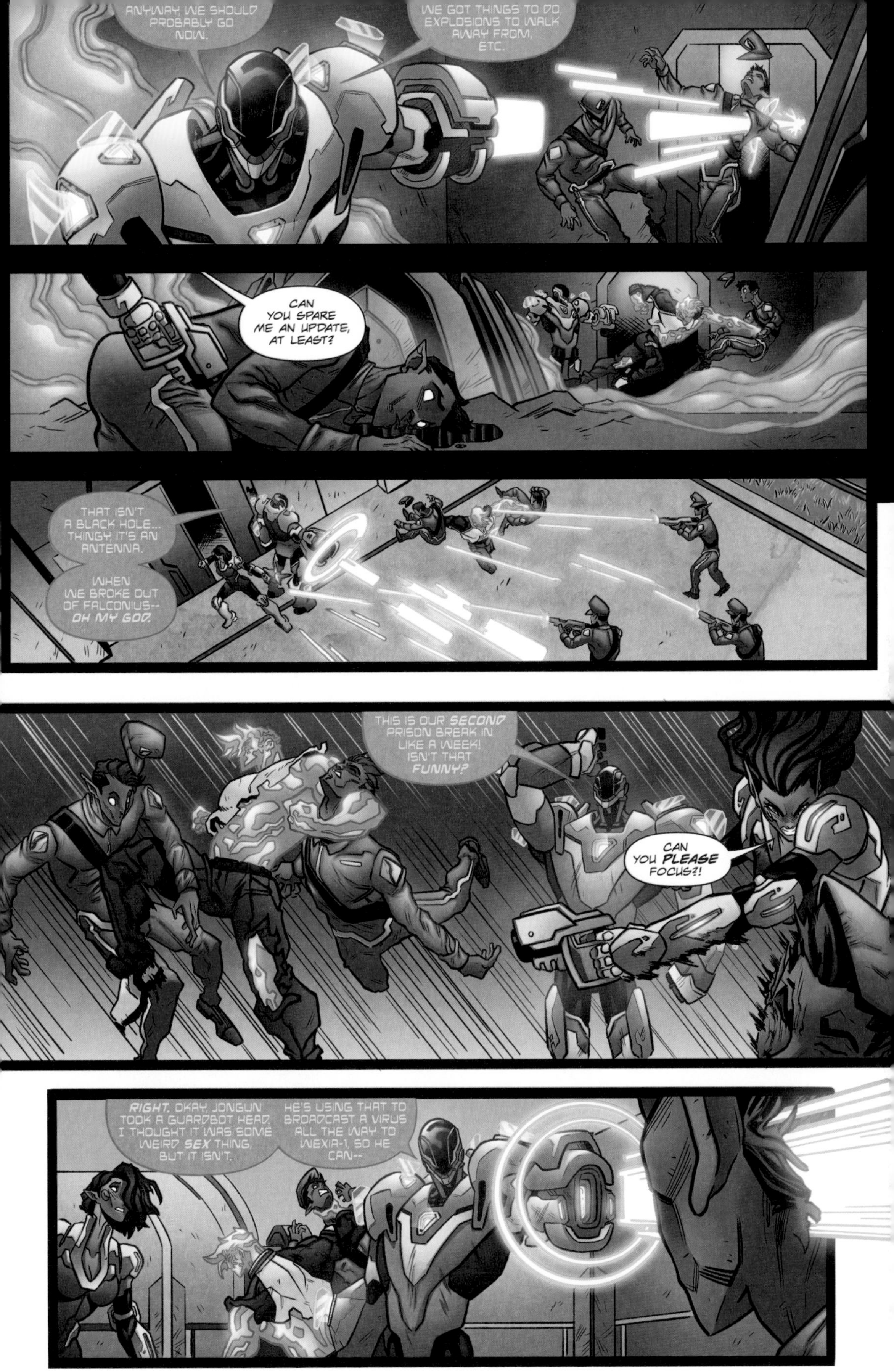
ANYWAY WE SHOULD PROBABLY GO NOW.
WE GOT THINGS TO DO, EXPLOSIONS TO WALK AWAY FROM, ETC.
CAN YOU SPARE ME AN UPDATE, AT LEAST?
THAT ISN'T A BLACK HOLE... THINGY, IT'S AN ANTENNA.
WHEN WE BROKE OUT OF FALCONIUS-- OH MY GOD.
THIS IS OUR SECOND PRISON BREAK IN LIKE A WEEK! ISN'T THAT FUNNY?
CAN YOU PLEASE FOCUS?!
RIGHT. OKAY, JONGUN TOOK A GUARDBOT HEAD. I THOUGHT IT WAS SOME WEIRD SEX THING, BUT IT ISN'T.
HE'S USING THAT TO BROADCAST A VIRUS ALL THE WAY TO WEXIA-1, SO HE CAN--

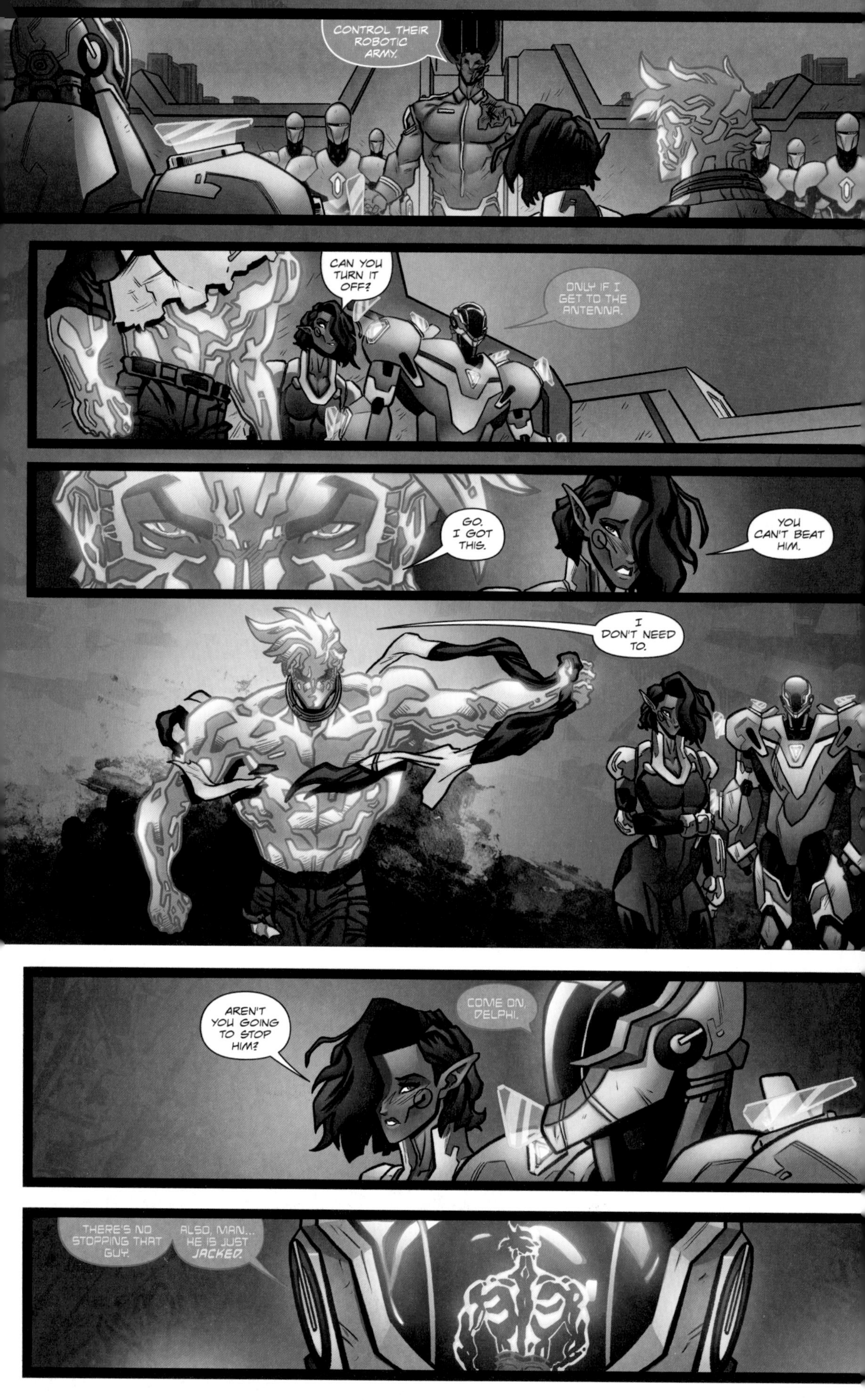
CONTROL THEIR ROBOTIC ARMY.
CAN YOU TURN IT OFF?
ONLY IF I GET TO THE ANTENNA.
GO. I GOT THIS.
YOU CAN'T BEAT HIM.
I DON'T NEED TO.
AREN'T YOU GOING TO STOP HIM?
COME ON, DELPHI.
THERE'S NO STOPPING THAT GUY.
ALSO, MAN... HE IS JUST JACKED.

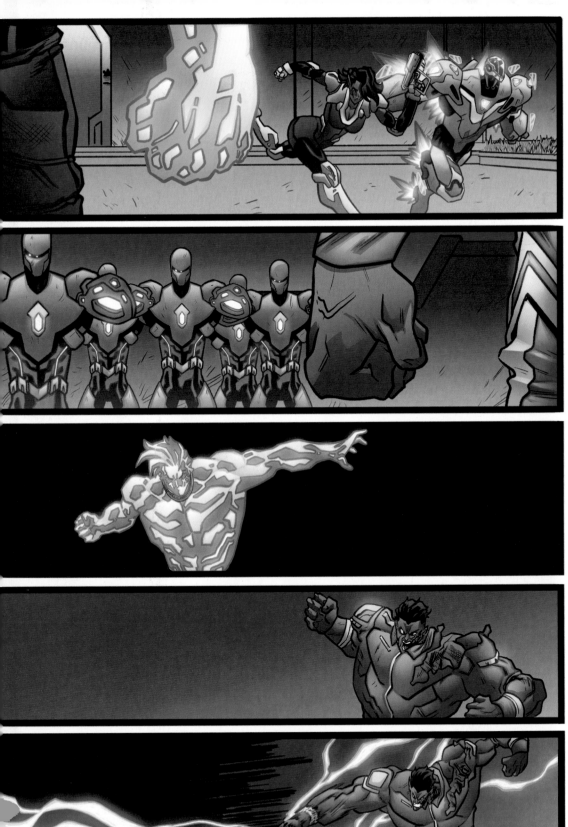

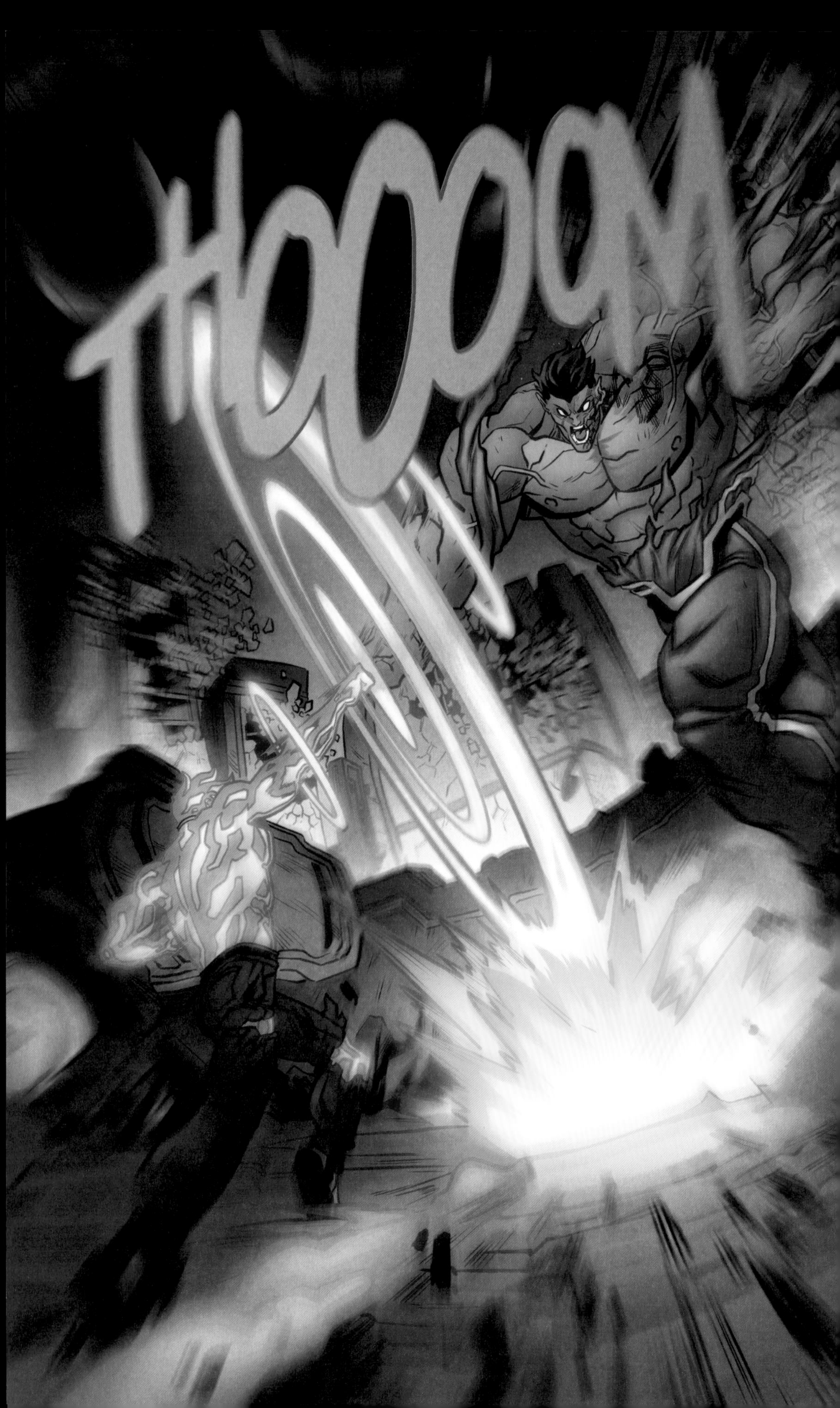
THOOOM

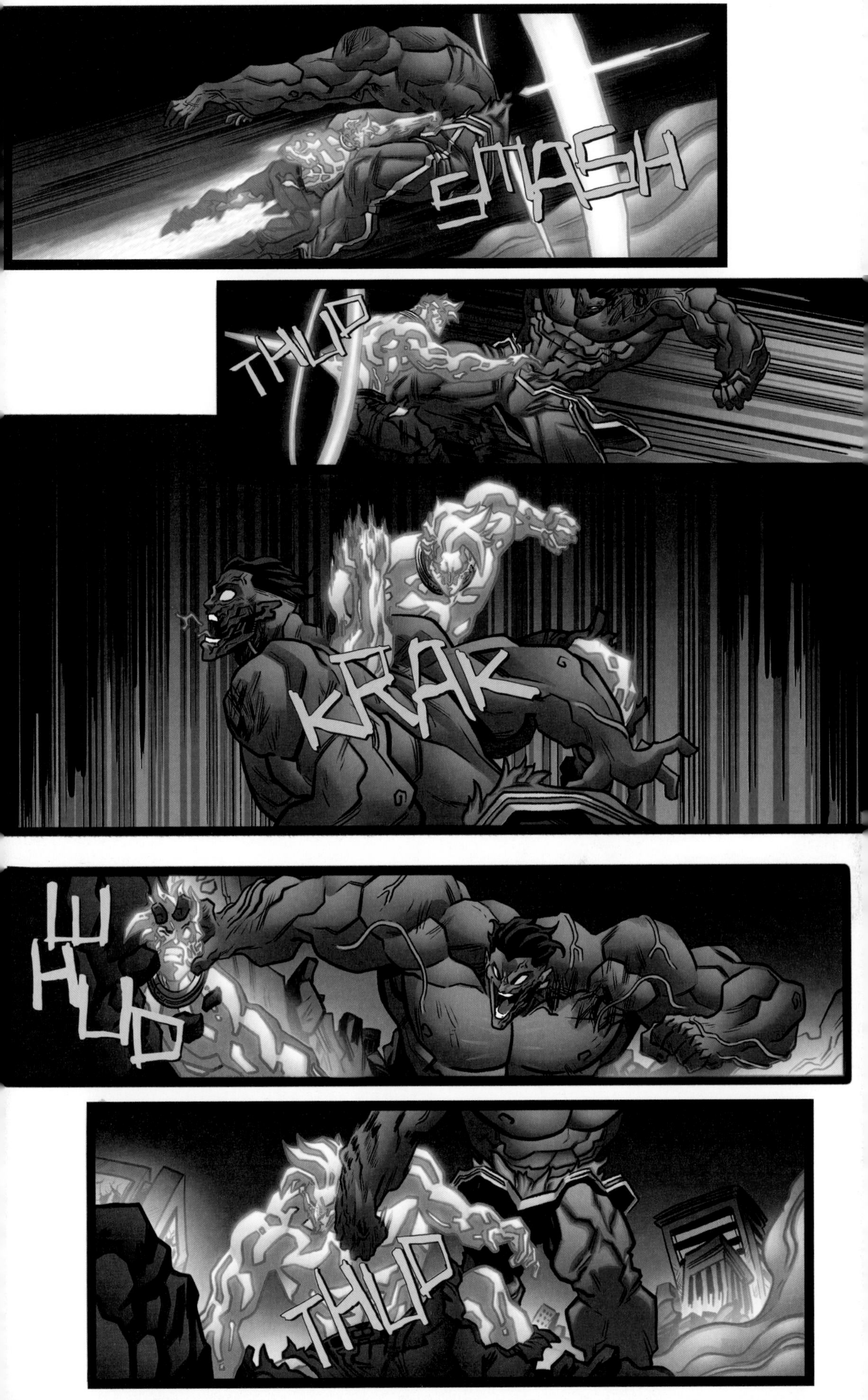
SMASH
THUD
KRAK
WHUD
THUD

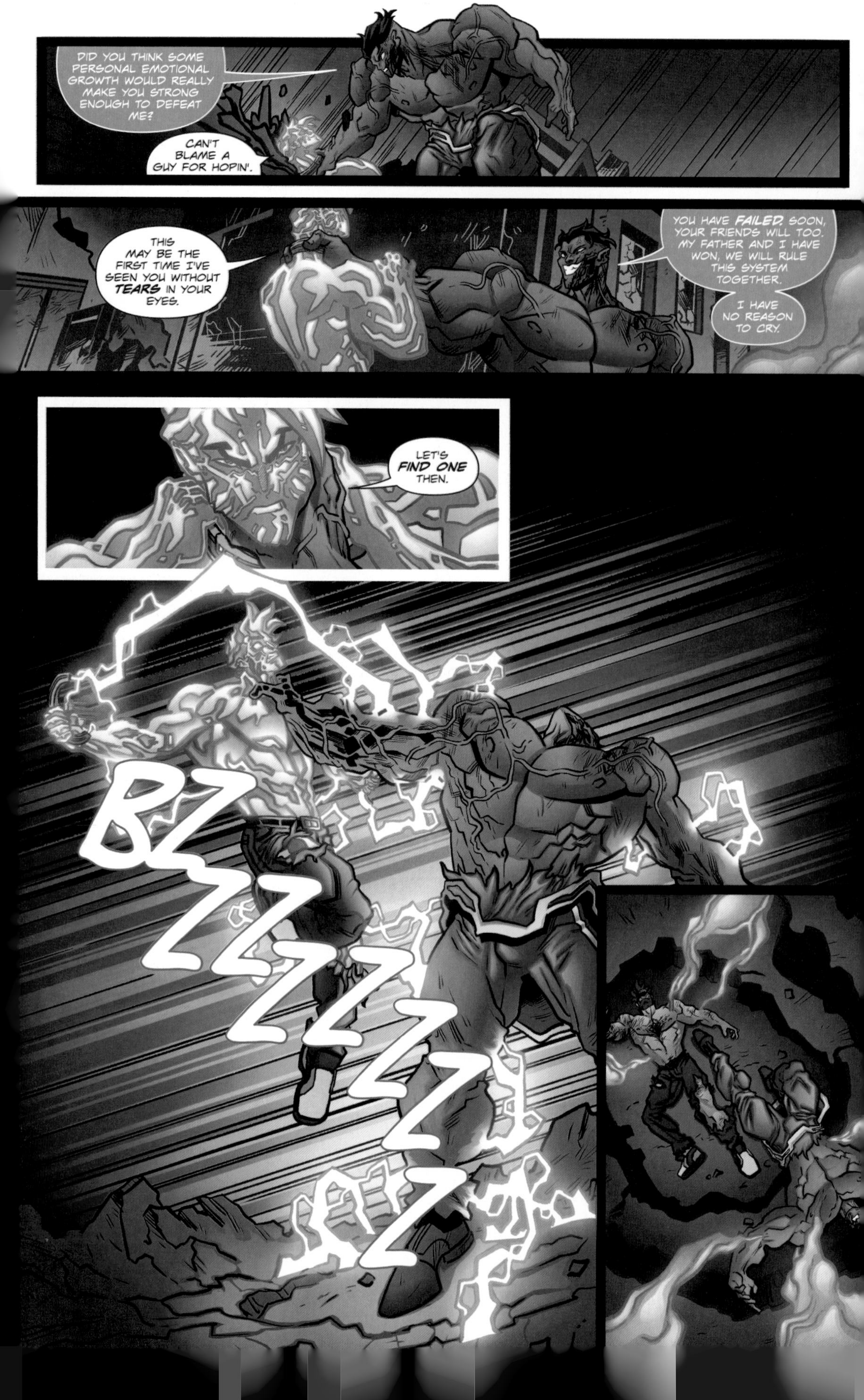
DID YOU THINK SOME PERSONAL EMOTIONAL GROWTH WOULD REALLY MAKE YOU STRONG ENOUGH TO DEFEAT ME?
CAN'T BLAME A GUY FOR HOPIN'.
THIS MAY BE THE FIRST TIME I'VE SEEN YOU WITHOUT TEARS IN YOUR EYES.
YOU HAVE FAILED. SOON, YOUR FRIENDS WILL TOO. MY FATHER AND I HAVE WON, WE WILL RULE THIS SYSTEM TOGETHER.
I HAVE NO REASON TO CRY.
LET'S FIND ONE THEN.
BZZZZZZZZ

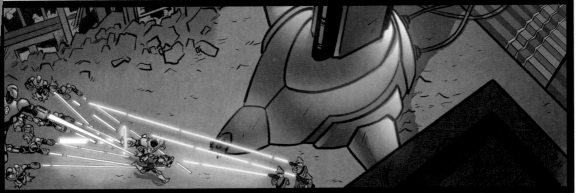

DELPHI--I CAN'T SHOOT AND HACK THIS AT THE SAME TIME.

MY ARMOR IS SECURED, BUT IT'LL JUST BE YOU--

THEN BE FASTER THAN LAST TIME, YEAH?!

TROY 3.0 UPLOADED

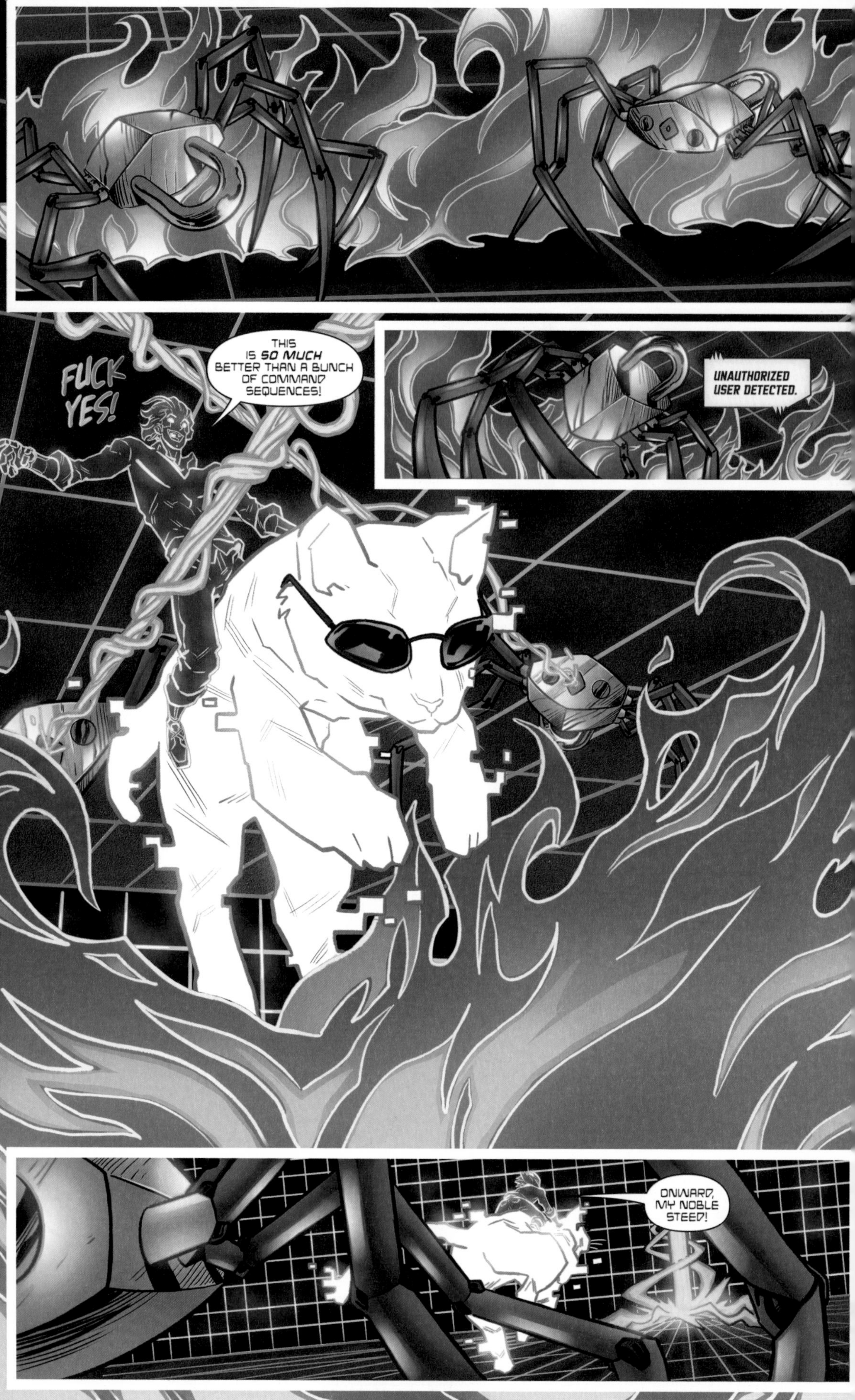
FUCK YES!
THIS IS SO MUCH BETTER THAN A BUNCH OF COMMAND SEQUENCES!
UNAUTHORIZED USER DETECTED.
ONWARD, MY NOBLE STEED!

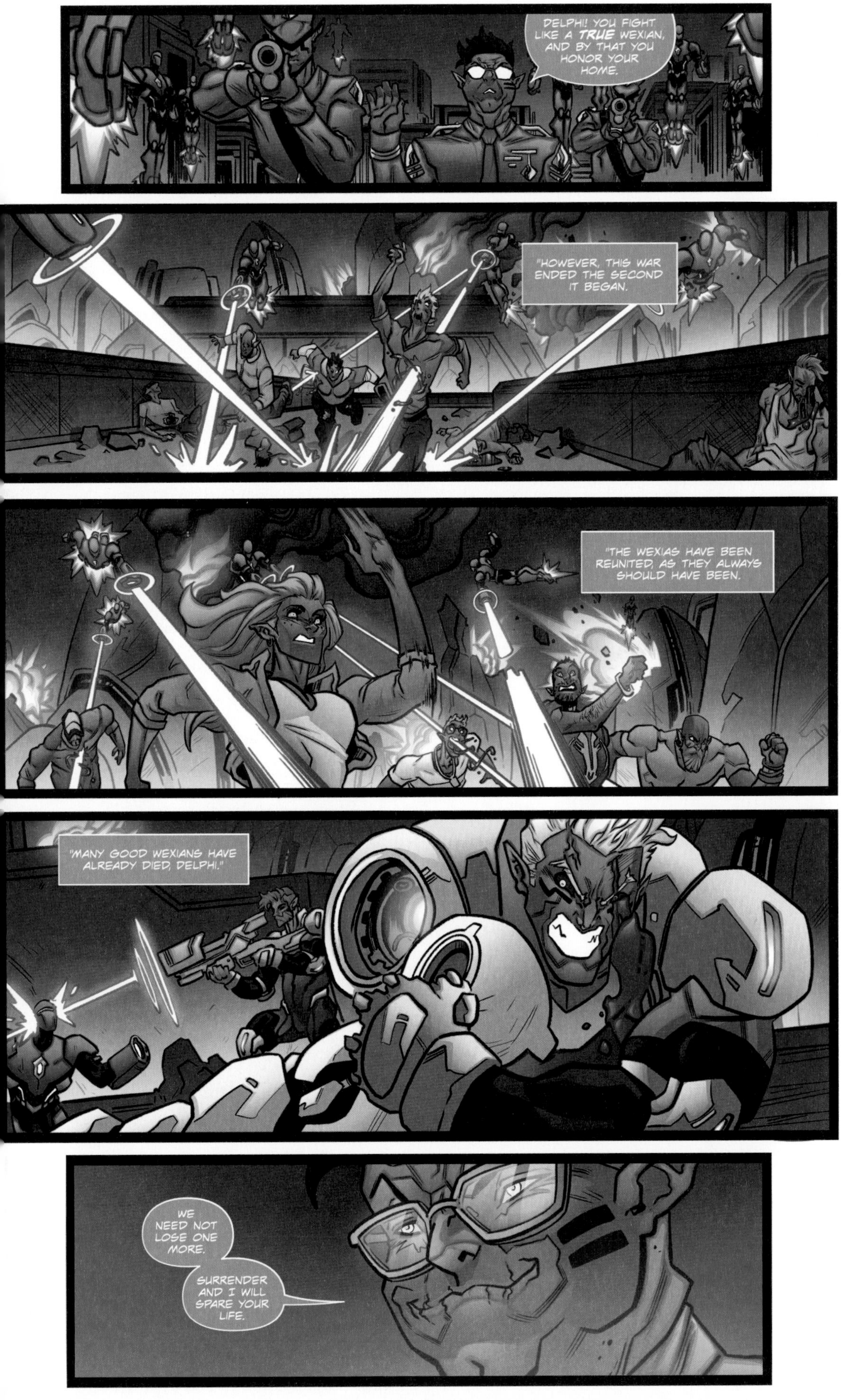
DELPHI! YOU FIGHT LIKE A **TRUE** WEXIAN, AND BY THAT YOU HONOR YOUR HOME.
"HOWEVER, THIS WAR ENDED THE SECOND IT BEGAN.
"THE WEXIAS HAVE BEEN REUNITED, AS THEY ALWAYS SHOULD HAVE BEEN.
"MANY GOOD WEXIANS HAVE ALREADY DIED, DELPHI."
WE NEED NOT LOSE ONE MORE.
SURRENDER AND I WILL SPARE YOUR LIFE.

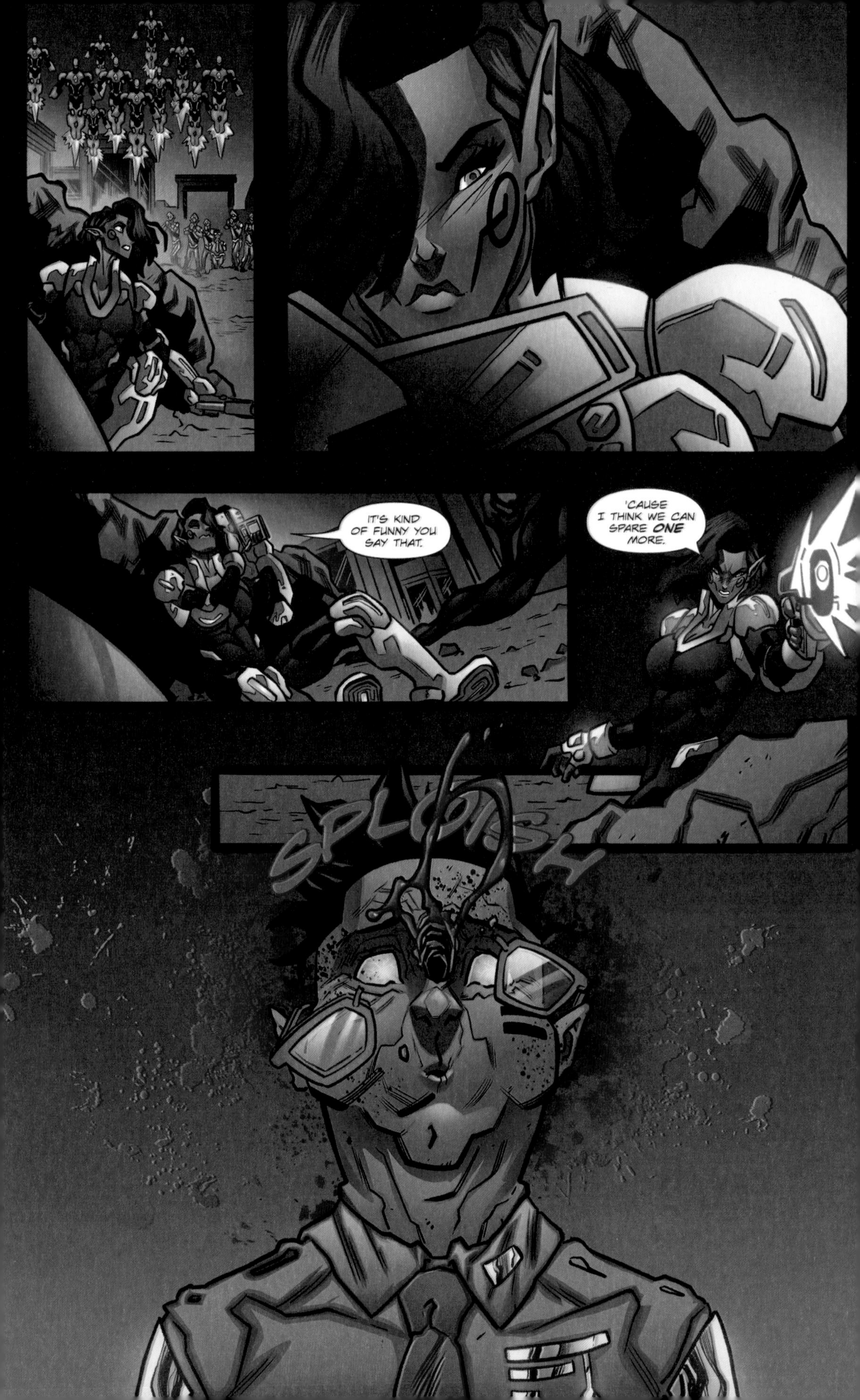
IT'S KIND OF FUNNY YOU SAY THAT.
'CAUSE I THINK WE CAN SPARE **ONE** MORE.
SPLOISH

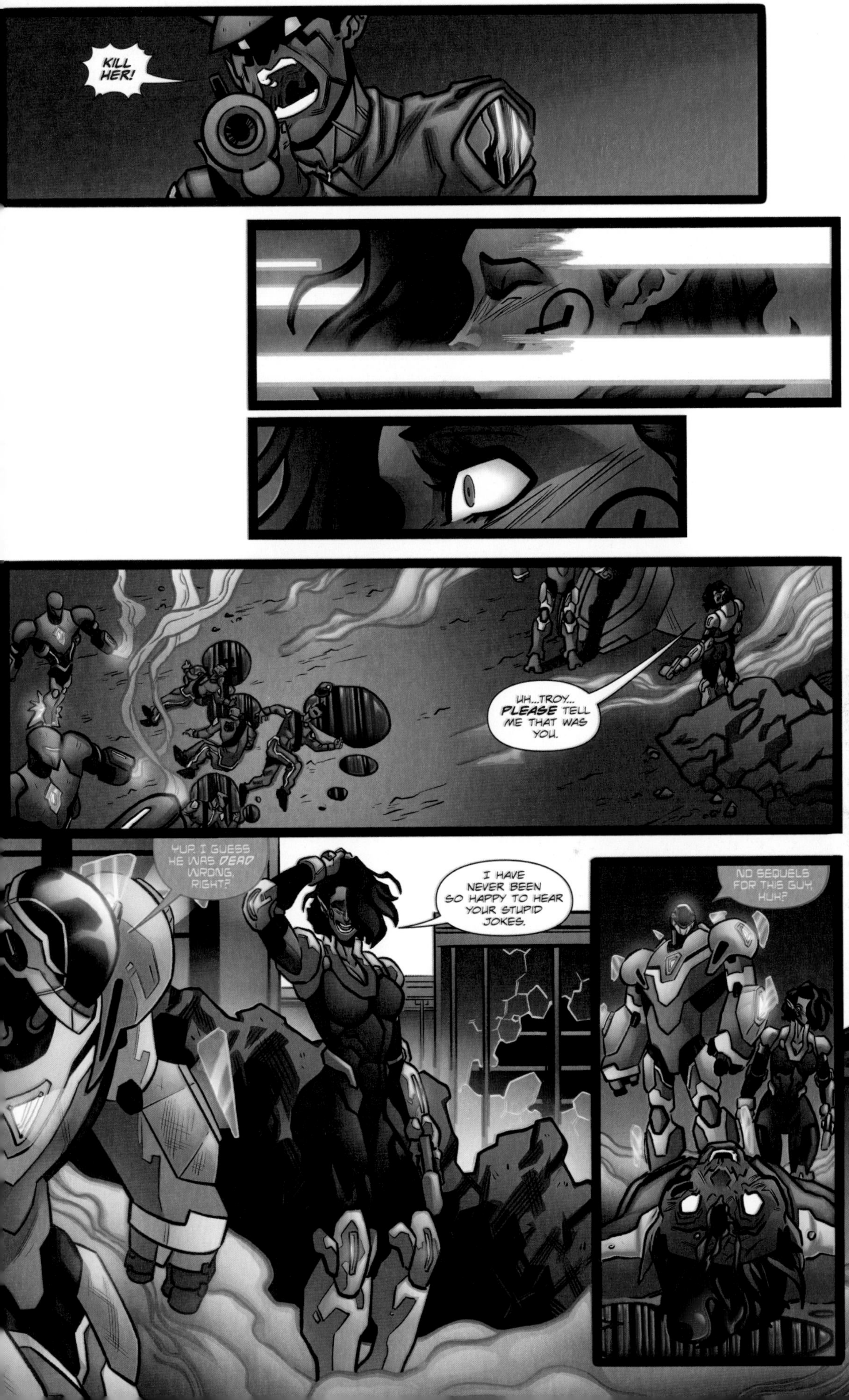
KILL HER!
UH...TROY... PLEASE TELL ME THAT WAS YOU.
YUP. I GUESS HE WAS DEAD WRONG. RIGHT?
I HAVE NEVER BEEN SO HAPPY TO HEAR YOUR STUPID JOKES.
NO SEQUELS FOR THIS GUY, HUH?

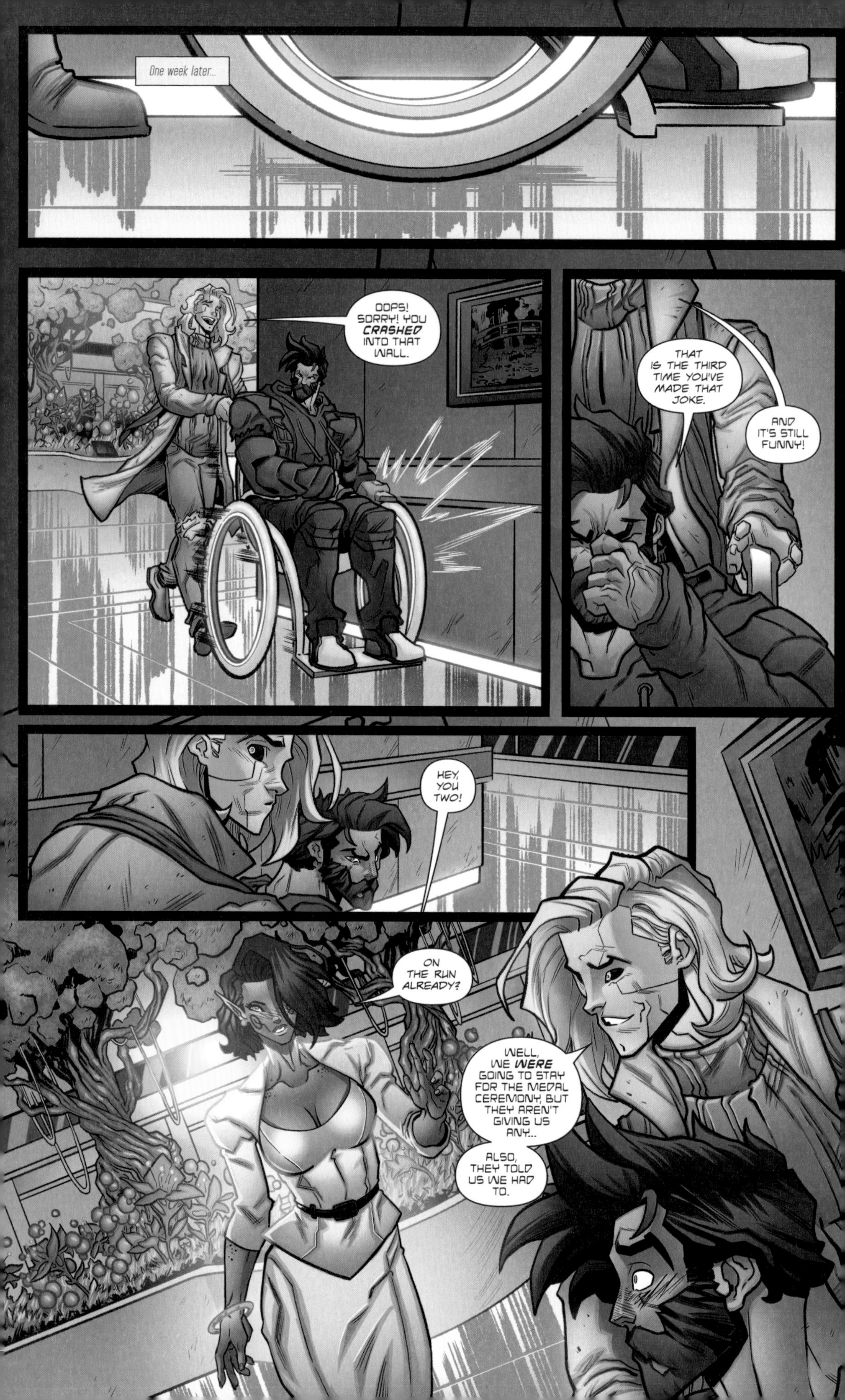
One week later...
OOPS! SORRY! YOU CRASHED INTO THAT WALL.
THAT IS THE THIRD TIME YOU'VE MADE THAT JOKE.
AND IT'S STILL FUNNY!
HEY, YOU TWO!
ON THE RUN ALREADY?
WELL, WE WERE GOING TO STAY FOR THE MEDAL CEREMONY, BUT THEY AREN'T GIVING US ANY...
ALSO, THEY TOLD US WE HAD TO.

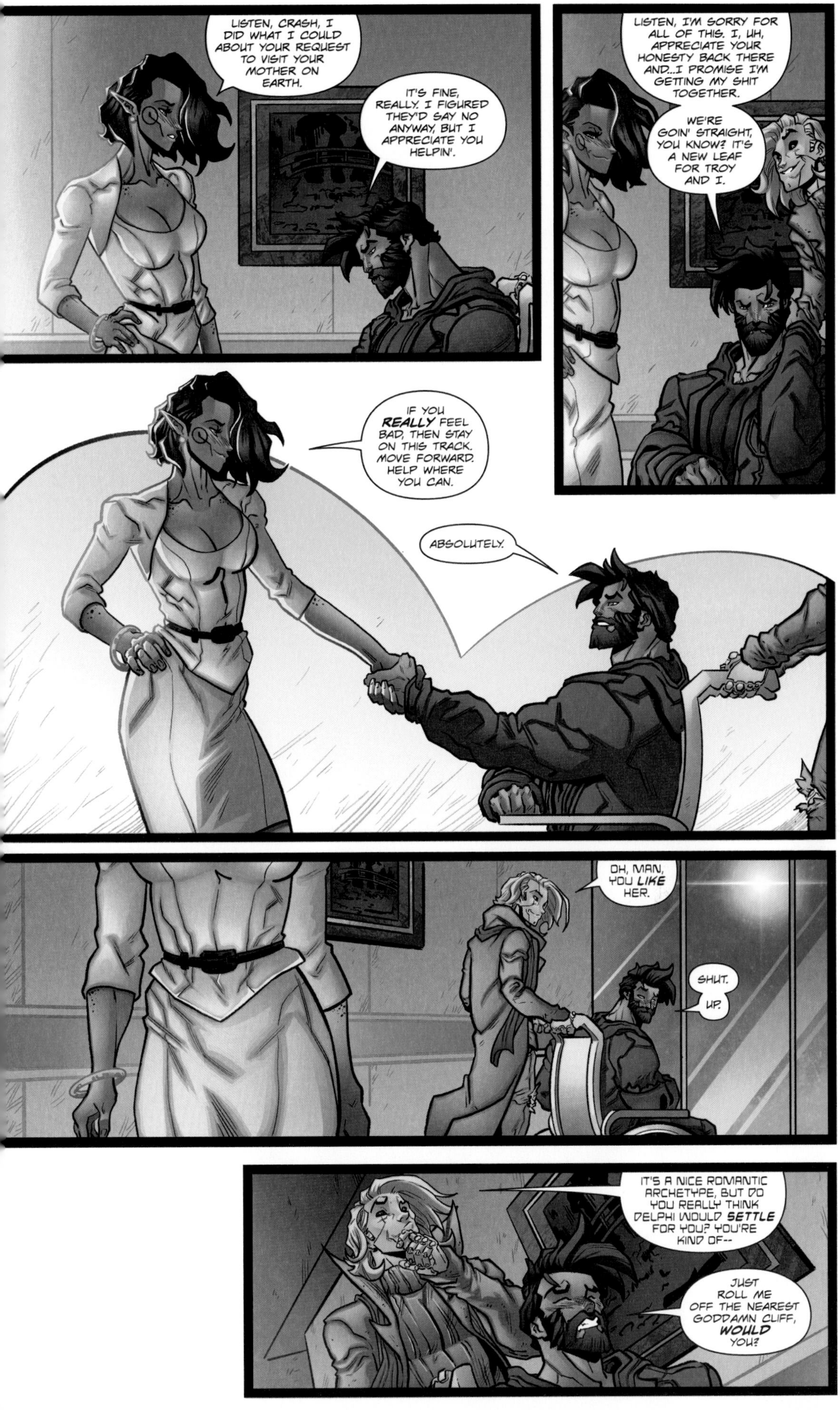

LISTEN, CRASH, I DID WHAT I COULD ABOUT YOUR REQUEST TO VISIT YOUR MOTHER ON EARTH.
IT'S FINE, REALLY. I FIGURED THEY'D SAY NO ANYWAY, BUT I APPRECIATE YOU HELPIN'.
LISTEN, I'M SORRY FOR ALL OF THIS. I, UH, APPRECIATE YOUR HONESTY BACK THERE AND...I PROMISE I'M GETTING MY SHIT TOGETHER.
WE'RE GOIN' STRAIGHT, YOU KNOW? IT'S A NEW LEAF FOR TROY AND I.
IF YOU **REALLY** FEEL BAD, THEN STAY ON THIS TRACK. MOVE FORWARD. HELP WHERE YOU CAN.
ABSOLUTELY.
OH, MAN, YOU **LIKE** HER.
SHUT.
UP.
IT'S A NICE ROMANTIC ARCHETYPE, BUT DO YOU REALLY THINK DELPHI WOULD **SETTLE** FOR YOU? YOU'RE KIND OF--
JUST ROLL ME OFF THE NEAREST GODDAMN CLIFF, **WOULD** YOU?

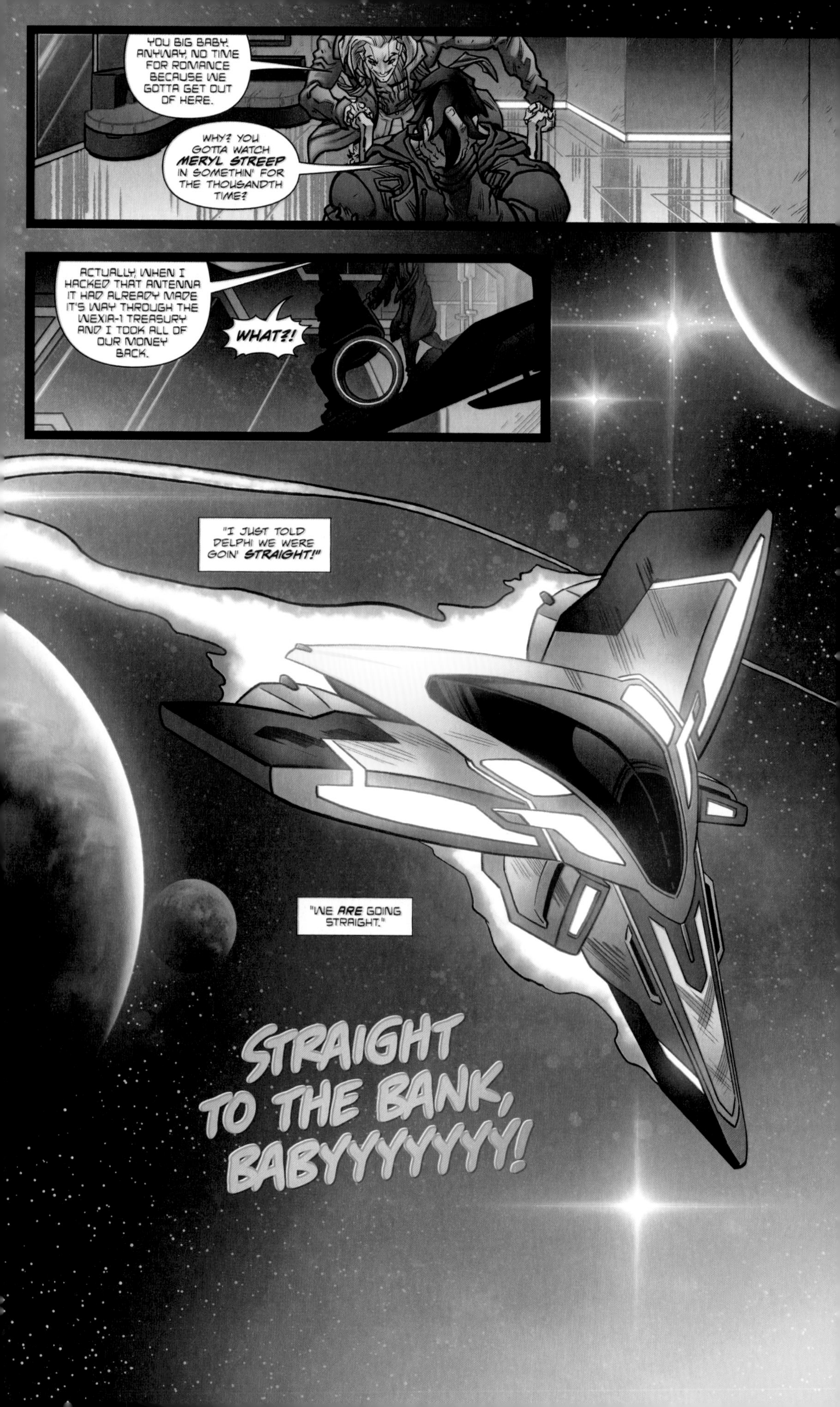

YOU BIG BABY. ANYWAY, NO TIME FOR ROMANCE BECAUSE WE GOTTA GET OUT OF HERE.
WHY? YOU GOTTA WATCH MERYL STREEP IN SOMETHIN' FOR THE THOUSANDTH TIME?
ACTUALLY, WHEN I HACKED THAT ANTENNA IT HAD ALREADY MADE IT'S WAY THROUGH THE WEXIA-1 TREASURY AND I TOOK ALL OF OUR MONEY BACK.
WHAT?!
"I JUST TOLD DELPHI WE WERE GOIN' STRAIGHT!"
"WE ARE GOING STRAIGHT."
STRAIGHT TO THE BANK, BABYYYYYYY!

end [for now]

Character Designs

Commentary by *Jarred Luján* **and** *Kyler Clodfelter*

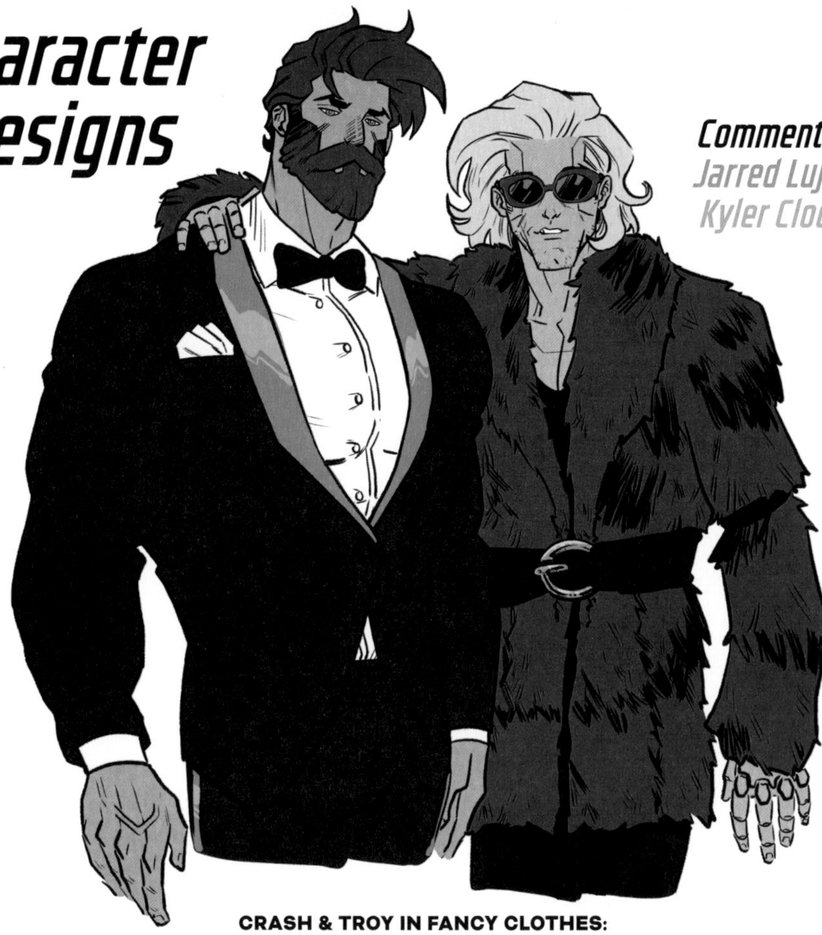

CRASH & TROY IN FANCY CLOTHES:

THE BEST PART OF TROY'S DESIGN IS THAT IT'S BASED OFF ONE OF MERYL STREEP'S OUTFITS IN **THE DEVIL WEARS PRADA.** IT STILL MAKES ME LAUGH. I WANTED TO SHOW THAT THERE'S SOME DEPTH TO CRASH OTHER THAN JUST "RUFF AND GRUFF," AND AFTER ALL, EVERY GIRL'S CRAZY 'BOUT A SHARPED-DRESSED MAN.

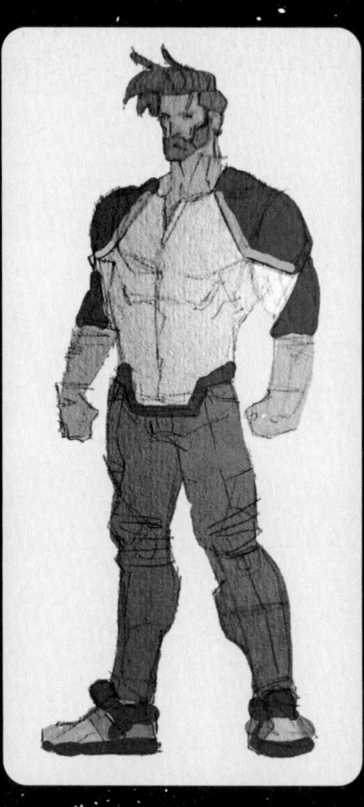

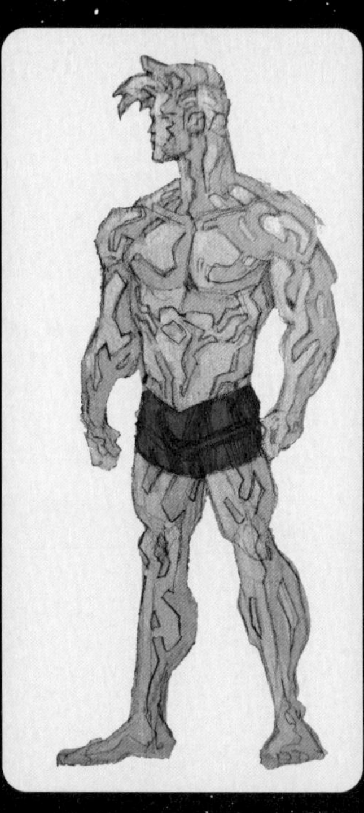

CRASH // REGULAR OUTFIT AND ROSE GOLD FORM:

ORIGINALLY, CRASH WAS JUST KINDA IMPERVIOUS ALL THE TIME, BUT KYLER RIGHTFULLY SUGGESTED MAKING IT A "FORM" SO HE'S MORE HITTABLE. I'M A SUCKER FOR MAIN CHARACTERS HAVING A TRANSFORMATION (THANKS TO MY LIFETIME OBSESSION WITH DBZ) AND WANTED ONE THAT WAS UNIQUE, YET FAMILIAR. SO, A ROSE GOLD COLOSSUS WAS BORN.

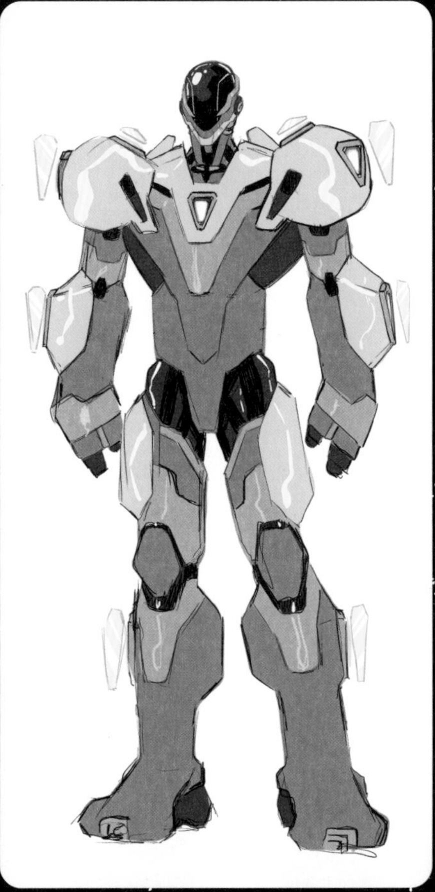

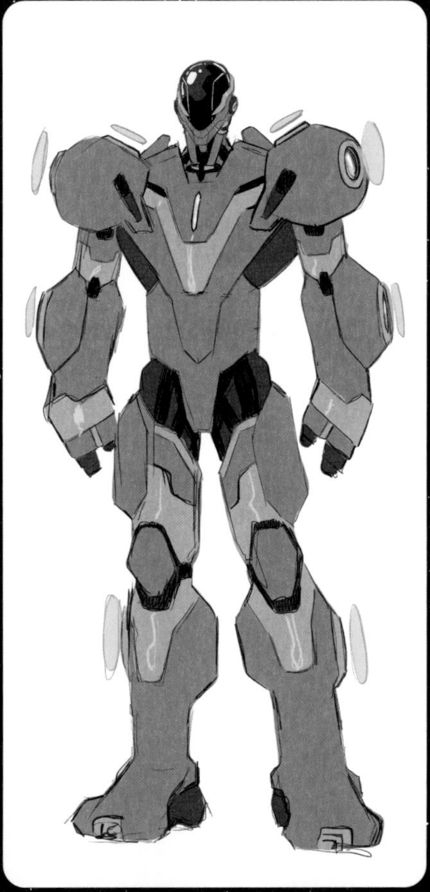

BATTLE TROY:
BATTLE TROY IS MY FAVORITE. IT'S SO OVER-THE-TOP AND RIDICULOUS FOR TROY, WHICH, IN TURN, MAKES IT THE MOST TROY THING IN THE BOOK. (BESIDES THE RED COAT.) HONESTLY, I JUST WANTED TO DRAW THE COOLEST ROBOT DESIGN I COULD WITHOUT WANTING TO DIE AFTER DRAWING IT OVER AND OVER AGAIN. I STILL LOVE THOSE SUPER OVER THE TOP SHOULDERS.

NEAR RIGHT (JONGIL):
THERE IS NO BETTER VILLAIN INSPIRATION THAN THE REAL WORLD, RIGHT? DUDE HAS A SUPER PUNCHABLE FACE, DON'T YA THINK?

RIGHT (DELPHI):
DELPHI'S ARMOR LETS HER BE AGILE WHILE PROTECTED. ANYBODY GOT A GLASS OF WATER? I'M SUDDENLY THIRSTY.

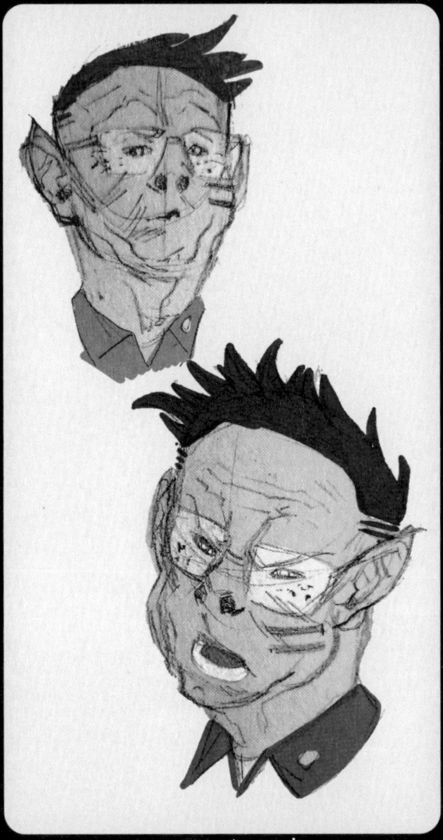

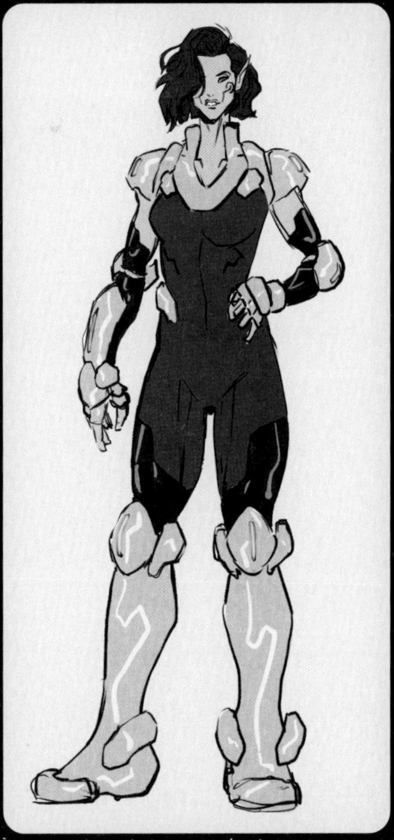

Cover Gallery

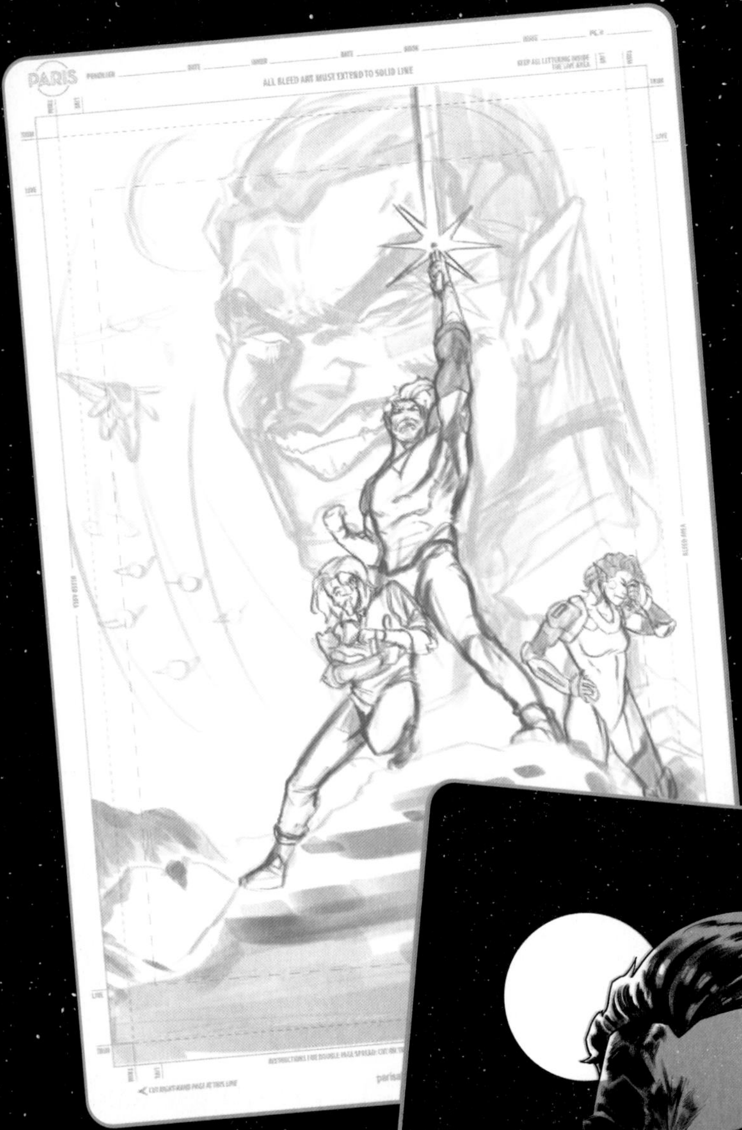

ALL BLEED ART MUST EXTEND TO SOLID LINE
KEEP ALL LETTERING INSIDE THE LIVE AREA

Layout, line art, and colors for the Star Wars homage cover for the first issue.

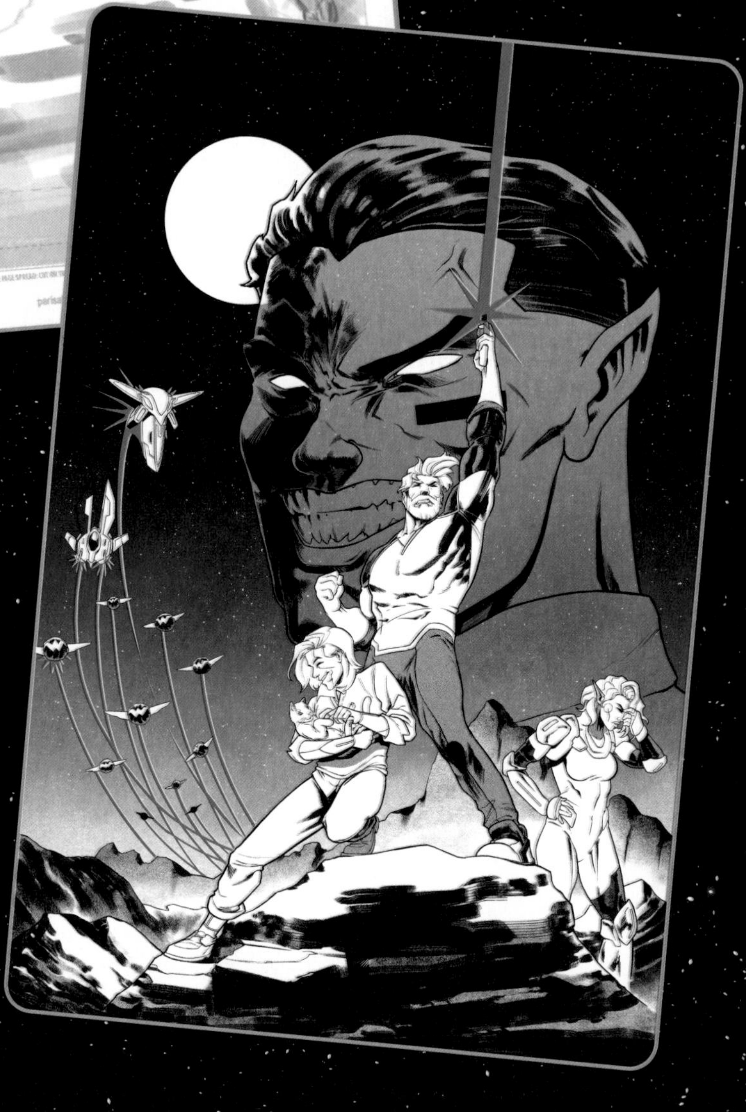

All artwork by Paris Alleyne.

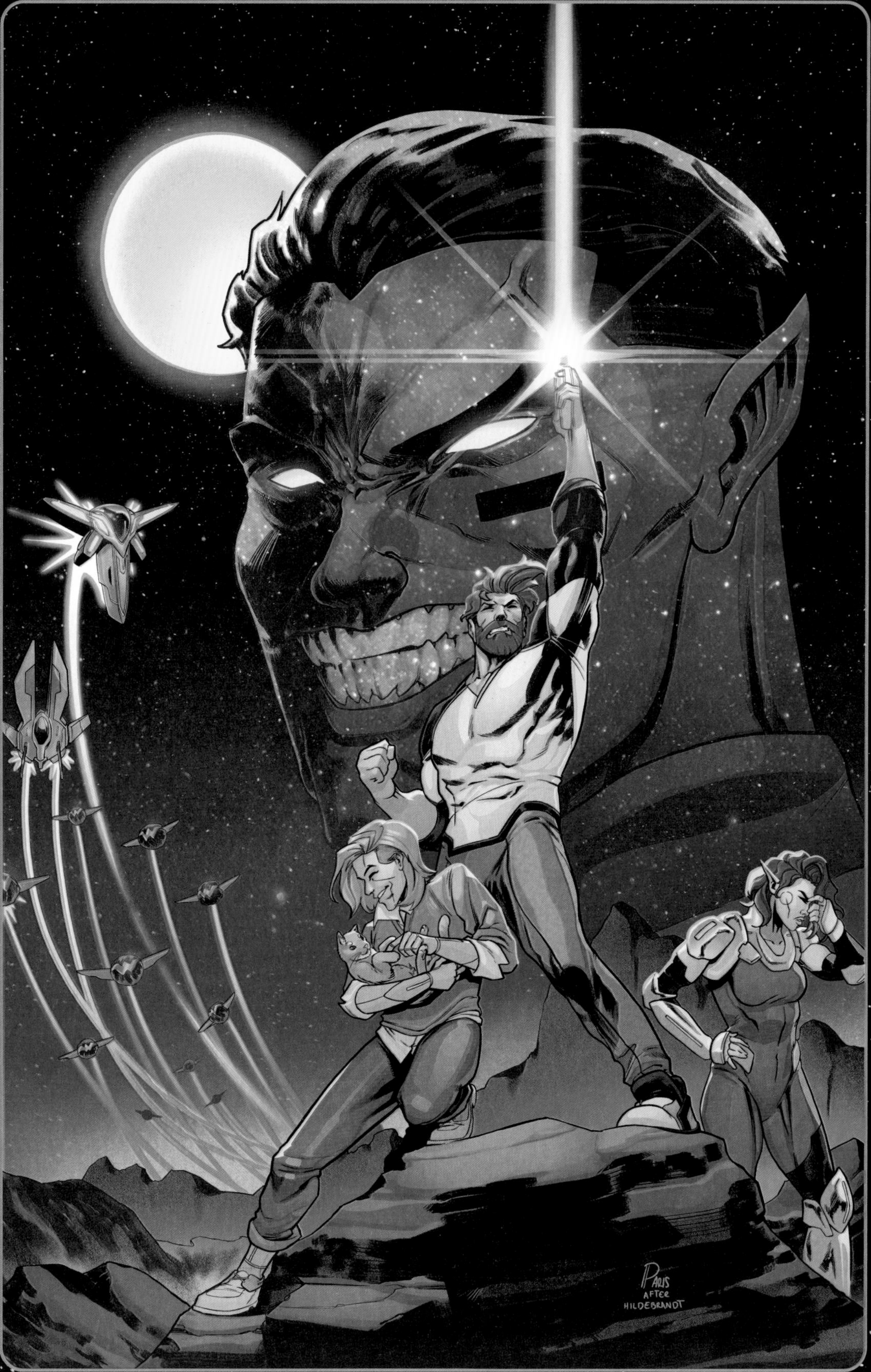
PARIS
AFTER
HILDEBRANDT

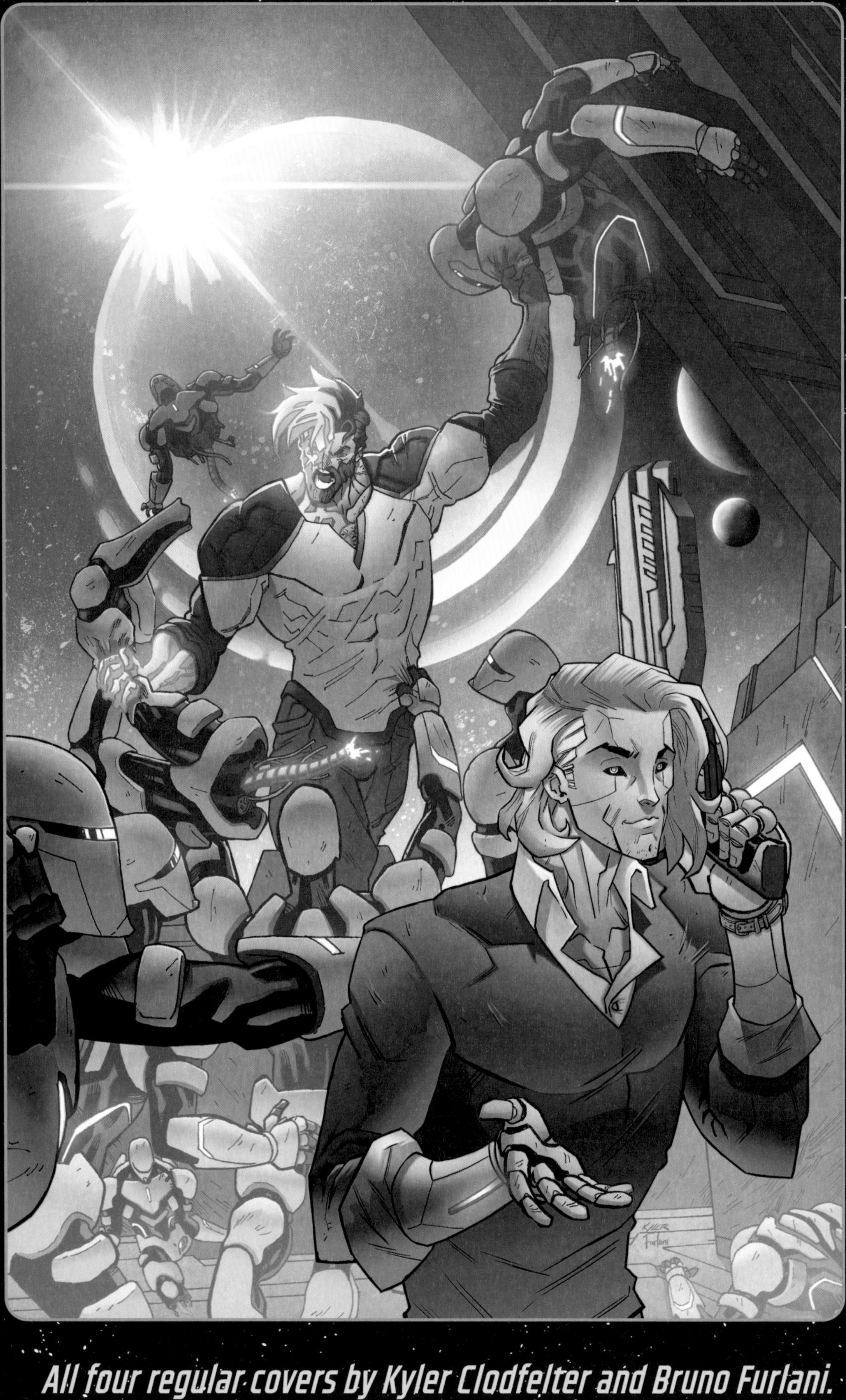

All four regular covers by Kyler Clodfelter and Bruno Furlani.

LEFT: cover #1

BELOW: cover #2

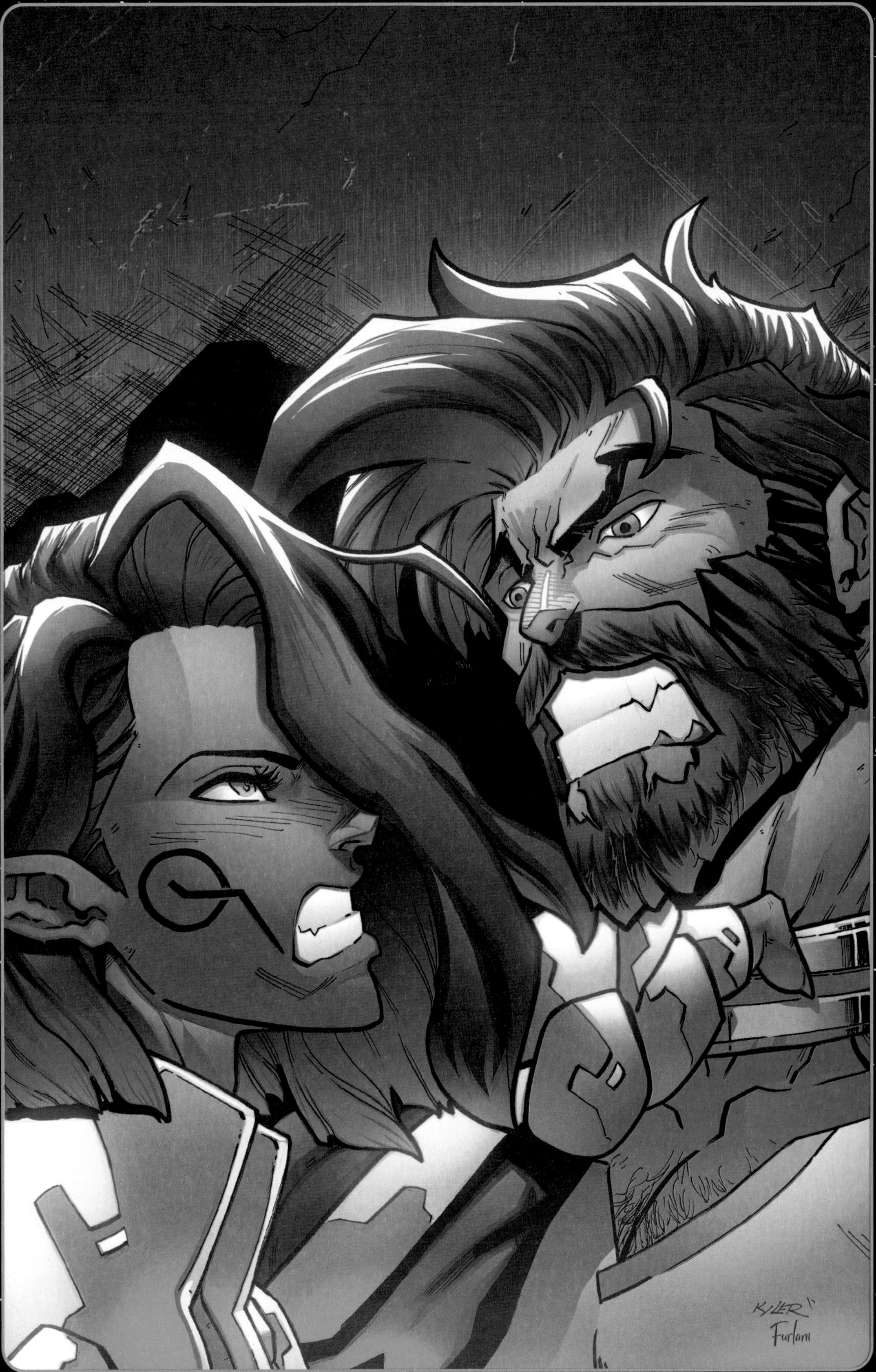
KYLER
Furlani

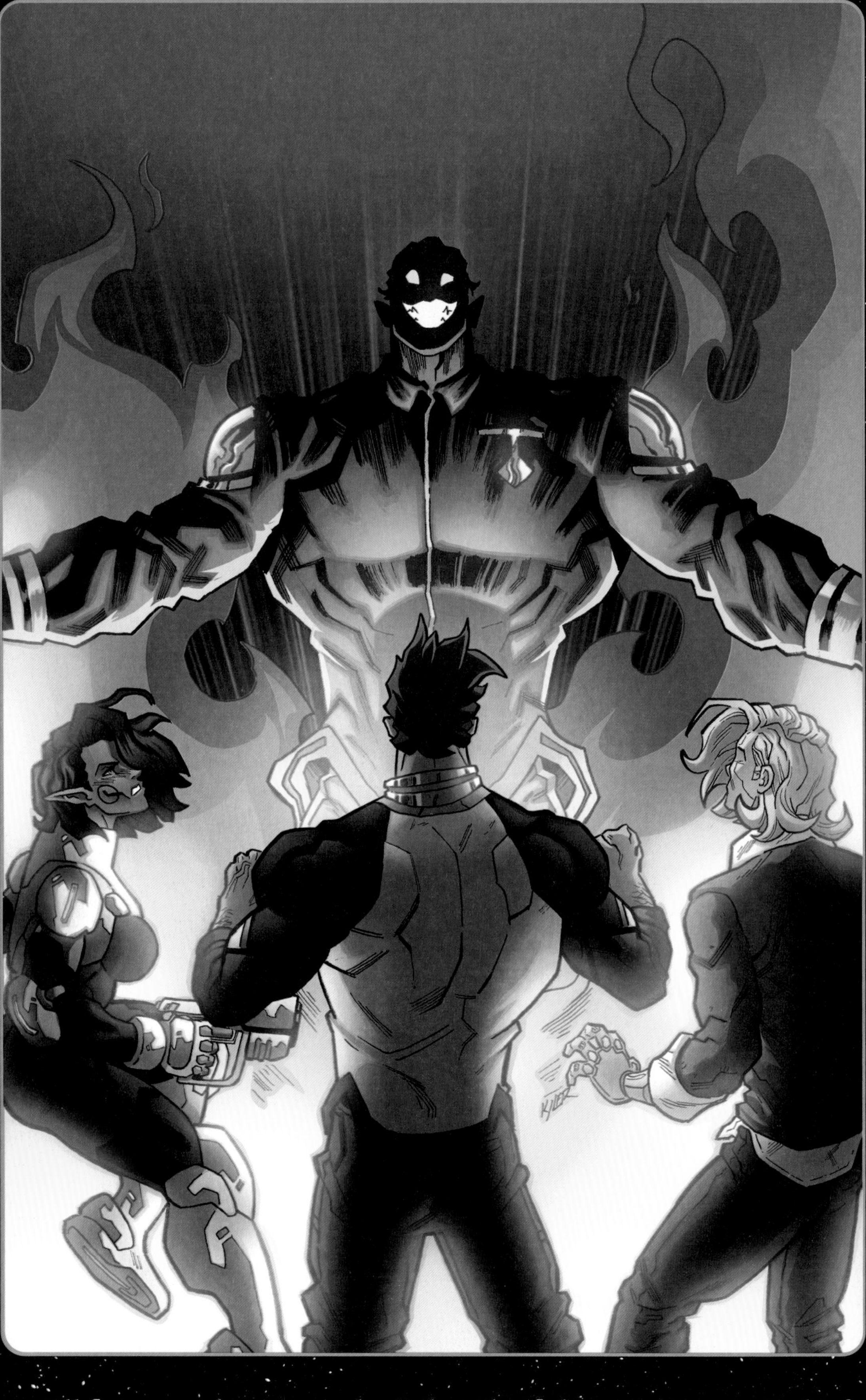
KYLER

All four regular covers by Kyler Clodfelter and Bruno Furlani.

LEFT: cover #3

BELOW: cover #4

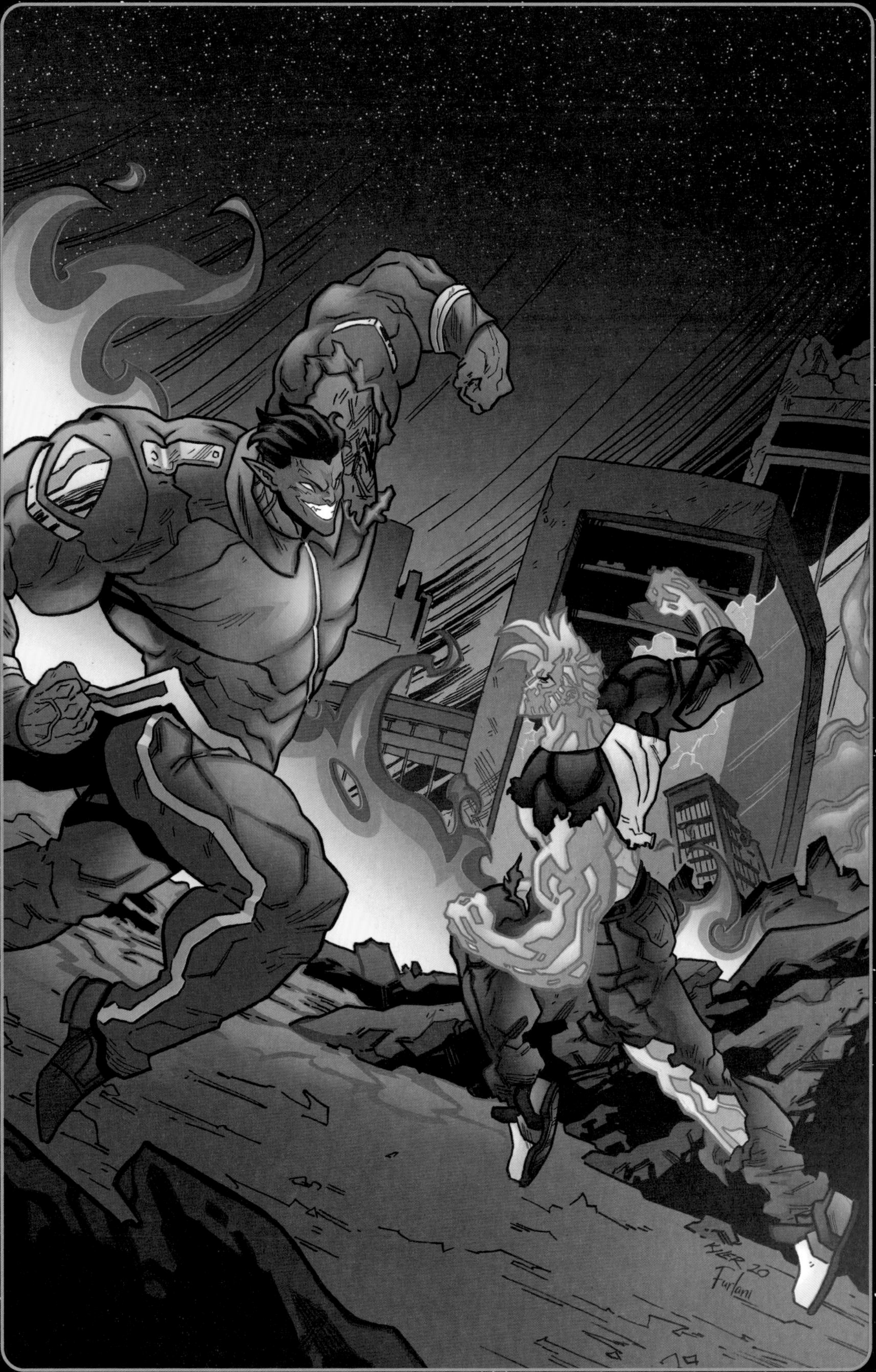
KYLER 20
Furlani

Trade Paperback Cover Process

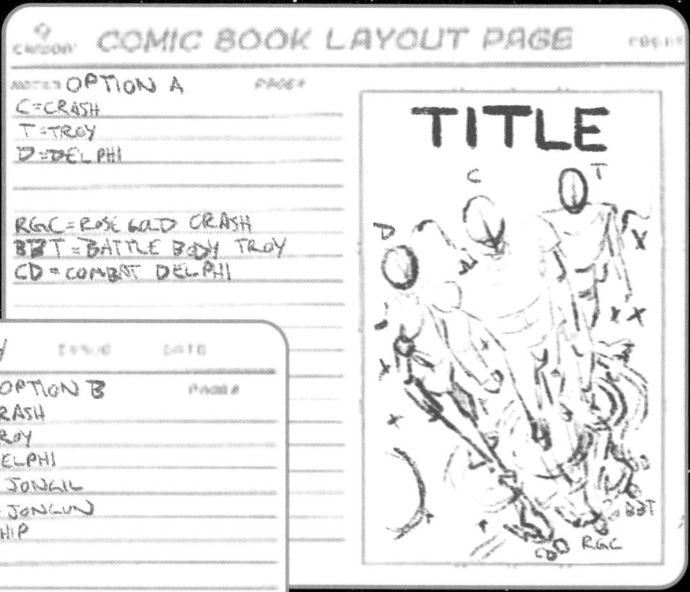
COMIC BOOK LAYOUT PAGE
OPTION A
C=CRASH
T=TROY
D=DELPHI
RGC=ROSE GOLD CRASH
BBT=BATTLE BODY TROY
CD=COMBAT DELPHI
TITLE

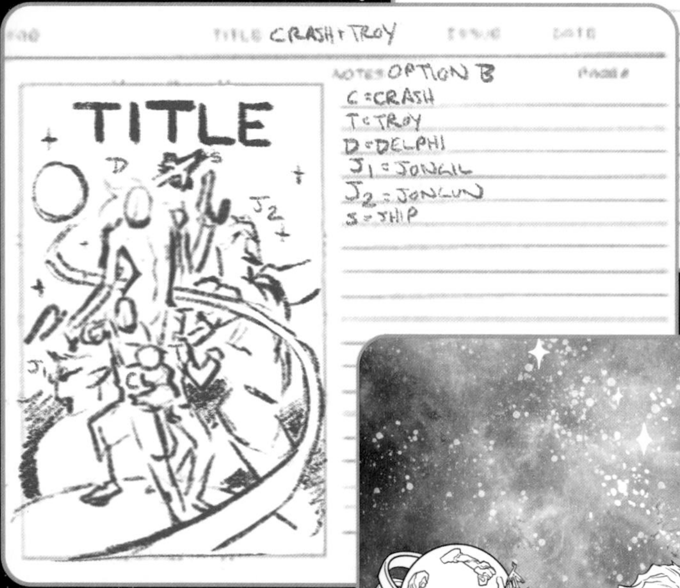
TITLE CRASH+TROY
OPTION B
C=CRASH
T=TROY
D=DELPHI
J1=JONGIL
J2=JONLUN
S=SHIP
TITLE

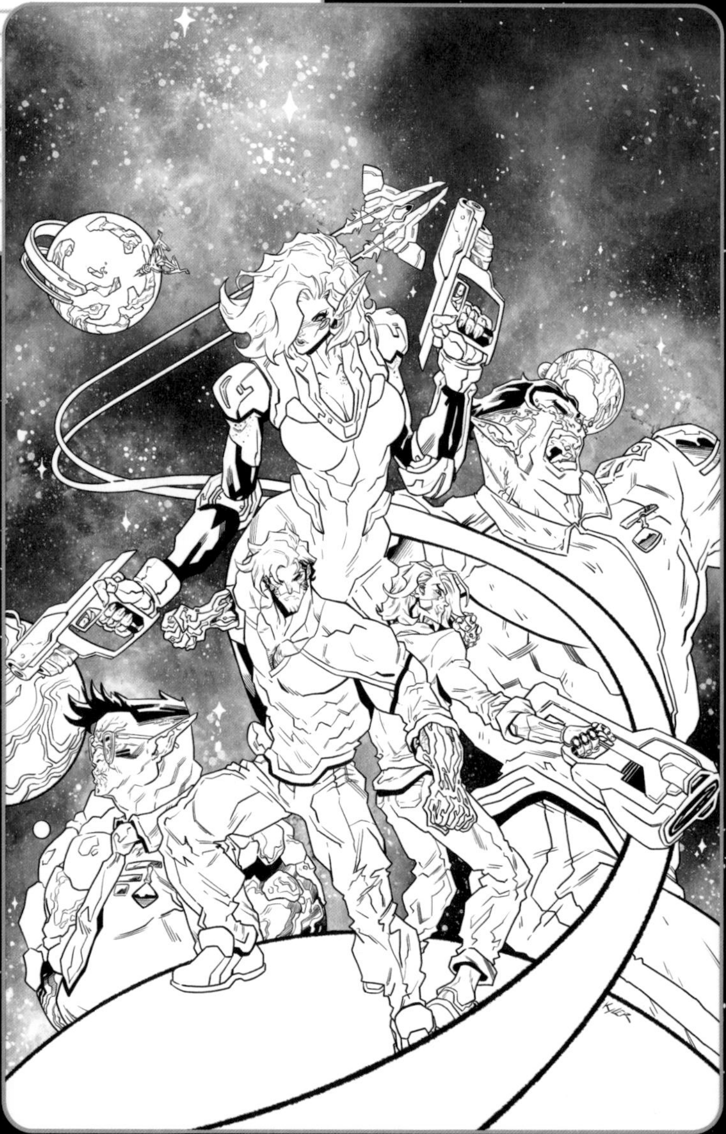

Concept drawings and line art by Kyler Clodfelter. Colors by Bruno Furlani.

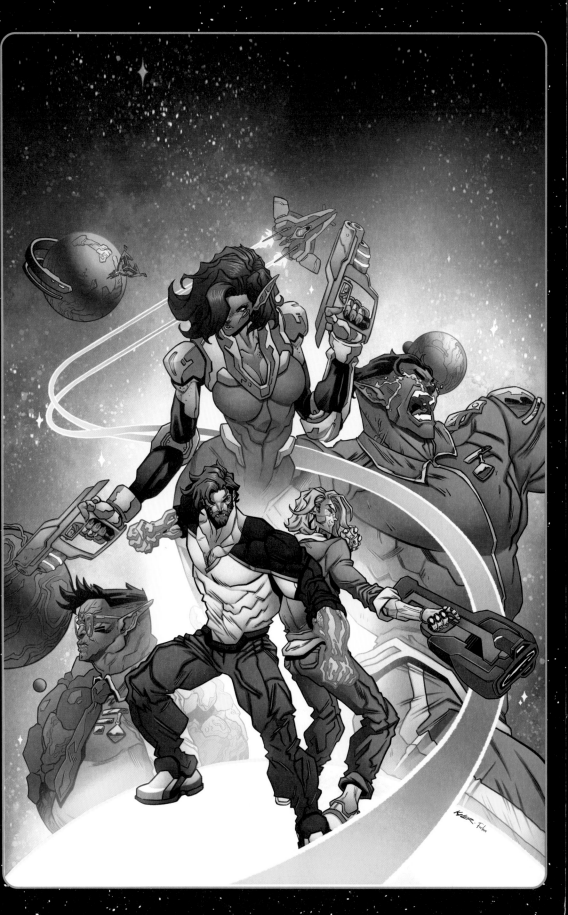

Jarred Luján

Jarred is a Mexican-American comic writer from the borderlands of Texas. He's a 2019 Mad Cave Studios Talent Search winner and a 2022 DC Milestone Initiate. He likes the Wu-Tang Clan, existentialism, and trying to convince his pets to be nice to him.

Kyler Clodfelter

Kyler Clodfelter is a comic book artist from Metro Detroit who loves fighting games, D&D, working out, anime and metalcore music played at ear splitting volumes. Inspired to draw comic books from a young age after reading titles such as Amazing Spider-Man and X-Men, he spent the next 20+ years honing his skills, ultimately attending College for Creative Studies (CCS).

Bruno Furlani

Bruno Furlani is a french freelance colorist who lives in the city of Rheims in France. He started coloring comics during high school. Bruno has a master's degree in geology but does not pursue this discipline. He decided to start as a professional colorist after Jarred offers him to join the project Crash & Troy. He is also the colorist of an issue of Dead Beats 2 with Kyler Clodfelter.

Buddy Beaudoin

Buddy Beaudoin is a comic book writer and letterer with lettering credits on titles from ActionLAB, Ominous Press, Scout Comics, A Wave Blue World, and more! He hopes you enjoy Crash & Troy as much as he does. If not, there's always cat videos.

Hernán Guarderas

Hernán Guarderas (he/him) is a comics writer and editor based out of New Jersey. He has written articles for Comic Book Resources, Newsarama, and Talking Comics. His recent comics writing has appeared in Power & Magic Press' Mañana Anthology. His editorial comics work has been in Kickstarter Project We Love Fog Line, and other indie shorts.